1863

LINCOLN'S PIVOTAL YEAR

Edited by Harold Holzer
and Sara Vaughn Gabbard

Southern Illinois University Press
Carbondale and Edwardsville

Publication of this book has been partially supported
by subvention from Friends of the Lincoln Collection
of Indiana.

Library of Congress Cataloging-in-Publication Data

1863 : Lincoln's pivotal year / edited by Harold Holzer
and Sara Vaughn Gabbard.
     pages   cm
Includes bibliographical references and index.
  ISBN 978-0-8093-3246-5 (cloth : alk. paper)
  ISBN 0-8093-3246-9 (cloth : alk. paper)
  ISBN 978-0-8093-3247-2 (ebook) (print)
  ISBN 0-8093-3247-7 (ebook) (print)
 1. United States—History—Civil War, 1861–1865.
 2. Lincoln, Abraham, 1809–1865—Military leadership.
 3. United States—Politics and government—1861–1865.
 I. Holzer, Harold. II. Gabbard, Sara Vaughn.
 III. Title: Lincoln's pivotal year.
 E470.A1169 2013
 973.7'33—dc23   2012040723

Printed on recycled paper. ♻
The paper used in this publication meets the minimum
requirements of American National Standard for Information Sciences—Permanence of Paper for Printed
Library Materials, ANSI Z39.48-1992. ∞

973.733
E

CONTENTS

Figures

1863

INTRODUCTION:
THE REMEMBRANCE OF A DREAM

HAROLD HOLZER

*T*hey have been called the most decisive, certainly the most revolutionary, twelve months of the entire Civil War. Indeed, only hours into the
new year of 1863, Abraham Lincoln guaranteed their reputation as such
by signing the first executive act ever aimed at destroying the stubbornly
intractable institution of American slavery.

It was a dramatic moment oddly shielded from public view. Lincoln
spent the better part of that eagerly anticipated holiday mingling with
hundreds of people at the annual White House New Year's reception. But,
as far as we know, emancipation was not mentioned to the large crowd of
visitors. Only when the president retreated to his second-floor office later
in the afternoon did he finally affix his name to the document—with but
a handful of associates on hand. Lincoln well understood that the moment
was epochal—perhaps the most important not just of the war but of the
entire nineteenth century—yet he was so worried about adverse public
reaction that he never considered turning it into the major public event it
deserved to be. Only later did he proudly point to it as the start of "a great
revolution in public sentiment."[1]

Other unforgettable moments did follow. The year 1863 also brought
the so-called Confederate High Water Mark in summer, an event that
climaxed nothing less than the most titanic battle that ever shook the
Western Hemisphere. And, in late autumn, that battle inspired the most
famous presidential speech in America's entire history. Earlier in the
year, lest we forget, Lincoln also established the uniform gauge for the

new Union Pacific Railroad, promising at last to connect the eastern and western shores of the vast continent. And that same month, the president cheered the admission of the new state of West Virginia to the Union, even though it had seceded from another state—one in active rebellion—in order to create itself. Once opposed to the exercise of vast presidential powers—that is, when a Democrat wielded them—Lincoln in 1863 became arguably the most powerful president in American history.[2] "Lincoln," complained Richmond's *Southern Illustrated News*, "is made Dictator of all the North, and vested with full power of the purse and the sword."[3]

All this said, when this momentous year ended, it nonetheless probably seemed, to many living in the North at the time, something of a disappointment. For 1863 brought not the end of the rebellion, as some hoped, but at most the end of the beginning. By the time the carnage ended at Gettysburg on July 3, the Civil War was only half over.

Historical perspective gives us the precious opportunity to view these crucial twelve months with more understanding and appreciation. But readers should never forget that even when the year began with Lincoln's thunderbolt decree against slavery, ending four score years of governmental tolerance of human bondage, the news was received with odd calm in most of white America. For all the upheaval it promised—or, to some, threatened—no parades, celebrations, or mass demonstrations ushered in this first, and biggest, event of 1863.

Writing from New Orleans, the special correspondent for the *New York Times* at least acknowledged the significance of the presidential order: "The first of January, 1863, is past, and the President's Proclamation, declaring Slavery abolished in the United States of America, has been given to the world;—it is an accomplished fact; it is history, and what is most, it is an irrevocable decree against human bondage ever again existing under the flag of the Union."

Then the reporter admitted, "It is astonishing to me, when I think of the vast consequences to follow to my own country and to the world, that a document so wonderful in its character could be issued without some attending miracle—some strange yet cheering natural phenomenon. So important, indeed, do I deem this proclamation of Mr. LINCOLN, that I consider it surpassed in the magnitude of its humanity only by the inspiration of the Sermon on the Mount."[4]

Not until November would Lincoln provide, at the Gettysburg Soldiers' Cemetery, the "sermon" to accompany the "miracle"—and even then, the indelible greatness of his words was initially overlooked by many Americans. True, the year 1863 has achieved a legendary place in American memory. We tend to forget, however, that it was far more difficult and confusing to endure at the time than to appreciate later. Characterizing the initial fuss over the Emancipation order as "silly trilling," for example, the *Brooklyn Eagle* predicted on the second day of the year, "We are of those who believe that Mr. Lincoln's proclamation will fail in its terrible purpose. We believe that a proclamation abolishing the pirate [ship] Alabama would have precisely the same effect." To the *Eagle*, often overlooked as an arbiter of public opinion but, in fact, one of the country's largest newspapers, serving one of its largest cities, "[W]e fear, the hope of a Union of a great, contented and happy people passes away like the remembrance of a dream."[5]

One reason for public uncertainty in 1863 may be that not only the nation but the North, too, remained bitterly divided that year. "I have too many *family* controversies, (so to speak) already on my hands, to voluntarily, or so long as I can avoid it, take up another," Lincoln wrote to one of his generals in late January. He was referring specifically to vexing military disputes within the chain of command, but he might as easily have been talking about the state of political affairs.[6]

Partisan politics remained white hot and ever-divisive throughout 1863. The president's popularity, though never officially measured (public-opinion polls had yet to be invented), surely varied unsteadily throughout the year, sagging after military defeats, rebounding after military triumphs—and certainly challenged anew by the inauguration of the first-ever military draft. In response, New York exploded with the worst racial violence in its history in what was perhaps the low point of the year. Amidst this backdrop, the government in Washington continued its unprecedented crackdown on individual liberty, as Democrats in the North bristled under what they claimed amounted to a Constitutional crisis. Meanwhile, Lincoln continued to search for a military commander who could inspire the Army of the Potomac to victory after its shattering loss to Robert E. Lee at Fredericksburg in the waning days of 1862.

The political situation in the Civil War North remains a particularly neglected subject, though recent books have begun at last to deal with this important subject.[7] One explanation for this neglect may be that 1863 commenced one year *after* the most recent congressional and many state elections. Thus, historians have tended to treat 1863 as politically anticlimactic, recognizing only that Lincoln's Republicans began the calendar year operating with a smaller majority in Congress and with fewer friendly governors and legislatures in Northern state houses. Lincoln wrote to one of the new class of opposition Democratic governors, Horatio Seymour of New York, in March, trying to woo him to the common purpose of "maintaining the nation's life and integrity." Lincoln modestly described himself in the communication as "for the time being . . . the head of a nation which is in great peril," adding of Seymour, "and you are at the head of the greatest State of that nation. . . . I assume, and believe, there can not be a difference of *purpose* between you and me"—only "as to the *means*."[8] As the year wore on, it became apparent that the two men differed so *much* in means that they would never find common ground.

Despite the president's olive branch, partisan political activity continued to percolate unabated throughout 1863. In fact, it witnessed at least one additional, momentous popular election—the contest for governor of Ohio, one of whose candidates was the quintessential "Copperhead"—the reigning term for antiwar Northern Democrats—former Congressman Clement Laird Vallandigham. Arrested earlier in the year for speaking out against the military draft, then tried by military tribunal, convicted, and exiled to the Confederacy, "Valiant Val," as his loyal supporters nicknamed him, emerged as something of a martyr candidate for governor, running for office without the ability to enter the state and campaign openly in his own behalf.

Whatever the nearly insurmountable handicaps to Vallandigham's electoral success, Lincoln remained extremely anxious about the Ohio race, fearful that a good showing for a man he believed to be an outright traitor would mark a stinging political rebuke for both the administration and the war effort. The president could hardly believe "that one genuine American would, or could be induced to, vote for such a man."[9] We principally recall the Lincoln of 1863 as an emancipator, warrior, and orator, but as the Vallandigham episode reminds us, he was also very much the active politician as well. In a letter to other Ohio Democrats in June, Lincoln could barely bring himself to mention Vallandigham by name: He repeatedly referred to him only as "Mr. V."[10] But as he later expressed it, he also knew the kind of country for which the Union was fighting could not postpone elections. "I have understood well," Lincoln acknowledged that year, "that the duty of self-preservation rests solely with the American people."[11] Vallandigham lost his 1863 governor's race in a lopsided vote, and Lincoln considered himself, and his policies, vindicated. Republicans won as well in Pennsylvania. But we should not underestimate how much time the president of a country "engaged in a great civil war" devoted to politics in 1863.

As the year progressed, however, the president shed some of the political timidity that marked his cautious introduction of emancipation. After risking (and enduring) political defeats when he issued his preliminary proclamation at the start of the election season in 1862, he bravely tested the limits of public opinion further in 1863 when he pressed hard for black enlistment. He did so with generally unappreciated sincerity and enthusiasm.

On March 26, he even appealed to Governor Andrew Johnson, military governor of Tennessee and certainly no friend of African American rights. "I am told you have at least *thought* of raising a negro military force," wrote Lincoln. This was just what he wanted to hear from "an eminent citizen of a slave-state, and himself a slave-holder. The colored population is the great *available* and yet *unavailed* of, force for restoration of the Union. The bare sight of fifty thousand armed, and drilled black soldiers on the banks of the Mississippi, would end the rebellion at once." In this hope, Lincoln was overconfident. The sight of black recruits did not end the rebellion in its tracks in 1863. But by summer, "armed, and drilled" black soldiers did bravely charge along the banks of South Carolina in the first wave of attack against Battery Wagner near Charleston. They died in great numbers and are now firmly enshrined in legend. The valor of the legendary 54th Massachusetts earned another significant place in the history of 1863. Some things were above politics, especially winning the war through every means available.

In a speech he prepared for delivery in his Springfield, Illinois, hometown in August—but which, ultimately, he assigned to one of his old neighbors to read while he remained glued to Washington—Lincoln wrote memorably about the Union and the soldiers fighting to defend it. "Thanks to all," he declared. "For the great republic—for the principle it lives by, and keeps alive—for man's vast future,—thanks to all."[12]

Such impassioned rhetoric would have served as a fit peroration for any of his great orations, and Lincoln was at the height of his rhetorical powers when he composed those words. But fearing his audience would be "over-sanguine of a speedy final triumph" and, more dangerously, opposed emancipation and black enlistment, he saw fit to add a final paragraph emphasizing his concerns. The war would continue, he pointed out, and if "the rightful result" was to be achieved, then white citizens had better get used to black soldiers fighting for both Union and their own freedom. Overshadowed by his elegiac triumph at Gettysburg less than three months later, the following must rank as one of the most unrestrained, underrated declarations of Lincoln's entire presidency:

> Peace does not appear so distant as it did. I hope it will come soon, and come to stay; and so come as to be worth the keeping in all future time. It will then have been proved that, among free men, there can be no successful appeal from the ballot to the bullet; and that they who take such appeal are sure to lose their case, and pay the cost. And then, there will be some black men who can remember that, with silent tongue, and clenched teeth, and steady eye, and well-poised bayonet, they have helped mankind on to this great consummation; while, I fear, there will be some white ones, unable to forget that, with malignant heart, and deceitful speech, they have strove to hinder it.[13]

As Lincoln acknowledged rather more prosaically in his annual message to Congress on December 8, "the war power is still our main reliance."

Looking back at the tumultuous year past, the president firmly believed that the army and navy, not the politicians, had "borne their harder part" in 1863, doing so both "nobly and well." To them, Lincoln generously insisted, "the world must stand indebted for the home of freedom disenthralled, regenerated, enlarged, and perpetuated."[14] As this book shows, their commander in chief deserves much of the credit as well.

This book is designed to revisit and recalibrate both the large and small dramas of this watershed year, in a series of assessments, written to mark its sesquicentennial, by some of the twenty-first century's most distinguished Civil War historians and Lincoln scholars.

John F. Marszalek, executive director of the Ulysses S. Grant Presidential Library, Mississippi State University, and historian Michael B. Ballard, archivist at Mississippi State University Mitchell Memorial Library and associate editor of the publishing projects of the Ulysses S. Grant Association, offer a comprehensive review of the military events of this crowded year. William C. Davis, professor of history at Virginia Tech, reminds us how difficult Lincoln's search for successful generals remained. Also on matters military, Craig L. Symonds, emeritus professor of history at the U.S. Naval Academy, demonstrates that some of the most important military engagements of 1863 were fought not on land but on water.

Edna Greene Medford, chair and professor of history at Howard University, provides a fresh perspective on how the breathlessly awaited news of Lincoln's emancipation edict changed life for African Americans in 1863. And Catherine Clinton of Queen's University Belfast in Northern Ireland, a noted biographer of Mary Lincoln, presents us a new and original look at the year through the private struggles of the president's own family.

As noted, perhaps the most shameful and frightening episode of the year occurred when New Yorkers violently rose up against military conscription in July—then quickly turned a so-called draft riot into a race riot. Historian Barnet Schecter, whose book on the subject remains one of the definitive accounts, here adds new research and analysis to the understanding of this horrific episode. And Orville Vernon Burton, professor of history at Clemson University, brings new understanding of Lincoln's most cherished and familiar two minutes—his oratorical triumph at Gettysburg on November 19.

Frank J. Williams, retired chief justice of the Rhode Island Supreme Court and a leading expert on Lincoln and the law of war, reminds us afresh that the sixteenth president navigated a constitutional minefield throughout 1863. Williams brings us closer than ever to the challenges Lincoln faced and overcame as he struggled to balance the concurrent roles of servant of the people and commander in chief.

Finally, two chapters of this book are devoted to one shelf of the historical archive long and undeservedly relegated to secondary importance: pictures. Bob Zeller, whose discoveries and commentary on Civil War photography have altered understanding of the medium's power during those years, examines 1863 through the lens of the cameras and cameramen that captured it. His essay reveals, among other points, just what their products meant to both technology and public opinion. I am proud to round out this collection with a chapter that examines what the evolving image of Lincoln's own increasingly iconic face—portraits in oil, print, and photograph—came powerfully to suggest to Northerners in 1863.

As all these chapters suggest, this is basically a book about the Civil War North in 1863—seen through the perspective of Lincoln, his cabinet, and his military and personal families, with a special focus on the president's decisions, remarks, and experiences. It does not pretend to provide a similar examination of the Confederacy in 1863 but not because of historical bias. It is not just that history belongs to the winners of wars, although surely the nation that emerged as the result of the sacrifices of 1863 remains more important than the sum of its divided parts between 1861 and 1865. More important, if we are to accept the premise that 1863 changed the war and changed society, we are obliged to keep the spotlight where it belongs: those who triumphed in behalf of Union and freedom.

But as these chapters powerfully remind us, even by the end of the remarkable year of 1863, victory and its resulting blessings were by no means assured. This book seeks not only to analyze a watershed year of history but also to illuminate the year as it unfolded to the people who lived through it. Abraham Lincoln contributed much to win, and define, the struggles of 1863, but as this book shows, many Americans did not know or appreciate it at the moment.

They were living through the "remembrance of a dream," all right, but they were still engulfed in its nightmare details.

Notes

1. Francis B. Carpenter, *Six Months at the White House with Abraham Lincoln: The Story of a Picture* (New York: Hurd and Houghton, 1866), 77, 269.

2. In 1848, Lincoln had protested the powers assumed by President James K. Polk during the Mexican-American War. See, for example, Lincoln to William H. Herndon, February 15, 1848, in Roy P. Basler, ed., *The Collected Works of Abraham Lincoln*, 9 vols. (New Brunswick, NJ: Rutgers University Press, 1953–55), 1:451. Hereafter cited as *Collected Works*.

3. *Southern Illustrated News* (Richmond, VA), March 14, 1863, reprinted in Herbert Mitgang, ed., *Lincoln as They Saw Him* (New York: Rinehart, 1956), 336.

4. *New York Times*, February 2, 1863.

5. *Brooklyn (NY) Eagle*, January 2, 1863.

6. Lincoln to John A. McClernand, January 22, 1863, *Collected Works*, 6:70.

7. See, for example, Mark E. Neely Jr., *Lincoln and the Triumph of the Nation: Constitutional Conflict in the American Civil War* (Chapel Hill: University of North Carolina Press, 2011).

8. Lincoln to Horatio Seymour, March 23, 1863, *Collected Works*, 6:145.

9. Gideon Welles, *Diary of Gideon Welles*, 3 vols. (Boston: Houghton Mifflin, 1911), 1:470.

10. Lincoln to Matthew Birchard and Others, June 29, 1863, *Collected Works*, 6:300–306.

11. Lincoln to the "workingmen of Manchester [England]," January 19, 1863, *Collected Works*, 6:64.

12. Lincoln to James C. Conkling, August 26, 1863, *Collected Works*, 6:410.

13. Ibid.

14. Annual Message to Congress, December 8, 1863, *Collected Works*, 6:52–53.

THE DAY OF JUBILEE

EDNA GREENE MEDFORD

$\mathcal{S}$ix days after President Lincoln issued the decree that promised freedom to all enslaved people held in areas under Confederate control, the *Richmond Daily Dispatch* boldly suggested that "no proclamation which the Yankees have issued, or may issue, will have the slightest effect upon the slave population of the South." Heretofore, it argued, the Union forces had carried off the enslaved population through kidnapping. "But beyond the lines of the Federal army, slavery will continue intact and impregnable as the rock of Gibraltar. It is a good deal older than any earthly Government, and it will last a good deal longer than any throne or republic of the earth. 'Cursed be Canaan; a servant of servants shall he be to his brethren,' is a proclamation which even the mighty Abraham Lincoln cannot abolish."[1] Doubtless, many of the newspaper's readers drew comfort from its prediction, but almost immediately, residents of the Confederacy found themselves facing an alternate reality. Their bound labor force had deserted plantation and farm, the able-bodied men among them had found dignity and self-worth in the ranks of the Union military, and those who chose to remain at home were facilitating the destruction of slavery from within. The Emancipation Proclamation would impact the South and its foundational economic institution in ways both predictable and unexpected. Before the end of the year, supporters and critics alike, in the North as well as the South, would be compelled to acknowledge its transformative nature.

Few would challenge the contention that New Year's Day 1863 was one of the most anticipated in American history. The nation had been at war with itself for more than a year and a half, with little indication of an impending resolution. The president's ultimatum, delivered one hundred days earlier, had threatened the rebellious South with forfeiture of its human property. For some, the day represented the potential for a new national beginning; others thought it likely to herald the permanent dissolution of the Union. No one better understood the importance of the day or the action that would be irrevocably linked to it than Lincoln. So when it came time to make good on his promise by affixing his signature to the proclamation, he placed the pen down long enough to steady a hand badly cramped from greeting well-wishers who had come to the White House, as was the tradition in those days. Of course, who could have blamed him if the unsteadiness of his hand *had* been caused by second-guessing this momentous act? Freeing three million enslaved people could rightly cause one's hands to shake, especially in a nation where the vast majority of the citizens were either indifferent to the suffering of people in bondage or gave tacit acceptance of their condition as long as whites were unaffected by their presence. The political, economic and social implications of the president's action were enormous. Instead of saving the Union, as it was intended to do, it could have served as the deathblow to the Northern cause. Lincoln accepted the gamble, knowing that the blame for failure would be directed to him.

But the president was not alone in appreciating the gravity of the moment. Despite the bravado from the Southern press, Confederates recognized that an emancipating document issued by the national president would compromise their cause. They had already lost thousands of laborers to the Union; those absconding often carried valuable information on troop movements and other military information that advantaged the North.[2] The vulnerability of the Confederacy to Union influence over their bondmen and women led Southerners to charge the North with inciting insurrection among the enslaved, an accusation that was repeated with even greater certainty after Lincoln issued the proclamation.[3]

Arguably, having more to lose than either Lincoln and the North or Jefferson Davis and the Confederacy were the 4.5 million men and women of African descent, nearly 4 million of whom were legally property. Since the beginning of the war, they had tied their fate to Northern success. Free men and women of color—constrained by prejudice against them as a result of their membership in a "servile" race—had hoped that white Americans would recognize the disruptions that slavery had caused the nation and put an end to the heinous institution once and for all. Their spirit had been buoyed by the preliminary proclamation of September 22, but they could not be certain that Lincoln had the will to go through with his threat. His heretofore lukewarm support of congressional actions regarding enslaved labor did little to allay black fear that this president was no friend of freedom. Hence, when he issued the preliminary proclamation,

African Americans and their supporters greeted the news with hopeful but cautious anticipation. The interval between the preliminary and final emancipation left famed orator and black abolitionist Frederick Douglass worried and elicited the complaint from him that Lincoln's words in the September document had "kindled no enthusiasm [and] touched neither justice nor mercy." Had the president linked the death of slavery with preservation of the Union, there would be greater confidence in the outcome. Instead, "[e]mancipation is put off—it was made future and conditional—not present and absolute."[4]

On the appointed day, African Americans and their abolitionist friends held vigils in major Northern cities and awaited the news that the final proclamation had been issued. In Boston, a crowd of three thousand or more gathered at Tremont Temple, where they passed the time listening to speeches by such prominent fighters for freedom as Douglass, William Wells Brown, Annie E. Dickinson, and J. Sella Martin. Predictably, the assembled crowd grew restless as the hours passed without any word from the president. Douglass described the transformation in attitude when word finally arrived: "At last, when patience was well-nigh exhausted, and suspense was becoming agony, a man . . . with hasty step advanced through the crowd. And with a face fairly illuminated with the news he bore, exclaimed in tones that thrilled all hearts, 'It is coming! It is coming! It is on the wires!' The effect of this announcement was startling beyond description, and the scene was wild and grand. Joy and gladness exhausted all form of expression, from shouts of praise to sobs and tears."[5] Too overjoyed to end the celebration at midnight, the revelers retired to the Twelfth Street Baptist Church, where they continued until daybreak.[6] Similar gatherings sprang up all over the North and Midwest. In New York, Henry Highland Garnet's Shiloh Presbyterian Church hosted a meeting for an overflowing audience. When the announcement was made that the president would issue the proclamation at midnight, those assembled raised three cheers each for Lincoln and for freedom.[7] In Chicago, the sole black survivor of John Brown's raid on Harpers Ferry, Osborne Perry Anderson, reminded the audience of the martyr's commitment to black freedom.[8] At Washington, a vigil was led by contrabands, who passed the day in song and in prayer for the president and the Union army and in praise for God. When the news of the proclamation reached the city's Israel Bethel A.M.E. Church, "Men squealed, women fainted, dogs barked, white and colored people shook hands; songs were sung. . . . Every face had a smile and even the dumb animals seemed to realize that some extraordinary event had taken place."[9]

Praise for Lincoln was nearly universal in the African American community, but the man who would be anointed "the Great Emancipator" had to share the day with a higher authority. Blacks in the Union understood the president's motivations for issuing the proclamation and were quick to distinguish between humanitarianism and "military necessity." Speakers at an emancipation celebration in Philadelphia alluded to the belief prevalent among some African Americans "[t]hat we are indebted to the President for the emancipation of the slave." They argued that Lincoln's efforts to save the Union and his willingness to embrace the destruction of slavery when all else failed earned for him "our highest esteem, admiration, and best wishes for his success and prosperity during his administration." But the credit for "this great deliverance" was God's alone. It was he who "defeated the purposes of men, and brought the blessing of freedom to the larger portion of our oppressed race."[10]

Circumstances dictated that those free and enslaved men and women behind the Confederate lines remain reticent about the proclamation. Many a bondman or woman who heard the good news on New Year's Day feigned ignorance of the event or pretended to be upset at the prospect of having the chains of bondage removed. But in places where the Union army maintained control, enslaved men and women felt it safe enough to celebrate. Although they had been exempted from the proclamation's provisions, thousands of black men and women in Norfolk, Virginia, lined the streets as Union troops and other black residents of the city marched in recognition of the great event.[11]

At Port Royal in South Carolina, early Union occupation had begun to facilitate the transformation from slavery to freedom. Here, black men and women had been introduced to a free-labor system and to the respon-sibilities attending free status. Here was located Camp Saxton, where many soldiers had received their first instruction in reading. The camp was home to the 1st South Carolina Volunteers, the first regiment of former slaves raised on Southern soil. As the soldiers and newly freed celebrated the news of emancipation together, the regiment's commander, Colonel Thomas Wentworth Higginson, observed the moment when those as-sembled became "Americans." The proclamation was read to the crowd.

The very moment the speaker had ceased, and just as I took and waved the flag, which now for the first time meant anything to these poor people, there suddenly arose, close beside the platform, a strong male voice (but rather cracked and elderly), into which two women's voices blended, singing, as if by an impulse that could no more be repressed than the morning note of the song sparrow.—

"My country, 'tis of thee,
Sweet land of liberty,
Of thee I sing!"

Higginson noted with amazement that this was "[t]he first day they had ever had a country, the first flag they had ever seen which promised anything to their people."[12]

Emancipation celebrations continued for the next several weeks as black leaders delivered impassioned speeches expressing gratitude to God and to the president and gave voice to expectations for material improvement. Reverend Jonathan C. Gibbs of the First African Presbyterian Church of Philadelphia reminded his congregation that the proclamation was ushering in a new era:

> The morning dawns! The long night of sorrow and gloom is past, rosey-fingered Aurora, early born of day, shows the first faint flush of her coming glory, low down on the distant horizon of Freedom's joyful day. O day, thrice blessed, that brings liberty to four million native-born Americans. O Liberty! O sacred rights of every human soul! . . . Today, standing on the broad platform of the common brotherhood of men, we solemnly appeal to the God of justice, our common Father, to aid us to meet manfully the new duties, the new obligations that this memorable day will surely impose. The Proclamation has gone forth, and God is saying to this nation by its legitimate constitute head, Man must be free.

By any reckoning, Reverend Gibbs was a man of privilege. Born free in Philadelphia, he studied at Dartmouth College and later at Princeton Theological Seminary and had attained one of the most honorable positions open to a man of his or any era. Yet, he was a member of a despised and deprecated race. So when the proclamation was issued, Gibbs and other free black men and women embraced it as their own moment of liberation, not just the day of freedom for the enslaved. He encouraged white Americans to support the proclamation and thereby give the government the assistance it needed to win the war. "Or in a short time," he warned, "the question will not be whether black men are to be slaves, but whether white men are to be free!"[13]

Douglass saw the proclamation in similar fashion. In an address at the Cooper Institute, now Cooper Union, a few days after it was issued, he declared it to be "the greatest event of our nation's history." Since the first of January, the nation had pledged itself to protect Americans of all colors, while black men and women were given a "stake in the safety, property, honor, and glory of a common country." In Douglass's estimation, all were liberated by Lincoln's edict, whites as well as African Americans. While some criticized its foundation in military necessity, Douglass viewed it as a "grand moral necessity." To the objection that the proclamation only abolished slavery in the states in rebellion, Douglass argued that with its demise in the Confederacy, it could not long continue in the Border States.

"Strike it at either extreme . . . and it dies." If some thought the proclamation mere "ink and paper," he challenged them to make it "iron, lead
and fire, by the prompt employment of the negro's arm in this contest."[14]

Throughout the North, African Americans embraced the proclamation
as the first step in returning dignity and respect to a people who had been
debased by slavery. Marriages would be legalized, black women could be
protected from the licentiousness of white men, and parents could gain
authority over their children. Freedom would end "oppression, cruelty, and
outrage, founded on complexion" and ensure "unerring justice."[15]

Over the course of the year, news of the proclamation reached enslaved
people in Confederate-controlled territory by various routes and at different times. While a few may have learned the news directly from Southern
Unionist owners who had gathered their human property together and read
the proclamation to them, most would have come upon the knowledge by
way of the ubiquitous slave grapevine or by eavesdropping on conversations
among white people—by listening at open windows at night, by overhear-
ing dinner conversation as they served meals to owners and their guests,
or by catching bits of information from letters and newspapers. Enslaved
men and women often got the first word through rumors passed along by
the extraordinary communications network that linked far-flung communities. "We done heard dat Lincum gonna turn de [Negroes] free," Susie
Melton recalled. "Ole missus say dey warn't nothin' to it. Den a Yankee
soldier tole someone in Williamsburg dat Marse Lincum done signed de
'Mancipation. Was winter time an' moughty cold dat night, but ev'ybody
commence gittin' ready to leave. Didn't care nothin' bout Missus—was
goin' to de Union lines." All that night the enslaved laborers celebrated,
and at daybreak, they piled their meager belongings on their backs and
set out to test their freedom. As the sun came up, Melton recalled, the
freed people began to sing.

> Sun, you be here an' I'll be gone.
> Bye, bye, don't grieve arter me
> Won't give you my place, not fo your'n
> Bye, bye, don't grieve arter me
> 'Cause you be here an' I'll be gone.[16]

Others learned of the provisions of the proclamation as their bondage
was being deepened. For example, Benjamin Holmes discovered the news
while housed in a slave pen, awaiting transport out of South Carolina after
his owner had sold him to a trader. The announcement was printed in a
local newspaper, and Holmes, who was literate, shared the information
with all held in the facility. "Such rejoicing as there was then!" he recalled a
decade later. "One old man held a prayer meeting right there in the mart."[17]

Of course, Holmes and his fellow bondmen remained enslaved, despite the proclamation's stipulations. He did not get his freedom until a year later, ironically, after he had been transported to Tennessee, a state exempted from the provisions of the proclamation.

Lincoln understood that in order to secure the freedom promised by his decree, action had to be taken either by the enslaved themselves or the Union military. They would have to be convinced to "come boldly over from the rebel side to ours."[18] Although it is virtually impossible to determine how many were actually induced to flee upon learning of the proclamation, one can get a sense of its effect in Captain Charles Wilder's report to his superiors just a few months after the decree was issued. As superintendent of the contrabands at Union-held Fortress Monroe in southeastern Virginia, he estimated that ten thousand or more fugitives had made their way to his camps. Many of them had fled during the early months of the war, arriving from nearby farms and plantations. But more recently, "They came here from all about, from Richmond and 200 miles off," he wrote. Some of those who came from as far away as North Carolina "knew all about the Proclamation and they started on the belief in it."[19] Although untouched by its provisions, the Border States lost enslaved laborers as well. By the spring of 1863, military commanders in these states complained routinely of the great influx of fugitives into their camps. "Whole families of them are stampeding and leaving their masters," one reported, including those of loyal Unionists.[20] A contemporary had described the decree as "a pillar of flame, beckoning the [enslaved] to the dreamed of promise of freedom."[21] The frequency with which black men and women flocked to the Union camps proved him right.

Men who had fled the Confederacy to secure their own freedom often returned to liberate those left behind. A few weeks after the proclamation went into effect, white residents of Edenton, North Carolina, requested protection from the "outrages" of Union military laborers who were carrying off furniture, bedding, and fellow black persons. Regarded as "indolent in their conduct" by the petitioners, the black men had threatened to "have the town shelled" if they were challenged.[22]

In issuing the proclamation, Lincoln had instructed the freed people to "abstain from all violence, unless in necessary self-defence."[23] Most did, but a lifetime of violence perpetrated against them virtually ensured that some would ignore the directive. In August 1863, military officials reported from Donaldsonville, Louisiana, that several government plantations were controlled by scores of unsupervised black men who were destitute and idle. They acquired horses and mules and purportedly rode through the countryside threatening local white residents and committing crimes.[24] A few weeks later, in Texas, white citizens grew alarmed at the news that an alleged conspiracy had been uncovered between a few white men and black men "to murder indiscriminately all the whites, except known Abolitionists." The residents were told that the plot extended to several counties in northern Texas. In response to the perceived threat, authorities arrested more than a dozen black men alongside a half dozen white ones.[25] Meanwhile, in Mississippi, "marauding bands" of "freed negroes" were reported to be "desolating neighborhoods in the Valley of the Mississippi, and citizens of Mississippi have been murdered at their homes by them."[26] Military men and civilians seemed thoroughly convinced that a full-scale rebellion of enslaved laborers was imminent. "We are invaded north, south, and west by a vindictive foe, who is desolating our borders, burning our dwellings, insulting our people, and inciting our slaves to insurrection," Charles Clark, the new governor, warned his fellow Mississippians, "Regiments of the latter have already been embodied and armed to fight against their masters." Clark, who had won election in 1863 on an antipeace platform, warned that compromise with the enemy would lead to confiscation of slave property, immediate emancipation, and the unthinkable—equality for black men. Rather than have the Confederacy come to this end, Clark preferred to see the last young man sacrificed on the battlefield and the remaining population of old men, women, and children "join hands together, march into the sea, and perish beneath its waters."[27]

Although they feared an unmanaged black presence, Confederate officials and civilians were similarly concerned about the danger posed when black men escaped to the federal lines. Shortly before he turned his office over to Clark, Governor John J. Pettus had recommended to the state legislature that all able-bodied black men be removed from areas vulnerable to Union raids and perhaps placed in the employ of the Confederate government. When within reach of the Union army, these men became instruments for the subjugation of the Southern people: "Every able-bodied negro man that falls into the hands of the enemy is not only a laborer lost to the country in the production of supplies for the support of our armies in the field, but he is also, under the present policy of the United States Government, a soldier gained to its Army."[28]

Confederates had every reason to fear the power of black men to give military advantage to the Union. Aside from promising freedom to the enslaved in rebel-held territories, the proclamation had provided for the recruitment of black men into the military as soldiers. Although written, some might argue, almost as if an afterthought, the authorization of black troops was a huge shift from the Lincoln administration's earlier policy. A few black units had been formed in the Union-occupied South before the proclamation, but now the government was committed to a full-fledged program. By mid-1863, a system had been established for the recruitment and training of these men, and several units had been given the opportunity to prove themselves on the battlefield. By the end of the year, black Union soldiers were more than fifty thousand strong.[29]

The extent to which the federal government prioritized the recruitment and enlistment of black soldiers is evident in an order issued in the Department of Virginia and North Carolina in December 1863. Believing that every able-bodied black man who fled the Confederacy deprived the enemy of critical labor to sustain the rebellion while adding to the strength of the federal cause as either soldiers or laborers, military personnel were ordered to aid all who attempted to come into the Union lines. Anyone found guilty of obstructing recruitment by discouraging or preventing freed persons from coming into the lines or, for the men, from enlisting in the military would be "punished with military severity." The order clearly expressed preference that such black men would be recruited for military service rather than put to nonmilitary labor, since, it was thought, "the best use during the war for an able-bodied colored man, as well for himself as the country, is to be a soldier." Military personnel were directed that no black man between the ages of eighteen and forty-five who could pass the medical examination would be employed as a farm laborer on a government farm.[30] Black men still held in bondage in the Border States were technically exempt from such recruitment, but as need increased, federal policy was eased. Military personnel ignored directives to seek the permission of loyal owners before recruiting their laborers, and laws passed that guaranteed freedom to black men who served not just for themselves but for their families challenged the authority of the owner and weakened slavery.

Generally, black men were as eager to enter the Union ranks as the North was eager to enlist them. Real-life concerns (the well-being of families left behind, uncertainty about the soldier's fate if captured by Confederate forces, and the likelihood of death) sometimes dissuaded men otherwise inclined to take that step toward donning the Union blue. But those who did were motivated by factors at once varied and complex. Men compelled to cower before their owners welcomed the opportunity to prove their manhood on the battlefield. For others, the personal satisfaction of successfully challenging one's self was sufficient motivation. But most were willing to risk their all for the opportunity to be considered fully recognized Americans, with all the rights and privileges enjoyed by others. Every battle engaged, every sacrifice shouldered, brought them closer to their goal. Douglass had encouraged enlistment for the long-term benefits: "Whether you are or are not entitled to all the rights of citizenship in this country has long been a matter of dispute to your prejudice. . . By enlisting in the service of your country at this trial hour, and upholding the National Flag, you stop the mouths of traducers and win applause even from the iron lips of ingratitude. Enlist and you make this your country in common with all other men born in the country or out of it."[31] Black men heeded Douglass's call. Their performance in combat quickly and emphatically dispelled the notion that men accustomed to lowering their gaze in the presence of white men would be unable to face former owners on the battlefield. Lincoln himself had suggested early in the war that arming black men would be disastrous for the Union. However, Northern need for black men's service and their valor in combat had already convinced him by mid-1863 that they would play a crucial role in the winning of the war. In a letter to long-time friend James C. Conkling, Lincoln expressed the sentiment that when the war was over, "there will be some black men who can remember that, with silent tongue, and clenched teeth, and steady eye, and well-poised bayonet, they have helped mankind on to this great consummation; while, I fear, there will be some white ones, unable to forget that, with malignant heart, and deceitful speech, they have strove to hinder it."[32] By the end of the war, approximately two hundred thousand soldiers and sailors would serve; thirty-eight thousand would give their lives in battle or have succumbed to the diseases pervasive in the camps.

Indicative of the black soldier's understanding of the imperative to fight was Meunomennie Maimi, a twenty-eight-year-old from Connecticut. In March 1863, Maimi became ill and considered returning home. In a letter to his concerned wife, he explained why he was eager to stay in the fight. Since January 1, the Union cause had been linked to "whether we are to have freedom to all or slavery to all." The soldier worried that a Confederate victory could lead to the expulsion of free blacks or even result in their enslavement. Contrarily, if the federal government prevailed, all would be free. The Emancipation Proclamation, he believed, was the government's first step in removing the obstacles to black advancement. "When slavery passes away," he argued, "the prejudices that belonged to it must follow." But in order to destroy the institution, the government would need the help of the black man. As for himself, Maimi was determined to return from war as "a free man, of a free country, and a free flag, and my brothers free," but he was prepared to "rest in death on the battlefield, with my face to the slaveholder, a continual reproach and curse upon him."[33]

Maimi's sentiments were shared by his brothers-in-arms—free born and freed—who since Lincoln's proclamation of freedom had been given not just an opportunity but a *reason* to join the federal forces. For them and for other African Americans who remained at home, the proclamation held unlimited promise. It deepened their expectations and encouraged them to challenge injustice and discrimination wherever they found it. In the first year after the decree was issued, black men and women worked steadfastly to make the document's perceived promise a reality.

When not confronting the rebel armies, black fighting men battled discrimination within the Union ranks. Barred from field-grade positions, forced to accept white commanding officers, and disadvantaged by unequal pay and excessive fatigue duty, they questioned the government's commitment to freedom. Especially troubling was the requirement that black men would receive ten dollars per month, three of which would be held back as a clothing allowance, while white soldiers of the same rank received thirteen. When soldiers of the 54th Massachusetts Regiment refused their pay until they were guaranteed the same compensation as whites, one of their number decided it was time to appeal directly to the president. Corporal James Henry Gooding reminded Lincoln of the valor black men showed just weeks before at Fort Wagner, where they had continued to advance in the face of horrific casualties: "The patient, trusting descendants of Afric's Clime have dyed the ground with blood, in defense of the Union, and Democracy. We have done a Soldier's duty. Why can't we have a Soldier's pay?"[34]

When he visited the White House in August 1863, Douglass posed a similar question to the president. In response, Lincoln counseled patience and assured him that the matter would be addressed at an appropriate time.[35] And it was, when a year later Congress passed a measure that made the pay of black soldiers equal to that of whites. Unfortunately, Corporal Gooding did not survive to enjoy this victory. He died that same month at Andersonville, the infamous prison camp in Georgia.[36]

As black men fought Confederates on the battlefield and battled prejudice and discrimination behind Union lines, those who remained at home pressed for an extension of their rights as well. In Michigan, a group of black leaders tied a willingness to fight for the Union under the state's banner to their treatment at home. They acknowledged that black men should play a role in suppressing the rebellion, and they proclaimed their readiness to come to the defense of their country whenever necessary. But they expressed their disinclination to "serve a State while it concedes all that is due to others and denies much, if not the most, that is due to us." They demanded that Michigan extend voting rights to them, that it remove the designation "white" from the state constitution, and that it abolish those laws that referred to color.[37]

In New York, black residents took the occasion of the July 1863 draft riot to make a statement about what they would and would not tolerate in an America where black men were fighting to save the Union and secure freedom. In March, Congress had passed conscription legislation that disadvantaged poor whites. It enabled the wealthy to avoid service by securing a substitute or by paying a $300 fee. Drafted to fight a war whose goal since January 1 included freedom for enslaved blacks, poor whites (many of whom were recently arrived immigrants) did not bear the burden gracefully. Racial hatred inflamed by economic competition and an American culture that encouraged immigrants to denigrate black persons had resulted in long-standing antagonisms between certain groups of white people and African Americans. During the five days of rioting, the mob burned the draft building, destroyed black-owned property, torched a home for orphaned black children, and murdered scores of people—both black people and those sympathetic to them.[38]

The response from the African American community was swift and uncompromising. Speaking on behalf of black New Yorkers as well as those throughout the country, James W. C. Pennington, a black Presbyterian minister, reminded the rioters that "a part of this country BELONGS TO US. . . . We claim the right to buy, hire, occupy and use houses and tenements, for legal consideration; to pass and repass on the streets, lanes, avenues, and all public ways." As for the willingness of black men to fight in the current war, Pennington reminded the nation, "We are doing so with the distinct understanding that WE ARE TO HAVE ALL OUR RIGHTS AS MEN AND AS CITIZENS, and that there are to be no side issues, no RESERVATIONS. . . . In this struggle we know nothing but God, Manhood, and American nationality, full and unimpaired."[39]

Lincoln's actions on January 1, 1863, had been motivated by the desire to resolve the crisis of disunion. Ultimately, his strategy succeeded; the national impediment to peace and unity—slavery—was destroyed. As an unintended consequence, African Americans seized the opportunity to challenge the nation's commitment to its founding principles. They had always done so, but the exigencies of war positioned them to fight discrimination and prejudice more effectively. The black soldier's service to the nation earned for him the right to be heard, and his plight gave the civilian population additional weapons with which to fight its own war on the home front. On January 1, Confederate officials, military men, and civilians alike doubtless sensed the broader implications of the proclamation. But a war that they had enthusiastically embraced had led them to this moment. Is it any wonder, then, that the *Richmond Daily Dispatch* chose to ignore the changes that had already begun to sweep through the Confederacy?

Notes

1. "Lincoln's Emancipation Programme," *Richmond (VA) Daily Dispatch*, January 6, 1863, http://dlxs.richmond.edu/d/ddr/browse.html.

2. General Robert E. Lee to Lieutenant Colonel J. Critcher, Commanding Fifteenth Virginia Cavalry, Fredericksburg, May 26, 1863, in *The War of the Rebellion: A Compilation of the Official Records of the Union and Confederate Armies*, 128 vols. (Washington, DC: GPO, 1880–1901), ser. 1, 25:826. CD-ROM. Hereafter cited as *OR*.

3. Jefferson Davis had charged Lincoln with attempting "the most execrable massacre recorded in the history of guilty man." "Jeff Davis's Message," *Harper's Weekly*, January 31, 1863, 67.

4. "January 1, 1863," *Douglass's Monthly*, January 1863, microfilm, Library of Congress, Washington, DC.

5. Frederick Douglass, *Frederick Douglass: Autobiographies*, ed. Henry Louis Gates Jr. (New York: Library of America, 1994), 791.

6. Ibid., 792.

7. "Grand Emancipation Jubilee," *New York Times*, January 1, 1863, http://www.nytimes.com/1863/01/01/news/grand-emancipation-jubilee-night-watch-freedom-shiloh-church-great-excitement.html?scp=1&sq=Grand+Emancipation+Jubilee&st=p, accessed October 30, 2011.

8. "Remarks of O. P. Anderson," *Anglo-African*, January 10, 1863.

9. Henry McNeal Turner, quoted in *Speak Out in Thunder Tones*, ed. Dorothy Sterling (New York: Da Capo, 1973), 316.

10. "Letter to the Editor on the Emancipation Proclamation from S.Q.R.," *Christian Recorder* (Philadelphia), March 14, 1863, Newspaper Microfilm Reading Room, Harvard Library, Cambridge, Massachusetts.

11. "Later from Norfolk—An African Demonstration," *Richmond (VA) Daily Dispatch*, January 7, 1863.

12. Thomas Wentworth Higginson, *Army Life in a Black Regiment* (New York: Collier, 1969), 59–61.

13. Reverend Jonathan C. Gibbs, "Freedom's Joyful Day," *Christian Recorder*, January 17, 1863.

14. Frederick Douglass, ""The Proclamation and a Negro Army," *Douglass' Monthly*, March 1863, http://www.accessible.com.

15. "Speech of T. Morris Chester, Esq. of Liberia, in the Cooper Institute, New York, January 20, 1863," *Anglo-African*, February 7, 1863, Microfilm, New York City Public Library.

16. *The Negro in Virginia*, comp. Workers of the Writers' Program of the Work Projects Administration in the State of Virginia (Winston-Salem, NC: Blair, 1994), 233–34.

17. John Blassingame, ed., *Slave Testimony: Two Centuries of Letters, Speeches, Interviews, and Autobiographies* (Baton Rouge: Louisiana State University Press, 1977), 618.

18. "To Charles D. Robinson," August 17, 1864, in Roy P. Basler, ed., *The Collected Works of Abraham Lincoln*, 9 vols. (New Brunswick, NJ: Rutgers University Press, 1953–55), 7:500. Hereafter cited as *Collected Works*.

19. Charles Wilder, "Testimony before the American Freedmen's Inquiry Commission," May 9, 1863, in Ira Berlin, Barbara J. Fields, Steven F. Miller, Joseph P. Reidy, and Leslie S. Rowland, eds., *Free at Last: A Documentary History of Slavery, Freedom, and the Civil War* (New York: New Press, 1992), 107–9.

20. Ibid., 99.

21. "The Great Event," *Anglo-African*, January 3, 1863, microfilm, New York City Public Library.

22. Berlin, Fields, Miller, Reidy, and Rowland, *Free at Last*, 98. Eric Foner has suggested that Lincoln did not exempt those areas under Union occupation where the number of unionists was small. Hence, approximately fifty thousand enslaved people were immediately released from bondage. The Edenton case suggests that even with

a Union presence, enslaved people had to wait to be physically liberated. For discussion of Union-occupied areas not exempted in the Emancipation Proclamation, see Foner, *The Fiery Trial: Abraham Lincoln and American Slavery* (New York: Norton, 2010), 241–44.

23. The Emancipation Proclamation, January 1, 1863, *Collected Works*, 6:30.

24. N. A. M. Dudley, Acting Brigadier-General to Lieut. Col. Richard B. Irwin, Assistant Adjutant-General, Nineteenth Army Corps, Headquarters United States Forces, Donaldsonville, Louisiana, August 2, 1863, *OR*, ser. 1, 26:668.

25. Lieutenant Colonel Samuel A. Robert to Captain Edmund P. Turner, Assistant Adjutant-General, Houston, Texas, Headquarters Northern Sub-District of Texas, Bonham, August 29, 1863, *OR,* ser. 1, 26:187.

26. John J. Pettus, Governor and Commander-in-Chief to Gentlemen of the Senate and House of Representatives, November 3, 1863, *OR*, ser. 4, 2:922.

27. Governor Charles Clark to Fellow Citizens, Executive Office, Columbus, Mississippi, November 16, 1863, *OR*, ser. 4, 2:960–61.

28. John J. Pettus, Governor and Commander-in-Chief to Gentlemen of the Senate and House of Representatives, Columbus, Mississippi, November 3, 1863, *OR*, ser. 4, 2:922.

29. Leon Litwack, *Been in the Storm So Long: The Aftermath of Slavery* (New York: Vintage, 1979), 71.

30. R. S. Davis, Major and Assistant Adjutant-General, General Orders No. 46, Headquarters, Eighteenth Army Corps, Department of Virginia and North Carolina, Fort Monroe, Virginia, December 5, 1863, *OR*, ser. 3, 3:1139, 1141, 1142.

31. "Why Should a Colored Man Enlist?" *Douglass' Monthly*, April 1863.

32. Abraham Lincoln to James C. Conkling, August 26, 1863, *Collected Works*, 6:409.

33. Meunomennie L. Maimi to T. A. Maimi, March 1863, in C. Peter Ripley, Roy E. Finkenbine, Michael F. Hembree, and Donald Yacovone, eds., *Black Abolitionist Papers: The United States, 1858–1865*, 5 vols. (Chapel Hill: University of North Carolina Press, 1992), 5:187–88, 191.

34. Corporal James Henry Gooding to President Abraham Lincoln, September 28, 1863, in Berlin, Fields, Miller, Reidy, and Rowland, *Free at Last*, 462.

35. Gates, *Frederick Douglass*, 784–87.

36. Herbert Aptheker, ed., *A Documentary History of the Negro People in the United States: From Colonial Times through the Civil War* (New York: Citadel, 1951), 1:484n.

37. "Michigan State Convention," *Anglo-African*, March 7, 1863.

38. For a discussion of the New York draft riots, see Iver Bernstein, *The New York Draft Riots: Their Significance for American Society and Politics in the Age of the Civil War* (New York: Oxford University Press, 1990).

39. J. W. C. Pennington, "The Position and Duties of the Colored People," in Philip S. Foner and Robert Branham, eds., *Lift Every Voice: African-American Oratory, 1787–1900* (Tuscaloosa: University of Alabama Press, 1998), 402.

2

UNDER COVER OF LIBERTY

FRANK J. WILLIAMS

*A*s the country entered its third year of war, 1863 began with a blow louder than any cannon fired on the battlefield. President Abraham Lincoln had at last signed the order that would change America. With his January 1, 1863, order, slaves were, at least in theory, emancipated in all areas still under Confederate control.

The Emancipation Proclamation came in the form of a war measure, replete with legal, political, and cultural significance. Months before, in his preliminary emancipation proclamation, Lincoln had made a commitment to emancipating slaves, but in that document, he had not fully developed a legally sound argument to justify his authority to take such a measure. Lincoln had initially believed that he was constitutionally bound, as president, to take no action against the "peculiar institution" of slavery, having written to Horace Greeley, editor of the *New York Tribune*, "If I could save the Union without freeing *any* slave I would do it, and if I could save it by freeing *all* the slaves I would do it; and if I could save it by freeing some and leaving others alone I would also do that. . . . I have here stated my purpose according to my view of *official* duty, and I intend no modification of my oft-expressed *personal* wish that all men every where could be free."[1] Even with this equivocation, a draft Emancipation Proclamation was in the president's desk.

Wishes are one thing, though, and actions another. And, more than anything else, what changed between the first year of the war, when Lincoln was silent on the subject of slavery, and the second, when he issued the Emancipation Proclamation, was the political climate. Lincoln himself later insisted in defense of his position that he did not claim to have controlled events—but, rather, events had controlled him.

Lincoln had reason to defend his position. After all, it was he who in 1861 had issued an order revoking General John Charles Frémont's public proclamation calling for the confiscation of the real and personal property of those who took up arms against the United States.[2] When Senator Orville Hickman Browning wrote to Lincoln to protest his decision, the president replied:

> Genl. Frémont's proclamation, as to confiscation of property, and the liberation of slaves, is *purely political*, and not within the range of *military* law, or necessity. If a commanding General finds a necessity to seize the farm of a private owner, for a pasture, an encampment, or a fortification, he has the right to do so, and to so hold it, as long as the necessity lasts; and this is within military law, because within military necessity. But to say the farm shall no longer belong to the owner, or his heirs forever; and this as well when the farm is not needed for military purposes as when it is, is purely political, without the savor of military law about it. And the same is true of slaves. If the General needs them, he can seize them, and use them; but when the need is past, it is not for him to fix their permanent future condition. That must be settled according to laws made by law-makers, and not be military proclamations. . . . Can it be pretended that it is any longer the government of the U.S.—any government of Constitution and laws,—wherein a General, or a *President*, may make permanent rules of property by proclamation?[3]

Lincoln's response to Senator Browning seemingly would present a problem for his later issuance of the Emancipation Proclamation. One year to the day of his letter to Browning, Lincoln issued the preliminary Emancipation Proclamation, in which he proposed doing precisely what he had stated was not within the range of military law of necessity. But, circumstances had changed, as had necessity.

After the Battle of Antietam, a Union victory—albeit a costly one with total casualties exceeding twenty-six thousand in one horrifying day—Lincoln knew it was time to act. Already expecting heavy criticism from some quarters for leaning toward emancipation, he knew that if the Union army's fortunes took another turn for the worse, he could miss the opportunity to act. With something resembling a victory, he could push ahead. The cries of radical Republicans and governors who wanted an end to slavery had risen to a fever pitch, and sentiment was turning their way.

Five days after the Union's victory at Antietam, Lincoln issued the preliminary Emancipation Proclamation, foreshadowing his January 1, 1863, order:

That on the first day of January in the year of our Lord, one thousand eight hundred and sixty-three, all persons held as slaves within any state, or designated part of a state, the people whereof shall then be in rebellion against the United States shall be then, thenceforward, and forever free; and the executive government of the United States, including the military and naval authority thereof, will recognize and maintain the freedom of such persons, and will do no act or acts to repress such persons, or any of them, in any efforts they may make for their actual freedom.[4]

When his intentions between September 1862 and January 1863 did not change, he was able to develop more fully his position, even given the fact that nothing in the Constitution gave Congress or the president the authority to confiscate property without compensation. By January 1, 1863, Lincoln had determined that, as commander in chief, his action could be justified as a war measure that would weaken the enemy. His basic legal argument was: Under law, slaves were considered to be property. (The valuation of each slave was written next to his name in the books of tax assessors.) Confiscation of such property would inevitably aid in quelling the rebellion. Necessity now warranted the use of the war powers to weaken the enemy. One historian complains that the Emancipation Proclamation had all "the moral grandeur of a bill of lading,"[5] but the president, with his legal background, wanted his reasoning to be well documented. While the Proclamation was crafted as a military order, it had, in addition, all the attributes of a legal and political statement.

I, Abraham Lincoln, President of the United States, by virtue of the power in me vested as Commander-in-Chief, of the Army and Navy of the United States in time of actual armed rebellion against authority and government of the United States, and as a fit and necessary war measure for suppressing said rebellion do, on this first day of January, in the year of our Lord one thousand eight hundred and sixty three, and in accordance with my purpose so to do publicly proclaimed for the full period of one hundred days, from the day first above mentioned, . . . order and declare that all persons held as slaves within said designated States, and parts of States, are, and henceforward shall be free; and that the Executive government of the United States, including the military and naval authorities thereof, will recognize and maintain the freedom of said persons.[6]

The president bolstered his argument that necessity warranted emancipation by directing that those slaves freed by the proclamation would "be received into the armed service of the United States to garrison forts, positions, and other places." Lincoln both strengthened his "necessity argument" and provided for additional manpower from this new source: the "great available and as yet unavailed of, force for restoring the Union."[7] In the end, nearly two hundred thousand African Americans served the Union.

There was little precedent for use of the war powers to take such extraordinary actions in the name of military necessity.[8] Therefore, Lincoln endorsed the concept of a constitutional amendment that would protect his actions should they be challenged. The resulting Thirteenth Amendment provided legal support for freedom.

The Emancipation Proclamation, as its title suggests, was a presidential proclamation, an "instrument that states a condition, declares a law and requires obedience, recognizes an event or triggers the implementation of a law (by recognizing that the circumstances in law have been realized)."[9] In this sense, it is a policy statement that does not carry the force of law unless acted upon by Congress. Apart from the Declaration of Independence, the Emancipation Proclamation may be the single most significant statement of policy issued by a governing authority in the history of the United States. It marks the end of governmental support for slavery, reversing a national pattern that considered the institution to be a domestic policy of the individual states, the operation of which existed outside the scope of federal power. It gave legal standing to the freedom already claimed by African Americans who were throwing off the shackles of bondage and moving to Union lines. And it shifted the moral tenor of the Civil War.

As the *New York Times* reported on the third day of the year:

> [Lincoln's proclamation] marks an era in the history, not only of this war, but of this country and the world. It is not necessary to assume that it will set free instantly the enslaved black of the South, in order to ascribe to it the greatest and most permanent importance. Whatever may be its immediate results, it changes entirely the relations of the National Government to the institution of Slavery. Hitherto Slavery has been under the protection of the Government; henceforth it is under its ban. The power of the Army and Navy, hitherto employed in hunting and returning to bondage the fugitive from service, are to be employed in maintaining his freedom whenever and wherever he may choose to assert it. This change of attitude is itself a revolution.[10]

Although crafted as a war measure in lawyer-like legalese so that it would survive challenges in court, the true meaning and purpose of the Emancipation Proclamation—the end of American slavery—was not hidden. The *New York Times* fully understood Lincoln's order and, in particular, his explanation of the authority upon which he based his order.

President Lincoln takes care, by great precision in his language, to define the basis on which this action rests. He issues the Proclamation as a "fit and necessary war measure for suppressing the rebellion." While he sincerely believes it to be an "act of justice warranted by the Constitution," he issues it "upon military necessity." In our judgment it is only upon that ground and for that purpose that he has any right to issue it at all. In his civil capacity as President, he has not the faintest shadow of authority to decree the emancipation of a single slave, either as an "act of justice" or for any other purpose whatever. As Commander-in-Chief of the army he has undoubtedly the right to deprive rebels of the aid of their slaves—just as he has the right to take their horses, and to arrest all persons who may be giving them aid and comfort,—as a "war measure" and upon grounds of military necessity.[11]

In the weeks that followed, the president stood by his position: "After the commencement of hostilities I struggled nearly a year and a half to get along without touching the 'institution'; and when finally I conditionally determined to touch it, I gave a hundred days fair notice of my purpose, to all the States and people, within which time they could have turned it wholly aside, by simply again becoming good citizens of the United States. They chose to disregard it, and I made the peremptory proclamation on what appeared to me to be a military necessity. And being made, it must stand."[12]

In a letter to James C. Conkling later that year, Lincoln further explained his argument: "You dislike the emancipation proclamation; and, perhaps, would have it retracted. You say it is unconstitutional—I think differently. I think the constitution invests its commander-in-chief with the law of war, in time of war. The most that can be said, if so much, is, that slaves are property. Is there—has there ever been—any question that by the law of war, property, both of enemies and friends, may be taken when needed? And is it not needed whenever taking it, helps us, or hurts the enemy? Armies, the world over, destroy enemies' property when they can not use it; and even destroy their own to keep it from the enemy."[13]

Even when pressed to expand the reach of the Emancipation Proclamation, Lincoln recognized that to do so would jeopardize the strength of his argument that the war powers authorized its issuance. In a letter to Salmon P. Chase, he said:

Knowing your great anxiety that the emancipation proclamation shall now be applied to certain parts of Virginia and Louisiana which were exempted from it last January, I state briefly what appear to me to be difficulties in the way of such a step. The original proclamation has no constitutional or legal justification, except as a military measure. The exemptions were made because the military necessity did not apply to the exempted localities. Nor does that necessity apply to them now any more than it did then. If I take the step must I not do so, without the argument of military necessity, and so, without any argument, except the one I think the measure politically expedient, and morally right? Would I not thus give up all footing upon constitution or law?[14]

Lincoln's journey as emancipator was not complete with the issuance of the proclamation; however, it was with this proclamation that the Great Emancipator truly made his name.

The year 1863 brought formidable constitutional controversies, which presented themselves in the midst of a bloody, tumultuous war. Like the president's issuance of the Emancipation Proclamation, measures taken later that year, which were said to impinge on the constitutional rights of some, were similarly justified as necessary wartime authority. Certain unalienable rights ("life, liberty, and the pursuit of happiness" in the Declaration of Independence) and later the constitutional right, including the right to freedom of speech and habeas corpus, were circumscribed for the sake of national security. While this was not popular or well accepted, it can be argued that the end of the war two years later is proof that such actions were necessary and, at least in part, played a role in ensuring both the nation's enjoyment of continued survival and its citizens' enjoyment of great liberties.

On March 16, 1863, Lincoln appointed Major General Ambrose Everett Burnside commanding general of the Department of the Ohio. (Burnside, a West Point graduate, who led the 1st Rhode Island Regiment—one of the first militia units to reach Washington in answer to President Lincoln's call for seventy-five thousand volunteers—had won early wartime glory with a successful expedition on the North Carolina coast. He served less successfully under George Brinton McClellan at Antietam. When Lincoln relieved McClellan on November 10, 1862, Burnside all but inherited command of the Army of the Potomac, a job for which he was temperamentally unsuited and, to his credit, reluctant to assume.) He took command of the Department of the Ohio at headquarters in Cincinnati, where wholesale criticism of the war was rampant. Agitated by such anti-administration speeches, General Burnside responded on April 13 by issuing General Order No. 38, authorizing imposition of the death penalty for those who aided the Confederacy and who declared "sympathies for the enemy." Burnside's order warned, "[T]he habit of declaring sympathies for the enemy will not be allowed in this Department. Persons committing such offenses will be at once arrested. . . . [T]reason, express or implied, will not be tolerated by this Department."[15]

Among those who particularly irked Burnside was former Ohio Demo-cratic Congressman and lawyer Clement Laird Vallandigham, the best known antiwar Copperhead[16] of the Civil War and perhaps Lincoln's sharpest critic.[17] Active in politics throughout most of his life, Vallandigham was elected to the House of Representatives from Ohio in 1856, 1858, and 1860. Burnside knew him well from several speeches Vallandigham had given while in Congress that had gained considerable publicity. Val-landigham charged Lincoln with the "wicked and hazardous experiment" of calling the people to arms without counsel and authority of Congress, with violating the Constitution by declaring a blockade of Southern ports, with "contemptuously" defying the Constitution by suspending the writ of habeas corpus, and with "cooly" coming before the Congress and plead-ing that he was only "preserving and protecting" the Constitution and demanding and expecting the thanks of Congress and the country for his "usurpations of power."[18]

Learning that Vallandigham was to speak again at a Democratic mass meeting in Mount Vernon, Ohio, Burnside dispatched two captains in civilian clothes to listen to the speech. As anticipated, Vallandigham lam-basted President Lincoln, referring to him as a political tyrant and calling for his overthrow.

Vallandigham proclaimed, among other things, that "the present war was a wicked, cruel, and unnecessary war, one not waged for the preserva-tion of the Union, but for the purpose of crushing out liberty and to erect a despotism; a war for the freedom of the blacks and the enslavement of the whites."[19] He argued that "if the administration had so wished, the war could have been honorably terminated months ago."[20] He also took an aim at General Order No. 38—the order that would provide the basis for his arrest—characterizing it as "a base usurpation of arbitrary author-ity" and inviting others to resist it: "[T]he sooner the people inform the minions of usurped power that they will not submit to such restrictions upon their liberties, the better."[21]

With General Order No. 38 as justification and at Burnside's direction, 150 Union soldiers arrived at the Copperhead's home in Dayton at 2:40 A.M. on May 5, 1963.[22] When Vallandigham refused to let the soldiers enter, they broke down his front door and forced their way inside.[23] They arrested him and escorted him to Kemper Barracks, a military prison in Cincinnati.[24]

Although he was a U.S. citizen, who would ordinarily be tried for criminal offenses in the civilian court system, Vallandigham was brought before a military tribunal a day after his arrest, where he was charged with "declaring disloyal sentiments and opinions, with the object and purpose of weakening the power of the Government in its efforts to suppress an unlawful rebellion."[25] Vallandigham, an attorney, represented himself before the military officers who presided over his case and protested that the commission had no authority to try him. While having been arrested for charging the president with violating the Constitution, Vallandigham invoked the provisions of the same document in hopes that it would afford him the right of a trial before a civilian court. Speaking on his own behalf, he argued:

> I am not in either "the land or naval forces of the United States, nor in the militia in the actual service of the United States," and therefore am not triable for any cause, by any such Court, but am subject, by the express terms of the Constitution, to arrest only by due process of law, judicial warrant, regularly issued upon affidavit, and by some officer or Court of competent jurisdiction for the trial of citizens, and am now entitled to be tried on an indictment and presentment of a Grand Jury of such Court, to speedy and public trial by an impartial jury of the State of Ohio, to be confronted with witnesses against me, to have compulsory process for witnesses in my behalf, the assistance of counsel for my defense, and evidence and argument according to the common laws and the ways of Judicial Courts.
>
> And all these I demand as my right as a citizen of the United States, and under the Constitution of the United States.[26]

Vallandigham's protestations fell on deaf ears, and the case before the tribunal proceeded. Vallandigham refused to enter a plea, and the tribunal found him guilty of violating General Order No. 38 and sentenced him to imprisonment "in close confinement in some fortress of the United States" for the duration of the war.[27]

After the trial, Democratic lawyer George Pugh, a former senator from Ohio, came to Vallandigham's aid, applying to the United States circuit court sitting at Cincinnati, for a writ of habeas corpus—a procedural method by which anyone accused of a crime has the right to hear and respond to the charges in a court of law. Pugh argued on Vallandigham's behalf that Vallandigham was not and could not be subject to military law because he was not a member of the armed forces. "This case before us . . . is the case of a citizen exempted from military arrest and jurisdiction, but who has, nevertheless, been arbitrarily and violently subjected to them. Can this be . . . according to the Constitution of the United States?" Pugh asked. Pugh further argued that Vallandigham's constitutional rights had been violated because Burnside was without the authority to make any law abridging freedom of speech or the press.[28]

In a patriotic opposition to Vallandigham's writ, Burnside argued concisely and logically:

If I were to indulge in wholesale criticisms of the policy of the Government, it would demoralize the army under my command, and every friend of his country would call me a traitor. If the officers or soldiers were to indulge in such criticisms, it would weaken the army to the extent of their influence; and if this criticism were universal in the army, it would cause it to be broken to pieces, the Government to be divided, our homes to be invaded, and anarchy to reign. My duty to my Government forbids me to indulge in such criticisms; officers and soldiers are not allowed so to indulge, and this course will be sustained by all honest men.[29]

Taking his hypothetical one step further, Burnside explained that in wartime the need to prevent such criticism is more pressing: "[I]t is my duty to my country . . . and the duty of the troops [of this army] to avoid saying any thing that would weaken the army . . . it is equally the duty of every citizen in the Department to avoid the same evil. Why should such speeches from our own public men be allowed?"[30] Burnside's argument was reminiscent of Lincoln's justification of the suspension of the writ of habeas corpus two years before. (President Lincoln first authorized the suspension of the writ by executive order along the rail lines between Washington and Philadelphia after the attack on Fort Sumter in April 1861. His actions were later ratified—and extended—by Congress, effectively widening martial law nationwide during the rebellion. Lincoln argued that suspension was a wartime necessity, authorized by the Constitution in times of civil war.) As Lincoln rhetorically asked in his speech to a special session of Congress, "Are all the laws, but one, to go unexecuted, and the government itself go to pieces, lest that one be violated?"[31]

Burnside's opposition was not dismissive of the Constitution and the freedoms it affords but recognized there is a demarcation of appropriateness that should not be crossed during wartime: "If the people do not approve of [the Administration's] policy . . . [l]et them freely discuss the policy in a proper tone; but my duty requires me to stop license and intemperate discussion, which tends to weaken the authority of the Government and army."[32]

Vallandigham's writ was denied.[33] In denying the writ, Judge H. H. Leavitt relied on a prior decision of the court that held that a writ should not be issued if the applicant has been detained or imprisoned under military authority.[34] Vallandigham later sought a writ of certiorari (which seeks an order from a higher court directing a lower court to send it the case record so the case may be reviewed) from the U.S. Supreme Court, which was likewise denied, the court ruling that it was without jurisdiction to review the military tribunal's proceedings.[35] In denying Vallandigham's petition, the Supreme Court stated, "Whatever may be the force of Vallandigham's protest, that he was not triable by a court of military commission, it is certain that his petition cannot be brought [under the Judiciary Act of 1789, which established the authority of the federal courts]; and further, that the court cannot, without disregarding its frequent decisions and interpretation of the Constitution in respect to its judicial power, originate a writ of certiorari to review or pronounce any opinion upon the proceedings of a military commission."[36]

The arrest, military trial, conviction, and sentence of Vallandigham aroused excitement throughout the country. The "wiley agitator," as Lincoln later obliquely described the Ohioan, found many supporters for his views in New York and, particularly, in heavily Democratic Albany.[37]

Sentiment in Albany held that Vallandigham's arrest was arbitrary and constituted an effort to exert military censorship of public discourse. Many New Yorkers felt that Vallandigham's arrest was a very real possibility for them, too. The Albany *Atlas & Argus*, an anti-administration, Democratic paper, reported that the arrest was an experiment conducted by the Lincoln administration to test how much the public would tolerate and reported the fears of those in New York: "[T]he blow that falls upon a citizen of Ohio to-day, may be directed at a Democrat of New York to-morrow. . . . The blow, therefore, is a threat at every Democrat." Four days later, the paper drove home this sentiment: "[T]he State of New York, and every citizen of the State, is equally threatened[.] We must make common cause with the citizens of other States, or we, too, are lost."[38]

Then the Democratic New Yorkers, incensed by Vallandigham's arrest, organized what the *Atlas & Argus* newspaper described as "[o]ne of the largest and most respectable meetings ever held at the Capitol," to protest against the case, which they believed was a "crime against the Constitution."[39] New Yorkers arrived at the Capitol in droves, and by 8 P.M., the broad walk leading to the Capitol steps and the adjacent grounds were packed with citizens.[40]

Although unable to attend the public meeting, Horatio Seymour, New York's Democratic governor, forwarded a letter that was read aloud to the spirited crowd of three thousand that filled the Capitol park.[41] Like many New Yorkers, Seymour was outraged at what he believed was a depredation of civil liberties: "The transaction involved a series of offences against our most sacred rights. It interfered with the freedom of speech; it violated our rights to be secure in our homes against unreasonable searches and seizures; it pronounced sentence without a trial, save one which was a mockery, which insulted as well as wrong. The perpetrators now seek to impose punishment, not for an offence against the law but for a disregard of an invalid order, put forth in an utter disregard of principles of civil liberty."[42]

At the rally, fiery speeches criticized Burnside for his action against Vallandigham. Among those who spoke were Judge Amasa J. Parker and U.S. Congressman Francis Kernan. Orator after orator expressed outrage against the allegedly arbitrary action of the administration. However, not everyone in attendance criticized the Lincoln administration's actions. Several soldiers who had just returned from the battlefield displayed great dissatisfaction with the meeting's purpose, breaking chairs into pieces and hurling them into the crowd. The *New York Times* reported that at one point during the disruption, it appeared as though the soldiers might seize control over the meeting. Their efforts were eventually thwarted, however, and the meeting returned to order.[43]

Ultimately, the attendees adopted a series of resolutions and ordered that a copy of the resolutions be transmitted to the president "with the assurance of this meeting of their hearty and earnest desire to support the Government in every Constitutional and lawful measure to suppress the existing Rebellion."[44]

The resolutions drove home the point that those who attended the meeting regarded Vallandigham's arrest and imprisonment as illegal and unconstitutional. In the Albany Democrats' opinion, "[the] assumption of power by a military tribunal, if successfully asserted, not only abrogates the right of the people to assemble and discuss the affairs of Government, the liberty of speech and of the press, the right of trial by jury, the law of evidence, and the privileges of *Habeas Corpus*, but it strikes a fatal blow at the supremacy of law, and the authority of the State and Federal Constitutions."[45]

On May 19, 1863, only days after this extraordinary public meeting, Erastus Corning, Albany's former Democratic mayor, who had been elected as president of the assemblage upon Henry S. Crandall's nomination, addressed the resolutions to Republican President Lincoln. Corning also enclosed a brief note signed by himself, as president of the assemblage, and by its vice presidents and secretaries.

In the days and weeks that followed the Albany meeting, similar meetings were held throughout the state of New York in protest of what organizers insisted was the administration's infringement upon the "most sacred rights of American freemen." Mass meetings occurred in Utica, Troy, and Waterloo, while in Brooklyn a subcommittee of the Democratic General Committee was appointed to "consider the subject of the recent arbitrary arrests by the Government, and draft resolutions expressive of the sense of the Union Democratic General Committee."[46]

These meetings were challenged, however, by those loyal to the Union and the Republican administration. In Albany, hundreds assembled on May 20, 1863, "to give expression to their patriotic loyalty, and to vindicate the

Capital of the State of New York from the imputation of indifference to the results of the war and to the integrity of the Nation." The *Albany Evening Journal* described the assemblage of the Albany Democrats as "a meeting to justify a bad man, and to denounce those who sought to punish him." The pro-administration paper continued, "The meeting was, and will be, recognized as a meeting to approve what a man, who is at heart a traitor, has said and done, rather than what its responsible managers will wish it to be deemed, viz.: a meeting to maintain the supremacy of the civil law."[47]

While protest meetings continued in Albany and in other cities, Lincoln himself dwelled upon the actions that had been taken against Vallandigham. On May 29, 1863, he telegraphed Burnside in code: "All the cabinet regretted the necessity of arresting, for instance, Vallandigham, some perhaps, doubting, that there was a real necessity for it—but, being done, all were for seeing you through with it."[48]

Committed to supporting Burnside's actions, Lincoln himself replied to the Albany Democrats, and he did so with an extremely long, closely reasoned document, constructed in lawyer-like fashion and sprawling over twenty pages of handwritten sheets. Lincoln justified the action of the administration in the arrest, trial, imprisonment, and banishment of Vallandigham and elaborated on his view that certain proceedings are constitutional "when in cases of rebellion or invasion, the public Safety requires them, which would not be constitutional when, in [the] absence of rebellion or invasion, the public Safety does not require them." More extraordinarily, Lincoln made sure copies of the letter went not only to Corning but to friendly newspapers like the *New York Tribune*. As early as June 5, Lincoln had read the letter to his cabinet, prompting Secretary of the Navy Gideon Welles to write in his diary that it "has vigor and ability and with some corrections will be a strong paper."[49] Mid-nineteenth-century presidents did not often deliver speeches, and Lincoln, a great communicator stifled by this tradition, found a new way to reach the public through the medium of the so-called public letter: a piece of ostensibly private correspondence that he released to the press so it could be widely published and broadly read.

In Lincoln's opinion, the framers of the Constitution were wise to include such a provision allowing for the suspension of the writ of habeas corpus "when in cases of Rebellion or Invasion, the public Safety may require it," as such a suspension was necessary to prevent "sudden and extensive uprisings against the government." Lincoln explained to the Albany Democrats that Vallandigham's arrest was not, as they mistakenly believed, premised on his criticism of the administration. Democrats in Albany had charged the Lincoln administration with arresting Vallandigham in an effort to silence him. The *Atlas & Argus* opined on May 12, 1863, "The arrest is a threat against every public man who refuses to advocate the extreme measures of the Abolition Cabinet." Lincoln sought to assure those who harbored such mistaken beliefs that they were incorrect. He explained that Vallandigham was arrested for his avowed hostility to the Union's war efforts, his laboring to prevent the raising of troops, and his encouragement of desertions from the army.[50]

Vallandigham's actions, aimed at damaging the army and leaving the Union without an adequate military force to suppress the rebellion, were intolerable to the administration and antithetical to the Union's attempt to preserve the nation. Lincoln contended that experience proved that armies cannot be maintained unless those who desert are punished by death. He believed that Vallandigham's efforts to encourage soldiers to desert the army were equally detrimental to the nation and should likewise be punished by death. With this came the most remembered passage of Lincoln's reply: "Must I shoot a simple-minded soldier boy who deserts, while I must not touch a hair of a wiley agitator who induces him to desert? . . . I think that in such a case, to silence the agitator, and save the boy, is not only constitutional, but, withal, a great mercy."[51]

Lincoln emphasized his belief that it was absolutely necessary to try insurrectionists, such as Vallandigham, before a military tribunal. In Lincoln's opinion, the civilian court system was woefully inadequate to handle such matters. He told Corning that "a jury too frequently have at least one member, more ready to hang the panel than to hang the traitor." Lincoln recognized that the civilian court system is properly suited for trying individuals of crimes that are well defined in the law but is ill suited for trying those charged with insurrection. Lincoln drove home the point, "[H]e who dissuades one man from volunteering, or induces one soldier to desert, weakens the Union cause as much as he who kills a union soldier in battle. Yet this dissuasion, or inducement, may be so conducted as to be no defined crime of which any civil court would take cognizance."[52]

On July 3, 1863, Corning replied to the president. Showing no signs of backing down, the committee charged Lincoln with "pretensions to more than regal authority" and insisted that he had used "misty and cloudy forms of expression" in setting forth his pretensions. It also took issue with Lincoln's description of the group as Democrats, despite that the assemblage used this self-description in its own resolutions. They now believed that the president should have described them as American citizens. To this, Lincoln, the "wiley" politician and astute lawyer in the White House, only peremptorily responded, offering only to further engage in the discussions if they made certain representations of support for the war.

Meanwhile, concerned about the harshness of Vallandigham's punishment and the potential criticism over Vallandigham's arrest, detention, and trial by military tribunal, President Lincoln commuted his sentence to banishment to the Confederacy.[53] Vallandigham managed to make his way to Wilmington, North Carolina, where he boarded a blockade runner and eventually arrived in Canada. Perhaps out of spite for the Lincoln administration, the Democratic Party of Ohio nominated Vallandigham for governor on June 11, apparently failing to recognize the difficulties Vallandigham would have campaigning from Canada. Vallandigham lost the November election.

Lincoln's perceptiveness in recognizing the need to try insurrectionists before a military tribunal, rather than the civilian court system—as argued in his letter to Corning—would help the Union win the Civil War. John Yoo, former legal counsel with the U.S. Department of Justice, has stated that without the ability to suspend the writ of habeas corpus, "the Union could not have fought the Civil War, because the courts would have ordered Abraham Lincoln to release thousands of Confederate POWs and spies."[54] Likewise, as Lincoln recognized, without the power to punish those who deserted the army or those who encouraged others to desert, the Union would have been unable to maintain its force in numbers, certainly inhibiting its success. Lincoln explained that the civil court system was wholly unable to prevent or punish such desertion. Recognizing this, Lincoln stepped outside the constitutional waters, taking measures that some would argue are extraconstitutional, for the sake of national security. Lincoln's recognition, much like Justice Robert H. Jackson's years later in his dissenting opinion in *Terminello v. Chicago, 337 U.S. 1* (1949), was that the Constitution ought not be a "suicide pact." Others similarly attribute the Union's success to Lincoln's suspension of the writ of habeas corpus and his willingness to try those detained before a military tribunal but for an altogether different reason. Historian Phillip Shaw Paludan surmises, "Lincoln kept the constitutional debate going throughout the war and thus propagandized to persuade the people that their constitutional system was adequate to survive and prosecute a war."[55]

Indeed, while issues concerning civil liberties of civilians were at the forefront of the minds of those in Albany, New York, similar issues surfaced that year on a different front.

As the Civil War progressed, a sideshow of guerilla-style hit-and-run attacks had begun to develop, especially during Major General Henry Wager Halleck's command of the Department of Missouri. Halleck had previously explained the predicament in Missouri: "The rebel authorities claim the right to send men, in the garb of peaceful citizens, to waylay and attack our troops, to burn bridges and houses, and to destroy property and persons within our lines. They demand that such persons be treated as ordinary belligerents, and that when captured, they have extended to them the same rights as other prisoners of war; they also threaten that if such persons be punished as marauders and spies, they will retaliate by executing our prisoners of war in their possession."[56] Faced with this dilemma, Halleck turned to Dr. Francis Lieber, a political philosopher and a political science professor who had immersed himself in the study of early-nineteenth-century warfare, to craft instructions on how soldiers should conduct themselves in wartime and to advise whether guerillas should be treated as ordinary belligerents and be given the same rights as prisoners of war.

After having first drafted a pamphlet titled "Guerrilla Parties Considered with Reference to the Laws and Usages of War," Lieber set out to draft a more complete set of "rules and definitions" to be used in the field as a guide to the laws and usages of war. Lieber completed his draft in February 1863, setting the stage for "Instructions for the Government of Armies of the United States in the Field," which was released as Army General Orders No. 100 and is now commonly referred to as the Lieber Code. On April 24, 1863, President Lincoln approved what Lieber had written and directed that it be published. The Lieber Code is the first comprehensive list of instructions on the laws of war. The instructions include 10 sections and 157 articles.[57] The sections ranged from martial law to property of the enemy and insurrection. The code was intended to be malleable enough so that wars could be won but also included more rigid standards designed to reflect basic human dignity.

> One legal historian has described the final product as follows: The Lieber Code may be said, without undue exaggeration, to be something of a legal masterpiece—a sort of pocket version of Blackstone's famous *Commentaries on the Laws of England*, though confined to the particular subject of the laws of land warfare. It is not simply a list of rules, as might be implied by the label "code." It was, in addition, a miniature commentary on those rules, explaining, if only in the briefest terms, the basic principles underlying the specific commands and prohibitions. As such, it made a lasting contribution to the development of the subject.[58]

The Lieber Code ultimately established the basis for later international conventions on the laws of war at Brussels in 1874 and at The Hague in 1899 and 1907.[59]

The Lieber Code defined "partisans" as "soldiers armed and wearing the uniform of their army, but belonging to a corps which acts detached from the main body for the purpose of making inroads into the territory occupied by the enemy." It followed Lieber's earlier writings by declaring that partisans were entitled to be treated as prisoners of war upon capture. On the other hand, unlawful guerrillas are described as "[m]en, or squads of men, who commit hostilities, whether by fighting, or inroads for destruction or plunder, or by raids of any kind, without commission [from any government], without being part and portion of the organized hostile army, and without sharing continuously in the war, but who do so with intermitting returns to their homes and avocations, or with the occasional assumption of the semblance of peaceful pursuits, divesting themselves of the character or appearance of soldiers." Such men "if captured, are not entitled to the privileges of prisoners of war, but shall be treated summarily as highway robbers or pirates."[60] Thus, under the Lieber Code, regular, uniformed army units who fight behind enemy lines are lawful belligerents, while nonmilitary persons who take up arms without authority and claim the protection due civilians while they are not fighting are unlawful guerrillas.

Perhaps most important, the code authorized the suspension of civil and criminal courts during wartime: "Martial law in a hostile country consists in the suspension by the occupying military authority of the criminal and civil law . . . and in the substitution of military rule and force for the same, as well as in the dictation of general laws, as far as military necessity requires this suspension, substitution, or dictation."[61]

Lieber set forth additional justification for the use of military commissions throughout the code, further recognizing, "Whenever feasible, martial law is carried out in cases of individual offenders by military courts. . . . Military offenses . . . [that are not governed by statute] must be tried and punished under the common law of war . . . by military commissions."[62]

In the words of one commentator, "[t]he Lieber Code, when viewed as a whole, sets forth a broad basis for trial by military commission. . . . By setting forth a much fuller description of the laws of war than had previously existed, the Lieber Code can be viewed as an important criminal directive, providing individual judge advocates guidance over the types of offenses that could be charged as violations of the laws of war." Importantly, "[t]he Code left many of the details of which offenses were triable by commission up to the individual department commanders, judge advocates, and the War Department, while still providing general guidance. The broad definition of the common law of war in the Code allowed the commissions to become a tool that could be molded to the particular needs of each department, rather than being closely defined in a limiting sort of way."[63]

In the wake of the Lieber Code, military commissions designed to try civilians sprang up across the United States. Indeed, within a month of the president's authorization of the Lieber Code, Vallandigham was imprisoned and stood trial.

Although the U.S. Supreme Court declined to review Vallandigham's imprisonment, it recognized the validity of Vallandigham's trial by military commission consistent with the Lieber Code: "General Burnside acted in the matter as the general commanding the Ohio Department, in conformity with the instructions for the government of the armies of the United States, approved by the President of the United States, and published by the Assistant Adjutant-General, by order of the Secretary of War, on the 24th of April, 1863." The code recognizes two types of military jurisdiction. The first type is that which is conferred by statute, and the second type consists of that which was recognized under the common law of war. The former must be tried in the manner directed by statute—by courts-martial; the latter must be tried and punished under the common law of war—by military commissions. The Supreme Court further recognized, "These jurisdictions are applicable, not only to war with foreign nations, but to a rebellion, when a part of a country wages war against its legitimate government, seeking to throw off all allegiance to it, to set up a government of its own."[64] Although the Supreme Court did not consider the merits of Vallandigham's case, the logical conclusion to be drawn from this recognition is that Vallandigham's trial by military commission was in its view lawful.

Although debates over these constitutional issues originated on different war fronts, the Lieber Code's recognition of the legality of military commissions had implications for the so-called wiley agitator, whose criticisms of the Lincoln administration risked "weaken[ing] the army."[65] The year 1863 may have been marked by what some would characterize as curtailments of certain inalienable rights, but such curtailments were constitutional, as Lincoln wrote in his letter to Corning, "when in cases of rebellion or invasion, the public Safety requires them."[66] As a result of this great debate and, in particular, the one Lincoln had with Corning, the sixteenth president in his wisdom in 1863 provided every future wartime president with an invaluable tool: a brilliantly crafted, highly accessible, tightly reasoned legal argument justifying the trial of insurrectionists or other enemy combatants.

Notes

1. Lincoln to Horace Greeley, August 22, 1862, in Roy P. Basler, ed., *The Collected Works of Abraham Lincoln*, 9 vols. (New Brunswick, NJ: Rutgers University Press, 1953–55), 5:388–89. Hereafter cited as *Collected Works*.

2. Burrus M. Carnahan, *Act of Justice: Lincoln's Emancipation Proclamation and the Law of War* (Lexington: University Press of Kentucky, 2007), 72–73.

3. Lincoln to Orville H. Browning, September 22, 1861, *Collected Works*, 4:531; emphasis added on *President*.

4. Emancipation Proclamation, September 22, 1862, *Collected Works*, 5:434.

5. Allen Guelzo, *Lincoln's Emancipation Proclamation: The End of Slavery in America* (New York: Simon and Schuster, 2004), 2.

6. Emancipation Proclamation, January 1, 1863, *Collected Works*, 6:29–30.

7. Preliminary Emancipation Proclamation, September 22, 1862, *Collected Works*, 5:433; Lincoln to Andrew Johnson, March 26, 1863, *Collected Works*, 6:149.

8. Carnahan, *Act of Justice*, 79.

9. Phillip J. Cooper, *By Order of the President: The Use and Abuse of Executive Direct Action* (Lawrence: University Press of Kansas, 2002), 116.

10. "The President's Proclamation," *New York Times*, January 3, 1863.

11. Ibid.

12. Lincoln to John A. McClernand, January 8, 1863, *Collected Works*, 6:48–49.

13. Lincoln to James C. Conkling, August 26, 1863, *Collected Works*, 6:408.

14. Lincoln to Salmon P. Chase, September 2, 1863, *Collected Works*, 6:428–29.

15. General Order No. 37 and General Order No. 38, in Benjamin Perley Poore, *The Life and Public Services of Ambrose E. Burnside, Solider-Citizen-Statesman* (Providence: Reid, 1882), 204, 206.

16. David S. Heidler and Jeanne T. Heidler, eds., *Encyclopedia of the American Civil War: A Political, Social, and Military History* (New York: Norton, 2000), 498–99. The term "Copperhead" is "borrowed from the poisonous snake of the same name that lies in hiding and strikes without warning. However, Copperheads regarded themselves as lovers of liberty, and some of them wore a lapel pin with the head of the Goddess of Liberty cut out of the large copper penny minted by the federal treasury." Frank J. Williams, "Abraham Lincoln and Civil Liberties in Wartime," Lectures, *Heritage Foundation*, 5n18, May 5, 2004, http://www.heritage.org/research/lecture /abraham-lincoln-and-civil-liberties-in-wartime, accessed July 7, 2012, pdf.

17. Poore, *Ambrose E. Burnside*, 208–9.

18. Cong. Globe, 37th Cong., 1st Sess. 57–59 (1861). See generally Frank L. Klement, *The Limits of Dissent: Clement L. Vallandigham and the Civil War*, North's Civil War Series, 8 (New York: Fordham University Press, 1998).

19. *Ex parte Vallandigham*, 68 U.S. 243, 244 (1864); *The Trial of Hon. Clement L. Vallandigham by a Military Commission and the Proceedings under His Application for a Writ of Habeas Corpus in the Circuit Court of the United States for the Southern District of Ohio* (Cincinnati: Rickey and Carroll, 1863), 32.

20. *Trial of Hon. Clement L. Vallandigham*, 32.

21. Ibid.

22. Michael Kent Curtis, *Lincoln, Vallandigham, and Anti-War Speech in the Civil War*, 7 Wm. and Mary Bill of Rts. J. 105, 107, 122 (1998). See also "Vallandigham Arrested," *Atlas & Argus*, May 6, 1863.

23. Ibid., 107.

24. Poore, *Ambrose E. Burnside*, 208; William H. Rehnquist, *All the Laws but One* (New York: Vintage, 1998), 65–66.

25. *Ex parte Vallandigham*, 68 U.S. at 244; see also Curtis, *Lincoln*, 105, 121; *Trial of Hon. Clement L. Vallandigham*, 31.

26. *Trial of Hon. Clement L. Vallandigham*, 29–30.

27. Ibid, 33.

28. Ibid., 52, 55.

29. Ibid., 41.

30. Ibid.

31. Message to Congress in Special Session, July 4, 1861, *Collected Works*, 4:430.

32. *Trial of Hon. Clement L. Vallandigham*, 42.

33. Ibid., 37–39.

34. Ibid., 262.

35. *Vallandigham*, 68 U.S. 251.

36. Ibid., 252.

37. "Lincoln to Erastus Corning and Others," June 12, 1863, *Collected Works*, 6:266.

38. "Revival of Arbitrary Arrests," *Albany (NY) Atlas & Argus*, May 12, 1863; "The Vallandigham Outrage: Meeting at the Capitol in Behalf of Personal Freedom," May 16, 1863.

39. "The Vallandigham Outrage: Immense Meeting at the Capitol," *Albany (NY) Atlas & Argus*, May 18, 1863.

40. Ibid.; *New York Times*, May 19, 1863.

41. *New York Times*, May 19, 1863.

42. *Albany (NY) Atlas & Argus*, May 18, 1863.

43. *New York Times*, May 17, 1863.

44. *Albany (NY) Atlas & Argus*, May 18, 1863.

45. Ibid.

46. Ibid., May 26, 1863.

47. *Albany (NY) Evening Journal*, May 19, 1863, May 21, 1863, and May 18, 1863.

48. Lincoln to Ambrose E. Burnside, May 29, 1863, *Collected Works*, 6:236.

49. "Lincoln to Erastus Corning and Others," June 12, 1863, *Collected Works*, 2:260, 267, 262. The portions from Lincoln's letter to Erastus Corning are reprinted in the *Collected Works* as the letter appeared in the *New York Tribune* on July 15, 1863. This version incorporates revisions that Lincoln made in the copy prepared for the press as well as the final copy sent to Corning. The original letter has not been located.

50. Ibid., 2:265, 266, 266.

51. Ibid., 2:266–67.

52. Ibid., 2:264.

53. Curtis, *Lincoln*, 109.

54. John Yoo, *War by Other Means: An Insider's Account of the War on Terror* (New York: Atlantic Monthly Press, 2006), 146.

55. Phillip Shaw Paludan, "'The Better Angels of Our Nature': Lincoln, Propaganda, and Public Opinion in the North during the Civil War," in *On the Road to Total War: The American Civil War and the German Wars of Unification, 1861–1871*, ed. Stig Forester and Jorg Nagler (Cambridge, MA: German Historical Institute, 1997), 357–76.

56. James G. Garner, General Order 100 Revisited, 27 Mil. L. Rev. 1, 5n13 (1965).

57. Francis Lieber, *Instructions for the Government of Armies of the United States in the Field* (Washington, DC: GPO, 1898), 3–45.

58. Stephen C. Neff, *Justice in Blue and Gray: A Legal History of the Civil War* (Cambridge, MA: Harvard University Press, 2010), 57–58.

59. Richard D. Rosen, "Targeting Enemy Forces in the War on Terror: Preserving Civilian Immunity," 42 Vand. J. Transnat'l L. 683, 695 (2009).

60. *Instructions for the Government of Armies of the United States in the Field, General Orders No. 100* (Washington, DC: War Department, Adjutant General's Office, April 24, 1863), articles 81–82.

61. Ibid., article 3.

62. Ibid., articles 12, 13.

63. Gideon M. Hart, *Military Commissions and the Lieber Code: Toward a New Understanding of the Jurisdictional Foundations of Military Commissions*, 203 Mil. L. Rev. 1, 39 (2010).

64. Vallandigham, 68 U.S. at 249.

65. *Trial of Hon. Clement L. Vallandigham*, 41.

66. Speech at Peoria, Illinois, October 16, 1854, *Collected Works*, 2:260, 267.

3

Lincoln at Sea

Craig L. Symonds

$\mathcal{B}$y 1863, Lincoln had schooled himself not only in the mysteries of land warfare but also in the even more arcane arena of nineteenth-century naval warfare. Given the absence of either a department of defense or a joint chiefs of staff, Lincoln was the only person in the government or its military establishment who had simultaneous command authority over both the army and the navy, and as a result, he was necessarily drawn into those aspects of the war where the two services had to cooperate: on the western rivers and along the Atlantic seaboard. In 1863, these two theaters of war coalesced around two politically and strategically important sites: Vicksburg, Mississippi, on the Mississippi River and Charleston, South Carolina, along the Atlantic coast.

By the fall of 1862, Vicksburg had become the buckle on the strap that held the two halves of the Confederacy together and the target of a major Union offensive. What made Vicksburg a daunting objective was its geography. The city sits on a high bluff 170 feet above the river's flood plain, and powerful guns atop that bluff commanded a hairpin turn in the river. Waterborne traffic could not move on the river so long as the Confederates held Vicksburg. Lincoln himself acknowledged, "Vicksburg is the key," adding, "the war can never be brought to an end until the key is in our pocket." Obtaining the key and unlocking the river required the Union army and navy to work together.[1]

Until October 1862, the Union's river gunboats—thinly armored, beetle-shaped craft, designed and built by bridge builder James Buchanan Eads—had operated under the tactical control of navy officers but the strategic control of an army officer: first, John Charles Frémont and then

Henry Wager Halleck. By 1863, however, those gunboats were no longer under the aegis of the army. The army accepted the reality that gunboats commanded by navy officers were part of the navy, and the army's gunboat flotilla became the navy's Mississippi squadron on October 1, 1862. The commander of this riverine force was Rear Admiral David Dixon Porter, an ambitious and supremely self-confident career officer who had spent more than two decades in a navy in which promotions came slowly if they came at all.

Lincoln had first met Porter under inauspicious circumstances back in the spring of 1861 during the Fort Sumter crisis. Secretary of State William Henry Seward had brought Porter to the White House along with army Captain Montgomery Meigs to discuss a plan to support and resupply Fort Pickens off the Gulf coast of Florida. Unaware that Secretary of the Navy Gideon Welles had already designated the U.S. steam warship *Powhatan* for the mission to Fort Sumter, Lincoln signed orders (written by Porter) to give Porter command of the *Powhatan* for the expedition to Florida, and the expedition to Sumter went forward without the *Powhatan*. Though many of Porter's fellow officers thought that Porter had behaved badly in this episode, Lincoln characteristically took all blame upon himself "for any apparent or real irregularity." Indeed, far from blaming Porter, the president had been impressed with the eagerness and confidence of the dark-bearded navy lieutenant, and eighteen months later, he willingly promoted him to rear admiral, jumping him over the heads of every captain in the navy, to give him command of the new Mississippi Squadron.[2]

Porter's army counterpart in the campaign for Vicksburg was Ulysses S. Grant, who experienced an even more meteoric rise in status and authority. Though he was a West Point graduate (class of 1843), Grant had left the army, where he had been unhappy serving in a variety of tiny frontier posts, to seek success in civilian life. It had eluded him. Like Porter, however, the onset of war brought new opportunities, which he quickly seized upon, and soon he was a rising star in the Union army. By 1863, he was the conqueror of Forts Henry and Donelson and the victor at Shiloh and charged with the capture of the rebel citadel at Vicksburg.

Porter was skeptical about the vague command arrangement in the western theater and downright suspicious of the army and its leaders ("I don't trust the army," he wrote to the Assistant Navy Secretary Gustavus Vasa Fox), and he was especially distrustful of West Pointers, whom he considered, as a class, "pedantic and impractical." He suspected that Grant's intention was to gobble up Vicksburg without seeking any help from the navy, though Porter noted smugly, "He can't do it." Grant and his second in command, William Tecumseh Sherman, managed to cajole and flatter Porter into a more cooperative frame of mind. Sherman especially, despite his subsequent reputation for ferocity, went out of his way to solicit Porter's cooperation, writing that he would "do anything possible . . . to comply with any request made by Admiral Porter." In the end, Porter, Grant, and Sherman made a compatible command team that demonstrated how effective joint operations could be when the commanders worked together.[3]

In the war so far, Lincoln had felt compelled to intervene in military planning and management far more than he had expected or desired. Circumstances had forced him to hire and fire a series of generals in the eastern theater—George Brinton McClellan, Ambrose Everett Burnside, John Pope, Joseph Hooker, and George Gordon Meade—and he had also become involved in the management of the river war, going so far as to determine which service paid for the powder and ball fired by navy warships operating within an army command. Now, however, with an apparently compatible command team in place in the west, he was content—indeed, quite pleased—to let his commanders work out their own plan of operations and run the war with no interference from him.

Part of the reason was simple geography. While Lincoln could—and did—make regular visits to the eastern army, the physical distance between the national capital and the western theater made such visits there not only difficult but nearly impossible. Another reason was that eastern newspapers focused most of their attention on the campaigns in Virginia, especially those in the one-hundred-mile corridor between Washington and Richmond, and as a result, the west seemed a distant backwater to most easterners. Once the Vicksburg campaign began in earnest, messages from Grant or Porter had to be sent upriver by steamboat, against the four-knot current, all the way to Cairo, Illinois, before they could be telegraphed to Washington, arriving in some cases weeks after the fact. All that made it easier for Lincoln to revert to his preferred role as commander in chief in regard to the western theater: that of a distant observer and supporter.[4]

Grant and Porter first tried to approach Vicksburg from the north and east. In December 1862, Grant moved his army overland through central Mississippi to attack the city from the east while Sherman and Porter threaded their way up the Yazoo River to assail the Chickasaw Bluffs north of the city. These efforts were undone when Confederate cavalry raids disrupted Grant's supply lines, and Sherman's assault was repulsed. After several unproductive and frustrating attempts to approach Vicksburg from the north along narrow and shallow tributaries, Grant next focused on trying to cut a canal across the bend in the Mississippi opposite Vicksburg. Lincoln appeared to be in favor of the canal in January 1863, probably because he was always interested in technical solutions.

By March, however, his interest had waned, perhaps because he had come to the conclusion that the canal was a waste of time. In the end, Grant finally decided that his best option was to strike at the city from the south, that is, from downriver.

Lincoln did not interfere with these plans, but he was skeptical of much of Grant's fruitless maneuvering, especially the unproductive forays up the sluggish backwaters north of the city. It reminded him too much of the meanderings by his eastern generals, who frequently sought to discover a way *around* the enemy instead of confronting him directly. Just as Lincoln had advised his eastern generals that an indirect approach only postponed the inevitable confrontation, he worried that all of Grant's marching to and fro was not seizing the bull by the horns.

Grant agreed, and in the early spring of 1863, he began the move that would result in the seizure of the rebel citadel. To get his army across the river and behind Vicksburg, Grant asked Porter to run a portion of his squadron past the rebel batteries at night. Though the Mississippi Squadron was not technically under Grant's command, Porter agreed to try it, and on April 16, he led ten ironclads and three army transports past the city. The Confederates lit bonfires on both sides of the river to illuminate the Yankee ships as they ran past. Porter noted, "The fire from the forts was heavy and rapid, but was replied to with such spirit that the aim of the enemy was not so good as usual." One of the transports was sunk, but the rest of the vessels made it with only minor damage.[5]

Grant, meanwhile, marched his men southward in a circuitous route through the marshy delta on the western side of the river in order to meet Porter at Hard Times Landing, forty-five miles below Vicksburg. Porter's fleet then escorted Grant's army across the river, and after another month of hard marching and hard fighting and a siege that lasted forty-seven days, Vicksburg fell to Union arms on July 4, 1863. Equally important, the commander of the rebel army defending Vicksburg, John C. Pemberton, was compelled to surrender his entire army.[6]

Throughout much of this, Lincoln remained doubtful of success. Even when Grant managed to get south of Vicksburg and across the river, Lincoln believed that the army should go southward to capture Port Hudson before moving inland. However, after Grant's siege resulted in a complete triumph that bagged both the city and its defending army, Lincoln was quick to admit his error and give all the credit to Grant on July 13: "I now wish to make the personal acknowledgement that you were right, and I was wrong." Indeed, when Lincoln heard the news of Vicksburg's fall, he was ecstatic. He threw his arms around Welles, who had brought him the news, and declared, "I cannot in words tell you my joy over this result. It is great, Mr. Welles. It is great." A month later, Lincoln was more poetic about the meaning of the campaign, writing in a public letter, "The Father of Waters again goes unvexed to the sea."[7]

In addition to Vicksburg, the other rebel citadel that held Lincoln's attention that summer was Charleston, South Carolina. This was not only because Charleston was the second most active blockade-running port on the Atlantic seaboard (after Wilmington, North Carolina) but also because it was a symbol of Southern rebellion. South Carolina was the state with the highest percentage of slaves in its population (58 percent), and its representatives had been the most tenacious and defiant in support of slavery in the decades before the war; South Carolina was the home of John C. Calhoun, who had promulgated the doctrine of state rights and spearheaded resistance to the national government during the nullification crisis of 1831–32; and in December 1860, South Carolina had been the first state to secede from the Union. Finally, Charleston Harbor was where the first shots of the war had been fired in April 1861. Many Northerners blamed South Carolina, and Charleston, in particular, both for causing and starting the war. As the *New York Tribune* declared in June 1862, "If there is any city deserving of holocaustic infamy, it is Charleston." For the blockaders, the rebel flag flying from the ramparts of Fort Sumter was an implied challenge and a continual affront. Gustavus Fox spoke for many when he wrote to one officer, "The fall of Charleston is the Fall of Satan's kingdom."[8]

Lincoln was drawn into the strategic planning for the capture of Charleston not only because of the city's symbolic importance but also because it soon became a political football in the rivalry between the Union army and navy, and, as in the river war, Lincoln had to play referee. Worried about the bad publicity the navy was getting due to the number of ships that were successfully running the blockade and because of the rampage of Confederate raiders, Welles and Fox were determined to make the capture of Charleston "purely naval" in order to win public credit and support. They urged Rear Admiral Samuel F. Du Pont, the Union navy commander off Charleston, to steam boldly into the harbor and seize the city without involving—or even informing—the local army commander. In a letter to Du Pont, Fox declared, "I feel my duties are two fold: first, to beat our southern friends; second, to beat the army."[9]

Both Welles and Fox thought such a vision within reach because of the advent of iron-armored warships. Since the previous March, when the original USS *Monitor* had battled the much-larger, rebel ironclad CSS *Virginia* (formerly the USS *Merrimack*) to a draw in Hampton Roads, Welles, in particular, had concluded that with a few such vessels, a determined naval commander could steam right past the Charleston forts and demand the surrender of the city. Welles and Fox told Lincoln that with a few ironclad warships, Du Pont "could go right into the harbor, with little or no risk, and destroy the Forts, batteries, and the Town itself." Given his experience with hesitant and cautious commanders in Virginia, Lincoln was no doubt encouraged to hear plans of such a direct approach.[10]

When Du Pont demurred at such a prospect, Fox pressed him. "If we give you the *Galena* and *Monitor*, don't you think we can go squarely at it by the [ship] Channel and make it [the attack on Charleston] purely navy?" No, as a matter of fact, he didn't. Du Pont had a much-lower opinion of the offensive capabilities of the new ironclads than Welles did. To be sure, the original *Monitor* had performed well in Hampton Roads back in March 1862, but soon after that, the *Monitor* and the USS *Galena* (the same two vessels that Welles now offered to Du Pont) had tried to fight their way up the James River past Drewry's Bluff below Richmond, and they had been ingloriously repulsed. Du Pont drew a clear lesson from that operation. To his wife, he wrote, "It was a very ill-advised and incorrect operation to expose those gunboats [at Drewry's Bluff] before the Army could take the fort in the rear." Now here was Fox urging him to do much the same thing at Charleston, where the enemy fortifications were vastly stronger than those on the James. Du Pont's preferred approach was to have the army assail the shore batteries first, which would open the way for the navy to enter the harbor.[11]

To Lincoln, Du Pont's apparent preference for a lengthy siege of the fortifications sounded altogether too much like the kind of thing he was hearing from McClellan, whose army was then stalled on the Virginia peninsula. Indeed, by now the very word "siege" conjured up presidential visions of delay and lost opportunity. Sensitive to Lincoln's concerns and eager to win laurels for the navy, Welles and Fox continued to push Du Pont to make a direct assault on the harbor forts with navy ironclads. If the *Galena* and the *Monitor* were insufficient, they offered to supply Du Pont with some of the newer, larger, and more powerful USS *Passaic*–class monitors. And, indeed, over the next six months, the navy department sent Du Pont one monitor after another, almost as fast as they could be built. By the end of 1862, Du Pont had seven of them, plus the giant iron-hulled frigate USS *New Ironsides* and an experimental armored warship called the USS *Keokuk*, which had two nonrevolving towers.

Du Pont was happy enough to receive these reinforcements, but he remained skeptical that even with nine ironclads he could smash his way past the rebel forts guarding Charleston Harbor and get past the obstructions in the inner harbor. Du Pont understood that for all their apparent invincibility, the monitors carried only two guns each, and their rate of fire was painfully slow. The massive 15-inch guns on the new *Passaic*-class monitors could fire only once every seven to ten minutes. For his part, Lincoln's expectations about what monitors could and could not do were heavily influenced by Welles and Fox. Like them, Lincoln was a champion of new technology, and he shared at least some of their confidence in the capability and invulnerability of the monitors. And, of course, the idea of a direct approach was a refreshing contrast to McClellan's indirect and, in Lincoln's view, unnecessarily complex, strategic plans.

Du Pont had a chance to make his case with the president on October 16, 1862, when he called on Lincoln in the White House during a brief trip away from the blockade. Unfortunately for Du Pont, their conversation took place at the peak of Lincoln's annoyance with McClellan's obstreperousness. Du Pont was surprised and somewhat taken aback when Lincoln began their conversation by reviewing the disappointments of McClellan's unhappy tenure of command in Virginia. Perhaps, Lincoln meant it as a cautionary tale for his reluctant admiral. In any case, Du Pont squandered the opportunity to explain his concerns about the plan of attack or the limitations of monitors to the president. Instead, he emphasized the "moral effect" that the presence of his squadron off the coast had on the enemy. "The iron grip we had on the coast," he assured Lincoln, "falsified the declarations of the chief promoters of the rebellion." He begged that "the government should not lose sight of us."[12]

Du Pont returned to his command off Charleston aware that the president and the navy department expected him to storm the harbor, but he remained doubtful that it could be done. To demonstrate this point and to test the capability of his monitors against shore fortifications, Du Pont ordered Captain John Worden, who had commanded the original *Monitor* in the Battle of Hampton Roads nearly a year before, to attack Fort McAllister on Ogeechee Sound ninety or so miles south of Charleston with three *Passaic*-class monitors. On the morning of January 27, 1863, Worden's monitors pounded the earthwork fort for nearly four hours until they ran out of ammunition. Afterward, Worden reported to Du Pont that the shelling had no serious effect on the enemy, and he asked for new orders. Du Pont saw this as a vindication of his assertion that the monitors had little offensive punch, reporting that the failure of the attack convinced him "that in all such operations to secure success troops are necessary." Welles, however, did not want troops involved and drew an entirely different conclusion, that "the turret vessels are strong and capable of great endurance."[13]

Welles tried to encourage Du Pont: "The Department will share the responsibility imposed upon commanders who make the attempt" to attack Charleston. The implication was clear: If Du Pont and his captains feared for their careers or their reputations, Welles was willing to accept the responsibility for failure. Du Pont did not respond directly to this suggestion, but his litany of requests and complaints continued. He reported that the machinery on the monitors was breaking down for lack of oil. He was short of almost everything, coal, in particular, but also "sugar, coffee, flour, butter, beans, and dried fruit." To Lincoln, Du Pont's letters sounded much like the letters that he had received from McClellan as excuses for refusing to advance.[14]

The year before, when Lincoln had sought to light a fire under McClellan, he had personally visited the army. Perhaps, he wished that he could do the same now with Du Pont, but as with the western theater, the logistics of a sea voyage to Charleston were daunting, to say nothing of the fact that since Lincoln suffered badly from seasickness, the prospect of a long sea voyage offered few charms. Instead, Lincoln suggested to Fox that Fox should go down to Charleston to make sure that Du Pont understood the administration's point of view. In the end, Fox didn't go either, but he did write to Du Pont, "*The idea of a siege meets with such disfavor that the President wished me to go down and see you*," underscoring the sentence for emphasis. Fox made it clear that the administration expected Du Pont to execute a purely naval attack—and soon. He described the attack as he saw it in his mind's eye: Imagine "carrying in your flag, supreme and superb, defiant, and disdainful, silent amid the 200 guns until you arrive at the centre of this wicked rebellion and then demand the Surrender of the forts." He reminded Du Pont, "The President and Mr. Welles are very much struck with this program," and begged Du Pont "not to let the Army spoil it."[15]

By the early spring of 1863, Lincoln was wondering if Du Pont was not simply a maritime version of McClellan. The admiral had been rock solid in organizing the blockade, and his capture of Port Royal in November 1861 had been swift and sure, but his constant requests for more ironclads, his gloomy reports, and especially his apparent preference for a lengthy siege rather than a bold dash into the harbor all sounded eerily familiar. As Du Pont no doubt hoped, his lugubrious reports lowered expectations in Washington, but they also lowered Du Pont's standing with the administration. Welles noted that, like McClellan, "Du Pont shrinks, dreads, the conflict he has sought," yet at the same time he was "unwilling that any other should undertake it." Welles concluded that Du Pont was simply being protective of his reputation. "I am disappointed," Welles confided to his diary, "but not wholly surprised." Lincoln agreed. That same day, Captain John A. Dahlgren, the commander of the Washington Navy Yard, noted in his diary, "Abe is restless about Charleston."[16]

Lincoln's restlessness and Du Pont's inaction may have contributed to the president's decision two days later to ask Welles to promote Dahlgren to the rank of rear admiral. Lincoln and Dahlgren had become quite close during Lincoln's frequent visits to the Navy Yard to witness the testing of one or another new weapon or simply to get away from the White House for a few hours. Dahlgren had made it clear to him that he was eager for both promotion and a fleet command, but so far, Lincoln had put him off, claiming that all such decisions resided with Welles and the Navy Department. Now, however, he simply told Welles to do it. A few days later, Dahlgren called on Welles to thank him for the promotion, but Welles told him candidly that it was not his doing, that he had advised against it, but that the president had insisted. Perhaps, by now, Lincoln was wishing that it was Dahlgren and not Du Pont who commanded the fleet off Charleston.[17]

Frustrated that his several letters had had no apparent impact on expectations in Washington, Du Pont resigned himself to making the naval attempt on Charleston that the administration expected. He wrote his wife, Sophie, "The president ought to know but does not that the work on the defenses of Charleston have gone on without intermission for twenty-three months." Apparently, it did not occur to him that if the president "ought to know" but did not, it was because Du Pont himself had not told him. A few days later, Du Pont wrote his friend Henry Winter Davis, "If the President knew what was involved in a failure he would never think of such a thing." Looking back at it later, Du Pont acknowledged that he might have stated his views "in more emphatic terms," and he justified his failure to do so by claiming that by laying out "all the facts . . . before the Department for its judgment and decision," he had done all that anyone should expect. Instead of forthrightly telling the president what he needed to know, Du Pont was content to send broad hints about the difficulties and adopt a martyr's role.[18]

That same month, Lincoln dropped in at the navy department to make one of the several impromptu visits that characterized one important aspect of his management style. As it happened, Navy Engineer Alban Stimers had just returned from a visit to Du Pont's fleet. Like Welles, Stimers was professionally invested in the success of the monitors, and he was as eager as Welles for them to demonstrate their prowess. Consequently, he painted Du Pont's lack of trust in the monitors as simply a lack of will. He told Lincoln that during a council of war aboard Du Pont's flagship, the planning had focused, once again, on how the army should seize the rebel shore batteries before Du Pont made any effort to run into the harbor.[19]

To Lincoln, this sounded like "the Peninsula all over again," and, somewhat alarmed, he asked Stimers if this meant "we were going into a *siege*." Lincoln muttered that Du Pont's "long delay" and especially his "constant call for more ships, more ironclads, was like McClellan calling for more regiments." He told Fox that if Du Pont wasn't going to use the monitors at Charleston, perhaps the vessels should be sent instead to Admiral

Farragut on the Mississippi River. Only "with difficulty" did Fox talk him out of this idea, and afterward, Fox wrote Du Pont to tell him about the president's suggestion, hoping no doubt that it would spur the admiral to quicker action.[20]

Privately, Lincoln told Welles that "he was prepared for a repulse at Charleston." "The President," Welles wrote in his diary, "who has often a sort of intuitive sagacity, has spoken discouragingly of operations at Charleston during the whole season. Du Pont's dispatches and movements have not inspired him with faith; they remind him, he says, of McClellan." After that, Welles told Du Pont again that he could have two more monitors, but he was to understand that he was not to wait for the army, nor was he to engage the rebel forts—he was to run past them and take command of the harbor. Even then, Welles was not sanguine that the orders would have much impact. Taking his cue from Lincoln, he wrote in his diary, "Du Pont is getting as prudent as McClellan."[21]

The impasse at Charleston had an impact on Lincoln's storied patience and equanimity. In March, Dahlgren was shocked by his friend's appearance and noted, "The President never tells a joke now." Lincoln seemed not himself, uncharacteristically complaining out loud and insisting, "They were doing nothing at Vicksburg and Charleston." He was distressed that "Dupont was asking for one iron-clad after another, as fast as they were built." He thought "the canal at Vicksburg was of no account, and wondered that a sensible man would do it." Dahlgren tried to cheer up his friend, putting an optimistic spin on the reports. But the president was inconsolable and expressed the fear that "the favorable state of public expectation would pass away before anything was done." Then, almost as if by a force of will, Lincoln dragged himself out of his mood, "leveled a couple of jokes at the doings at Vicksburg and Charleston," and left. Dahlgren's final comment in his diary that night was: "Poor gentleman."[22]

Unable to convince his superiors of the ill wisdom of a naval attack on Charleston and aware that he could delay an attack no longer, Du Pont finally led his ironclads into Charleston Harbor on April 7. Though Welles (and no doubt Lincoln, too) had envisioned a run past Fort Sumter into the inner harbor, the obstructions that the Confederates had laid across the harbor opposite Sumter compelled Du Pont to stop and take the fort under fire. At a range that varied from three hundred to five hundred yards, the Union ironclads exchanged fire with the fort for four hours. The slow rate of fire from the monitors meant that in all that time, they were able to get off a total of only 139 shots. The rebels, by comparison fired 2,209 shots, 520 of which struck a target. While the big shells from the monitors pockmarked the exterior brick face of the fort, they were unable to do it any serious damage. The monitors, on the other hand, took a terrific beating. The *Passaic*, namesake of its class, received two hits in quick succession near the base of its turret, jamming it so that it would no longer turn. Other shells so wrecked the USS *Nahant* that it could not maneuver. The USS *Patapsco* was hit forty-seven times, the *Nantucket* fifty-one times, and the *Weehawken* fifty-three times. Worst hit of all was the experimental *Keokuk*. Struck ninety times, it sank the next day in water so shallow the Confederates were able to recover its guns.[23]

Du Pont had intended to renew the attack later that night, and then he received the reports from his captains. Those reports revealed how badly the Union ironclads had been mauled. Du Pont forwarded the reports to Washington to justify his decision not to renew the attack. But instead of seeing this as a validation of Du Pont's good judgment, Welles saw it as proof that the admiral's loyal captains were willing to support him. McClellan's generals had always backed him up, too. After reading the reports, Welles summarized them, "It is the recommendation of all, from the Admiral down, that no effort be made to do anything."[24]

As for Lincoln, despite the mental association he had now made between Du Pont and McClellan, he was not yet ready to give up on his admiral. He wrote Du Pont to urge him to hold his position near the harbor entrance, "or if you have left it, return to it and hold it until further orders." What Lincoln hoped was that a continuing threat to Charleston would prevent the defenders of the city from sending reinforcements to Vicksburg, a thousand miles to the west where Grant was marching toward the Mississippi state capital at Jackson. Alas, Du Pont had already withdrawn from Charleston, and when he got Lincoln's letter, he took it as a rebuke.[25]

Lincoln was genuinely mystified by Du Pont's readiness to assume that his letter constituted a censure, in particular because he had taken care to write that "no censure upon you . . . is intended." But admirals, apparently, were as touchy as generals. For his part, Welles had already made up his mind that Du Pont had to go. More than Du Pont's apparent timorousness, it was his touchiness that convinced Welles that, as he confided to his diary, "I fear he can no longer be useful in his present command." Lincoln did not seek Du Pont's dismissal, but neither did he come to his defense. Like Welles, he was disappointed more by Du Pont's prickly attitude (again, so like McClellan) than by his failed attack on Charleston. The admiral seemed far more concerned that he might have to bear public blame for a failure than he was by the failure itself. In the end, the assignment went to Lincoln's old friend and new admiral Dahlgren.[26]

Dahlgren never captured Charleston either, and in time, he also became the target of newspaper complaints about the lack of progress in the effort to capture "Satan's kingdom." Nevertheless, throughout the rest of the summer of 1863, Dahlgren was energetic and conscientious. Aware that his masters in Washington craved regular information, he sent in near-daily status reports. Indeed, Dahlgren almost worked himself to death, as his health deteriorated to such a point that he could barely get himself out of bed. Dahlgren's work ethic and steadfast loyalty satisfied Lincoln that he had the right man on the spot.

In addition to his intense interest in events both at Vicksburg and Charleston, Lincoln also followed news of the war on the high seas, where a handful of Confederate commerce raiders were plundering Union merchant commerce despite the efforts of the navy to find the raiders and sink them. The opposition newspapers made much of the apparent helplessness of the navy to protect American commerce. The merchants of New York petitioned Secretary Welles to establish a system of convoys, but to do that, Welles would have to weaken the blockade, which he was unwilling to do. Lincoln backed him up mainly because he recognized that any intervention with the navy department about how to deploy its warships was a slippery slope that led to micromanagement. In this, as so many aspects of the war, Lincoln would simply have to bear the public criticism and encourage his subordinates to do their best.

On the whole, Lincoln's limited involvement with the naval war during 1863 reflected his notion of the proper role of a commander in chief: to provide matériel support and encouragement, promote the deserving, winnow out the hesitant, and sustain public support for the war. Throughout it all, he had to bear the slings and arrows of public disappointment: about the progress of the war, about emancipation, and, occasionally, about the naval war as well. In a public letter intended for his critics, Lincoln noted not only the recent progress in the war on land but also of recent naval successes: "Nor must Uncle Sam's web feet be forgotten. At all the watery margins they have been present. Not only on the deep sea, the broad bay, and the rapid river, but also up the narrow muddy bayou, and wherever the ground was a little damp, they have been and made their tracks."[27]

Whatever his mood may have been in the dark of the night, Lincoln continued his optimistic message in his annual message to Congress in December. There was, of course, the good news of both Gettysburg and Vicksburg to report, and he forecast brighter days ahead for the nation. He praised "the heroic men of the navy" who fought the ships, but he also remembered the "mechanics and artisans" who designed and built those vessels. He noted that "the resources of the nation have been developed and its power displayed in the construction of a navy" that has "rendered signal service to the Union."[28]

Notes

1. David Dixon Porter, *Incidents and Anecdotes of the Civil War* (New York: Appleton, 1885), 95–96. Porter is the only source for this oft-quoted passage, and it is not impossible that it was a postwar invention of Porter, who was prone to take creative license in his memoirs.

2. Lincoln to Gideon Welles, May 11, 1961, in Roy P. Basler, ed., *The Collected Works of Abraham Lincoln*, 9 vols. (New Brunswick, N.J.: Rutgers University Press, 1953–55), 4:366–67. Hereafter cited as *Collected Works*.

3. Porter, *Incidents and Anecdotes*, 125; Sherman to Porter, November 12, 1862, *Official Records of the Union and Confederate Navies in the War of the Rebellion*, 30 vols. (Washington, DC: GPO, 1894–1922), 23:473. Hereafter cited as *ORN*.

4. Craig L. Symonds, *Lincoln and His Admirals: Abraham Lincoln, the U.S. Navy and the Civil War* (New York: Oxford University Press, 2008), 107–17.

5. David Dixon Porter to Gideon Welles, April 17, 1862, *ORN*, 24:552–53.

6. The best one-volume history of the campaign is Michael B. Ballard, *Vicksburg: The Campaign That Opened the Mississippi* (Chapel Hill: University of North Carolina Press, 2004).

7. Lincoln to Ulysses S. Grant, July 13, 1863, *Collected Works*, 6:326; entry July 7, 1863, Gideon Welles, *Diary of Gideon Welles*, ed. Howard K. Beale, 3 vols. (New York: Norton, 1960), 1:364; Lincoln to James C. Conkling, August 26, 1863, *Collected Works*, 6:409.

8. *New York Tribune*, June 3, 1862; Gustavus V. Fox to Samuel F. Du Pont, June 3, 1863, Gustavus V. Fox, *The Confidential Correspondence of Gustavus Vasa Fox, Assistant Secretary of the Navy, 1861–1865*, 2 vols. (1920; reprint, Freeport, NY: Books for Libraries, 1920, 1972), 1:126.

9. Gustavus V. Fox to Samuel F. Du Pont, June 3, 1862, Fox, *Confidential Correspondence*, 1:126.

10. Salmon P. Chase, *Inside Lincoln's Cabinet: The Civil War Diary of Salmon P. Chase*, ed. David Donald (New York: Longman's, 1954), 138.

11. Gustavus V. Fox to Samuel F. Du Pont, May 12, 1862, Fox, *Confidential Correspondence*, 1:119; Samuel F. Du Pont to Sophie Du Pont, May 29, 1862, in John D. Hayes, ed., *Samuel F. Du Pont: A Selection from His Civil War Letters* (Ithaca, NY: Cornell University Press, 1969), 2:79.

12. Samuel F. Du Pont to Henry Winter Davis, October 25, 1862, and Samuel F. Du Pont to Sophie Du Pont, October 21, 1862, in Hayes, *Samuel F. Du Pont*, 2:253, 253n.

13. John Worden to Samuel F. Du Pont, January 27, 1863, Du Pont to Gideon Welles, January 28, 1863, and Du Pont to Worden, January 28, 1863, in *ORN*, 13:544–47; Welles, *Diary*, entry March 17, 1863, 1:248.

14. Samuel F. Du Pont to Gideon Welles, February 8 and 9, 1863, and Du Pont to Gustavus V. Fox, March 2, 1863, in *ORN*, 13:651, 655, 712.

15. Gustavus V. Fox to Samuel F. Du Pont, February 20 and 26, 1863, in Fox, *Confidential Correspondence*, 1:181, 186.

16. Welles, *Diary*, entry February 16, 1863, 1:236–7; entry February 14, 1863, Madeliene V. Dahlgren, ed., *Memoir of John A. Dahlgren, Rear Admiral, United States Navy* (New York: Webster, 1891), 388.

17. Welles, *Diary*, entry February 2, 1863, 1:239.

18. Samuel F. Du Pont to Sophie Du Pont, March 27, 1863, and Du Pont to Henry Winter Davis, April 1 and May 11, 1863, in Hayes, *Samuel F. Du Pont*, 2:250, 533, 3:302.

19. Alban Stimers to Gideon Welles, March 11, 1863, *ORN*, 13:729.

20. Welles, *Diary*, March 12, 1863, 1:247.

21. Ibid., April 2, 1863, 1:259.

22. Dahlgren, *Memoir*, February 6 and March 29, 1863, 387, 389.

23. John Johnson, *The Defense of Charleston Harbor* (Charleston, SC: Walker, Evans, and Cogswell, 1890), 58–59; "Abstract of Expenditure of Ammunition," *ORN*, 14:27.

24. Welles, *Diary*, April 20 and 21, 1863, 1:276–77.

25. Lincoln to Samuel F. Du Pont, April 13, 1863, *ORN*, 14:132; Du Pont to Sophie Du Pont, April 13, 1863, *Samuel F. Du Pont*, 3:21.

26. Lincoln to Samuel F. Du Pont, April 13, 1863, *ORN*, 14:132; Welles, *Diary*, April 30, 1863, 1:288.

27. Lincoln to James C. Conkling, August 23, 1863, *Collected Works*, 6:409–10.

28. Lincoln, Annual Message to Congress, December 8, 1863, *Collected Works*, 7:44.

4

Military Drafts, Civilian Riots

Barnet Schecter

"*W*e are contending with an enemy who, as I understand, drives every able bodied man he can reach, into his ranks, very much as a butcher drives bullocks into a slaughter-pen." So wrote Abraham Lincoln to Horatio Seymour, the Democratic governor of New York, in August 1863. "No time is wasted, no argument is used.... It produces an army with a rapidity not to be matched on our side, if we first waste time to re-experiment with the volunteer system." Lincoln was adamant about resuming the federal conscription as soon as possible in the wake of devastating antidraft riots that had convulsed New York City for almost a week in July, nearly destroying the commercial, financial, and industrial hub of the Union. Lincoln promised that excessive quotas for heavily Democratic districts would be reduced and that he would not hinder a U.S. Supreme Court ruling on the constitutionality of the draft law, but he would "not consent to lose the *time* while it is being obtained." Lincoln wrote that his goal was to be "just and constitutional; yet practical, in performing the important duty . . . of maintaining the unity, and the free principles of our common country."[1]

The Confederacy had acted first in resorting to conscription, a year earlier, in April 1862. Lincoln's administration had followed by implementing the Federal Militia Draft a few months later, lengthening the time the federal government could call state troops into national service from ninety days to nine months. But this erosion of state control over military matters was just an intermediate step to bypassing the governors completely, with the first federal draft in U.S. history—"An Act for Enrolling and Calling Out the National Forces"—which Lincoln signed into law on March 5, 1863, two days after Congress passed it, largely along party lines.[2]

This measure alone marked a watershed in Lincoln's presidency and in American history. In colonial times and during the American Revolution, local and state governments enforced compulsory military service. With the federal draft, the hallowed notion of the homegrown militia as a bulwark against tyranny by a centralized power or dictator—a Cromwell or Napoleon—handed down from the Whig tradition in England, had been cast aside. Lincoln's opponents lashed out in the Democratic press. In New York, Manton Marble, editor of the *World*, likened Congress to "an oligarchic conspiracy plotting a vast scheme of military servitude" and asserted that the Conscription Act was so oppressive that it "could not have been ventured upon in England even in those dark days when the press-gang filled English ships-of-war with slaves."[3] For the poor and working classes, the draft law was doubly outrageous because it exempted anyone who could pay $300—almost a year's salary—or present a substitute.

This aspect of the law enabled Peace Democrats to link the draft to Lincoln's most revolutionary act, the Emancipation Proclamation, issued on January 1, 1863. By freeing the slaves in the Confederacy by decree, Lincoln had transformed the war from a conservative effort to preserve the Union to a radical crusade for abolition. Benjamin Wood's pro-Democratic *New York Daily News* declared, "It is a strange perversion of the laws of self-preservation which would compel the white laborer to leave his family destitute and unprotected while he goes forth to free the negro, who, being free, will compete with him in labor. . . . Let the laboring population assemble peaceably in mass meeting and express their views upon the subject. . . . Let them make it a necessity with the Administration to give up its insane Emancipation scheme. Let them insist that in place of the conscription of white men to serve blacks, we shall have negotiation, compromise, and peace."[4]

Far from fostering peaceful mass protest, this linkage of emancipation and the draft—using inflammatory rhetoric to incite political, racial, and class conflict—would produce the largest civil insurrection in American history, the New York City draft riots in July 1863. The largest rebellion in American history apart from the Civil War as a whole, the riots caused an untold number of deaths, wrought extensive damage on New York City, and shattered its free black community. Instead of weakening the Northern war effort, however, the riots spurred the formation of African American regiments, which eventually constituted more than ten percent of the Union army. Ultimately, the destructive reach of the riots extended far beyond the war itself and well into the next century: The riots and their aftermath would play a critical role in the defeat of Reconstruction, making 1863 a pivotal year both for Lincoln and for American society.

Following the passage of the conscription act in March 1863, the Provost Marshal General's Bureau, a new office within the War Department, sent its personnel across the country, door-to-door, taking the names of draft-eligible men. Here the novelty of the law was felt acutely: For the first time, the distant federal government in Washington was able to reach directly into every household and workplace to draft men into a national army. Violent resistance sprang up, particularly in areas where workingmen gathered and had heard the denunciations of the draft by Democratic editors and orators: the marble quarries of Vermont; the coal fields of eastern Pennsylvania; and across the Midwest, where the Union blockade of the Mississippi River had stifled commerce, ruining numerous farms and businesses. Several draft officials and employers who cooperated with them were killed, and white mobs attacked African American neighborhoods and workers in New York City (March 6), Detroit, Michigan (March 6), and Buffalo, New York (first week of July).

Once the enrollment process was completed in the spring and early summer, officials were ready to conduct the draft lottery, the drawing of names to determine who would be compelled to serve in the Union ranks—or find a way out.[5] "There is a lurking mischief in the atmosphere that surrounds this unwelcome stranger," the *Daily News* declared of the draft on the morning of Saturday, July 11, when the drawing of names was set to begin in New York City at 9:00 A.M. At the ninth-district draft office, a four-story brick building at Forty-Sixth Street and Third Avenue, slips of paper, each "rolled tightly and bound with a ring of India-rubber," were placed in a cylindrical drum, which was rotated by a handle on the side in order to mix the names randomly. The *Daily News* dubbed it "the wheel of misfortune." But the lottery proceeded peacefully, and by 4:00 P.M., about half of the twenty-five-hundred-man quota for the district had been drafted. The office closed, and the draft was set to resume on Monday, July 13, at 9:00 A.M.[6]

The draft had also begun peacefully in Boston, Massachusetts; Providence, Rhode Island; New Haven, Connecticut; and Pittsburgh, Pennsylvania, among other cities. The *New Haven Journal* noted that the announcement of the draft and "explanation of the process" had helped relieve much of the public's "rising anxiety." That enrollment officers and provost marshals, blacks and whites, rich and poor, were all "so fortunate as to draw a prize" at the lottery argued for the fairness of the draft and promoted calm among the "very anxious and deeply interested" audience at the draft office, the *Pittsburgh Gazette* reported. However, the *Providence Journal* pointed out that workingmen who could not afford the $300 exemption would be the ones to actually serve, and their families would immediately become charity cases. "The families of such should be provided for at public expense," the paper declared, since a soldier's pay would "little more than pay the rent of a small tenement."[7]

By Sunday, with the first draftees' names published in the *Herald*, the apparent calm of the previous day's lottery in New York had already unraveled, and it dawned on many observers that starting the draft right before the Sabbath had been a serious mistake. As journalist Joel Tyler Headley pointed out, "To have the list of twelve hundred names that had been drawn read over and commented on all day by men who enlivened their discussion with copious draughts of bad whiskey, especially when most of those drawn were laboring-men or poor mechanics, who were unable to hire a substitute, was like applying fire to gunpowder." Men and women began stockpiling guns, clubs, stones, and bricks at numerous depots. In a barroom on East Broadway, a former army captain stirred up enthusiastic support when he declared he would rather "blow his own brains out than shoulder a musket in defense of an abolition administration."[8]

By 6:00 A.M., on Monday, July 13, when workers usually started their twelve-hour day at factories, shipyards, railroads, and other industries, small groups coming up from the southern end of Manhattan were walking up the west side along Eighth and Ninth Avenues. From the squatters' shacks filling the city's open lots and from the slums on the east side, new marchers quickly swelled the ranks, and clusters of women and children trailed behind them. The men entered factories and other workplaces and soon enforced a citywide labor strike. The crowds of striking workers mingled with the unemployed and converged on a large vacant lot just east of Central Park and north of Fifty-Ninth Street, pouring into it like "living streams," wrote Headley, who estimated the gathering at about ten thousand people.

After listening to several speeches, the mob, carrying placards painted simply with the words "NO DRAFT," set off south, down Fifth and Sixth Avenues in two columns, which joined after both turned east onto Forty-Seventh Street and "heaved tumultuously toward Third Avenue."[9] The mob's target was the ninth-district draft office, but some men stopped to cut down telegraph poles with axes stolen from a hardware store, and women pulled up the Fourth Avenue railroad tracks with crowbars. The loss of the poles and tracks threatened to cut off not only the links between the police central office and the precincts but also the city's communication with its suburbs and the rest of the country.[10]

Throughout the morning, officials reacted with small deployments of policemen, militia, and federal troops that were rapidly swept aside by the gathering mobs. Shouting "Down with the rich men!" the crowd stormed the ninth-district draft office, setting a fire that spread and burned down

the entire block. The mob then headed south to seize guns and ammunition stockpiled in two armories on Second Avenue. Soon, a second phase
of the riots began to unfold, as political protest combined with sabotage
of government targets gave way to street crime; attacks on individuals
and private property were suddenly tempting in the chaotic atmosphere.
Clusters of men, women, and children from the slums looted hungrily, with
few policemen to stop them. The metaphor of class warfare—exploited for
decades by Democrats like Fernando Wood and Isaiah Rynders to garner
immigrant votes—had become a literal, violent eruption, far bigger than
any they had provoked before.[11]

By Monday afternoon, the riots had escalated horrifically, becoming
a vicious racial pogrom targeting the city's free black community, which
consisted of a mere 12,500 people in a city of 800,000. "I don't know if the
niggers themselves is responsible for this here trouble, but by God there is
a war about 'm, damn 'm, and we'll pound 'm," a rioter told a reporter from
the *World*. "It's the abolitionists that have been pushing matters eternally,
and we won't stop it. We'll pound the God damn abolitionists as well as
the niggers." Smaller mobs broke off from the main one and roamed the
entire width of the island, attacking black persons wherever they could be
found and setting fire to their churches, homes, and businesses. Individuals
on the street, waiters in restaurants, families in mostly black tenements,
and seamen in boardinghouses were all hunted down. Eighteen black men
were lynched from lampposts, their bodies burned and mutilated, while
others were chased off of docks into the rivers. Some five thousand black
men, women, and children became homeless refugees, fleeing Manhattan
on foot and by ferry. According to one African American newspaper, 175
black persons were killed during the riots.[12]

On Forty-Fourth Street and Fifth Avenue, rioters looted the Colored
Orphan Asylum and burned it to the ground. The staff evacuated the 233
children and shepherded them to the nearest police station. Several young
Irish American streetcar drivers and firemen rescued about twenty of the
children who had been separated from the group and surrounded by the
mob, the *Times* reported. Ignoring threats from dozens of "fiends" who
shouted, "Murder the d[amne]d monkeys," and "Wring the necks of the
d[amne]d Lincolnites," the drivers and firemen brought the orphans to
the Twentieth Precinct station house.[13]

James McCune Smith, the attending physician at the orphanage, was
the first accredited black physician in the United States. He and other black
leaders, including the Reverend Henry Highland Garnet and Frederick
Douglass, were at the forefront of a generation that had been waging a
civil rights movement since the 1840s. The records of their state and national conventions were largely destroyed in the riots, and their aspirations

were dealt a serious setback. With the exodus of blacks from New York, membership in their organizations and churches would dwindle, and the leaders would have to focus on helping homeless refugees apply to the government and charitable groups for basic necessities and financial aid.[14]

The rioters essentially controlled the city at dusk on Monday; the night was hot, and columns of black smoke rose from burning structures all over town. At the Saint Nicholas Hotel, civic leaders from both parties had arrived, anxious to consult with Mayor George Opdyke and Major General John Wool. George Templeton Strong and other members of the Union League Club called for the immediate imposition of martial law and occupation of the city by federal troops. According to Strong, Opdyke and Wool each claimed that the other had sole authority to declare martial law in the city, and both refused to take action.[15]

Tammany Democrats—including County Supervisor William Tweed, District Attorney A. Oakey Hall, and the notorious agitator Rynders—argued that martial law would further enrage the rioters. They hoped to combine limited military force with persuasion, a sympathetic but firm voice urging obedience to the law and redress through the courts. Opdyke believed the worst of the rioting was over and was swayed by the Democrats.[16]

Opdyke promised the Union League Club representatives that he would keep the military option open and use it if the situation did not improve in the next few days. The staunch Republicans telegraphed President Lincoln from Wool's suite, pleading for "instant help in troops and an officer to command them and to declare martial law." Then they left the hotel in disgust. The culprits, they believed, were not only the agitators in the streets but Democratic politicians and editors.[17]

Indeed, in the midst of this acute crisis and despite the atrocities committed, the *World* continued to add fuel to the fire on Tuesday, claiming to speak for the people at large. Marble wrote, "Although the community generally condemns the plundering and cruelty perpetrated by some hangers-on of the mob, yet there is an astonishing deal of public and private sympathy with the one idea of resistance to the draft. The laboring classes say that they are confident that it will never be enforced in the city."

Marble proceeded to attack the administration's infringement of civil rights and to blame Lincoln for the riots: "Will the insensate men at Washington now at length listen to our voice? Will they now give ear to our warnings and adjurations? Will they now believe that Defiance of Law in Rulers breeds Defiance of Law in the people? Does the doctrine proclaimed from the Capitol that in war laws are silent please them [when] put in practice in the streets of New York?" The *World* insisted that the people wanted a war for "the Union and the Constitution"—

not for abolition—and that Lincoln had ignored them. Thousands of men had thronged Union Square two years earlier in support of the war effort, a situation Marble describes, "These are the very men whom his imbecility, his wanton exercise of arbitrary power, his stretches of ungranted authority have transformed into a mob."[18]

Across the North in communities where the draft lottery had not yet begun, provost marshals were hoping New York's authorities would put down the mob aggressively and set an example. In Detroit, a district provost marshal telegraphed his superior that anger over conscription "has become intensified to an alarming degree by the successful violence in the city of New York, compelling the draft to be deferred. A spark here would explode the whole and bring it into the most violent action." Rioting had broken out on a smaller scale in Newark, New Jersey, and tensions ran high in towns across New York state. Provost Marshal General James Fry suspended the draft in Buffalo on Tuesday while pushing forward with the lottery in some parts of Philadelphia and the rest of Pennsylvania. From Iowa City, Iowa, a telegram to Secretary of War Edwin M. Stanton spoke for all the rest: "The enforcement of the draft throughout the country depends upon its enforcement in New York City. If it can be successfully resisted there, it cannot be enforced elsewhere. For God's sake let there be no compromising or half-way measures."[19]

Following events from the South, ardent secessionist Edmund Ruffin came to a similar conclusion from opposite motives, writing hopefully in his diary that "the timidity & forbearance" of the authorities in New York would trigger rioting all over the North. Ruffin predicted that the damage from the New York riot to "Lincoln's government & Yankeedom" would be greater than the ravages of a hundred thousand Confederate troops; far worse would be the impact on the Union's reputation and moral standing in the eyes of the world. Ruffin wrote, "I shall await the consummation most anxiously—& earnestly, though but faintly hoping that the atrocity & rage of the mob may be so extended, & unrestrained, as [to] lay in ashes the whole of the great city of New York, with all its appendages & wealth, as just retribution for its share of the outrages perpetrated on the people of the South."[20]

General Robert E. Lee, defeated at Gettysburg, Pennsylvania, ten days earlier, had retreated to the Potomac River and by 11 A.M. on Tuesday, July 14, had managed to escape with almost his entire army across the river. However, Stanton was only willing to send five regiments of militia back to New York right away, and they would not arrive until late Wednesday night. In the interim, the mayor, the governor, the police, and the military had to cope—in their various ways—with the escalating violence in the streets.[21]

As mob rule gripped the city, Lincoln feared for the safety of his son Robert, who was en route to Washington via New York. On Tuesday, Lincoln sent him a telegram at the Fifth Avenue Hotel in Manhattan: "Why do I hear no more of you?" Robert eventually returned safely to the White House.[22]

Governor Seymour, who was traveling to see relatives in New Jersey when the riots broke out, took his time and did not arrive in Manhattan until Tuesday morning, sparking controversy over his tardiness and sympathy for the rioters. Tweed, who had been out on the streets since the riots began, trying to calm his constituents and keep abreast of events, met the governor at the ferry and escorted him to the Saint Nicholas Hotel, where they met with the mayor. At City Hall, the governor reportedly addressed the crowd as "My friends" at the beginning of his speech: "I call on the people to maintain law and order. If the conscription law will not bear the test of the courts and the Constitution, it will not be enforced, but if upheld by the courts, then the state and city authorities will combine for the purpose of equalizing the tax and making it bear proportionately on the rich and the poor." The crowd cheered loudly.[23]

After the speech, Seymour told local officials that he deemed martial law a last resort. Intent on forestalling federal intervention and keeping the city in Democratic hands, the governor then issued a proclamation that placed him in command of enforcing law and order in the city, the local authorities being overwhelmed. Seymour got into a carriage with Tweed, and "amid the cheers of the multitude that thronged about the vehicle," they set off on a tour of the city, accompanied by other Democratic officials. The governor was cheered throughout the excursion and gave two more speeches.

Aside from President Lincoln and federal officials, Seymour had the greatest power to determine the government's handling of the draft riots, and by his words and actions, he endorsed a conciliatory approach. He set up his own headquarters at the Saint Nicholas Hotel, where he conferred with Samuel Barlow, General George Brinton McClellan, and other prominent Democrats, many of whom he sent as his emissaries to flashpoints across the city, where they persuaded mobs to disperse. Uptown, small-business and property owners along with clergymen also addressed the mobs, offering help in opposing the draft's $300 clause in exchange for an end to the violence.[24]

Despite the occasional successes of Democratic leaders and Catholic priests in mollifying the rioters, the violence, on the whole, continued to escalate in Manhattan. By Wednesday, rioting had also broken out in New York's Albany, Troy, Yonkers, Hastings, Tarrytown, Rye, New Rochelle, Jamaica, and Staten Island. Hartford, Connecticut, and Boston had also erupted. Wednesday thus became a turning point at which the city had to be saved or fall to the mob completely. The hottest day of the year dawned with black smoke from sixty charred buildings, filling the air. The roads in Westchester County were jammed with refugees, as were the docks and railroad stations. People fled on the assumption that New York City would soon be destroyed. Many others could not flee because the rioters had torn up the railroad tracks. For those who remained in the city, especially black persons, danger lurked around every corner, particularly if they dared to show themselves on the street. The rioters continued to commit grisly murders as they purged the black neighborhoods.[25]

Some staunch Republicans not only wanted martial law but also appealed to Lincoln on Wednesday morning to send General Benjamin F. Butler to run the occupation and enforce the draft. Butler was known in the South as "the Beast" because of his ruthless tactics while military governor of New Orleans the previous year. Nearly all agreed that General Wool was incompetent, and a stronger officer was needed to win the battle against the rioters, on one hand, and the disloyal Democratic leadership, on the other. The belief had begun to spread among Republicans that the protest against the draft was "not simply a riot but the commencement of a revolution, organized by sympathizers in the North with the Southern Rebellion."[26]

"Let Barlow and Brooks and Belmont and Barnard and Wood and Andrews and Clancy be hung if possible. Stir the govt up to it," journalist Frederick Law Olmsted wrote to a friend. "I did not mean to omit Seymour." Talk of executing political opponents as traitors, in the private letters and diaries of Olmsted and Strong, may have constituted a serious policy goal or may have simply been a venting of anger. What is clear is that Union League Club members eventually hoped to reconstruct New York City much as radical Republicans in Congress would try to reconstruct the rebellious Southern states. For the moment, the club's top priority was to restore order in the city—with an unambiguous show of force.[27]

Anything less, they warned, would send a dangerous message to the rest of the country and to European powers, whose eyes were all fixed on New York. "The whole country is observing with interest the course of the Administration in dealing with the New York Conscription," a prominent Philadelphia Republican wrote to President Lincoln. "If not proceeded with, say, by an officer of known determination such as General Butler with military and naval forces to support him, the Union goes up in a blaze of States Rights. An exhibition of resolution will ensure Seymour's submission, the execution of the draft elsewhere, and avoidance of foreign intervention."[28]

Despite such advice, martial law was never declared in the city. Opdyke's fear, shared by other local leaders and the Lincoln administration, was that such a step would alienate Democratic leaders, who may have led the working classes into disloyalty but who could also bring them back into line again, as they were demonstrating through their speeches to the mobs across the city.[29]

During the final days of the riots, however, it was brute force that proved decisive in bringing the uprising to an end. Federal troops, brought in from the harbor forts, fired by platoons into the mobs and used artillery loaded with grapeshot and canister to clear the streets. By Wednesday night, rioters had gained control over parts of the east side by barricading them and setting up patrols on the perimeter. They searched house to house to kill off wounded policemen and soldiers. It would be the job of the militia regiments arriving from the Gettysburg front late Wednesday night and early Thursday morning to relieve the exhausted police and federal troops and to flush out the last pockets of resistance.

President Lincoln's choice of a Democrat, General John A. Dix, to replace General Wool on Friday, July 17, clearly disgusted those New Yorkers who had hoped for General Butler and a declaration of martial law. However, while Dix's appointment signaled that Lincoln was willing to work with the War Democrats of Tammany Hall instead of sweeping them aside, it also showed that the president intended to stop the rioting and enforce the draft in New York—and the Democrats would have to cooperate.

As commander of the Maryland Department, Dix had tolerated no disloyalty, a fact that recommended him for his new post. Dix, a New Yorker, had the confidence of the city's financial leaders, since he was himself an attorney and financier to whom they had turned before in moments of crisis. They had gotten him appointed secretary of the treasury in 1861 to help the feckless lame-duck president, James Buchanan as he stumbled through the secession crisis. At that time, Dix had also persuaded eastern capitalists to lend the federal government $5 million to shore up its finances.

The choice of a conservative War Democrat with a national reputation for integrity, nonpartisan leadership, and toughness as a military commander seemed to confirm President Lincoln's mastery of political compromise. Lincoln kept conservative, loyal Democrats in his war coalition and also pleased many ardent Republicans, who were happy to see power taken away from Governor Seymour.[30]

When New York Republicans asked Lincoln to launch a federal investigation of the riots and prosecute any Democrats who had fomented the uprising, the president was noncommittal. "Well, you see if I had said no," Lincoln told James Gilmore, "I should have admitted that I dare not enforce the laws, and consequently have no business to be President of the United States. If I had said yes, and appointed the judge, I should—as he would have done his duty—have simply touched a match to a barrel of gunpowder." Lincoln calculated that martial law in the city and a full investigation of the riots would provoke still more violence: "You have heard of sitting on a volcano. We are sitting upon two; one is blazing away already, and the other will blaze away the moment we scrape a little loose dirt from the top of the crater. Better let the dirt alone—at least for the present. One rebellion at a time is about as much as we can conveniently handle."[31]

The peaceful resumption of the draft in New York on August 19, 1863, was made possible not simply by the ten thousand Union troops and three batteries of artillery, supplemented by a division of militia stationed in the city; Tweed had also shown his flair for compromise, and Lincoln had agreed to his plan. The city floated $3 million in bonds to finance a Substitute Committee, run by Tweed, which would pay the exemption fee for any poor man who was drafted. The committee would also use the money to hire substitutes and reward volunteers so that Lincoln was guaranteed enough men for the Union ranks.

As the draft resumed, however, Lincoln faced further opposition to the Conscription Act in the state courts, where Democratic judges ruled against it, arguing that national conscription hollowed out the ranks of the militia, the institution that was the states' traditional and essential protection against excessive federal power. The Supreme Court of Pennsylvania, the highest court to issue a ruling on the Conscription Act during the Civil War, voted three-to-two along party lines in *Kneedler v. Lane* that the law was unconstitutional. With judges in several states using the writ of habeas corpus to release draft resisters from federal custody and military prisons, Lincoln was tempted to address the American people directly with an emphatic defense of the draft law and a call to arms.[32]

At some point in August or September 1863, he wrote out a detailed argument. He defended the constitutionality of the draft law by pointing to the power of Congress "to raise and support armies" and quoted from the Constitution that "this Constitution, and the laws made in pursuance thereof . . . shall be the supreme law of the land . . . anything in the constitution or laws of any State to the contrary notwithstanding."[33]

At least a million men had already volunteered, Lincoln said, but more were needed so that the "toil and blood" of these volunteers should not go to waste, and the country should not break apart: "There can be no army without men. Men can be had only voluntarily or involuntarily. We have ceased to obtain them voluntarily, and to obtain them involuntarily is the draft—the conscription. If you dispute the fact, and declare that men can still be had voluntarily in sufficient numbers, prove the assertion by yourselves volunteering in such numbers, and I shall gladly give up the draft."[34]

Lincoln went on to defend the specific provisions of the draft law: "Much complaint is made of that provision of the conscription law which allows a drafted man to substitute three hundred dollars for himself; while as I believe, none is made of that provision which allows him to substitute another man for himself." However, Lincoln argued, it should be the other way around: "The substitution of men is the provision, if any, which favors the rich to the exclusion of the poor. But this, being a provision in accordance with an old and well-known practice in the raising of armies, is not objected to. There would have been great objection if that provision had been omitted. And yet, being in, the money provision really modifies the inequality which the other introduces."[35] The $300 exemption, Lincoln argued, effectively capped the price of hiring a substitute (which would otherwise have been driven up much higher by competition among wealthy draftees), thus enlarging the pool of exempt men to include those of more modest means.

"The inequality could only be perfectly cured by sweeping both provisions away," Lincoln concluded. "This, being a great innovation, would probably leave the law more distasteful than it now is."[36] At the time, several monarchies and republics in Europe enforced universal selective service without exemptions, and while this would have been consonant with the American spirit of freedom and equality, Lincoln apparently perceived that Congress and the public lacked the political will to adopt such a system.

Noting that involuntary military service had been used in the Revolution and the War of 1812 (albeit at the state level), Lincoln asked, "Wherein is the peculiar hardship now? Shall we shrink from the necessary means to maintain our free government, which our grand-fathers employed to establish it, and our own fathers have already employed once to maintain it? Are we degenerate? Has the manhood of our race run out?" In September, Lincoln decided not to publish the document. Perhaps he did not want to push the fairness of the law too hard when the upper and middle classes were paying cash to avoid the battlefield. He may also have sensed that this vigorous statement of federal authority would only provide more fodder for his opponents to denounce him as a power-hungry tyrant. Instead, Lincoln focused on enforcing the draft.[37]

He called a special meeting of his cabinet on September 14, 1863. Gideon Welles, Secretary of the Navy, in his diary describes it: "The course pursued by certain judges is, he says, defeating the draft. They are discharging the drafted men rapidly under *habeas corpus*, and he is determined to put a stop to these factious and mischievous proceedings if he has the authority." The cabinet was divided as to whether Lincoln should take the potentially explosive step of suspending habeas corpus. "The President was very determined," Welles described, "and intimated that he would not only enforce the law, but if Judge Lowry [Chief Justice Walter H. Lowrie, Supreme Court of Pennsylvania] and others continued to interfere and interrupt the draft he would send them after Vallandigham." (Lincoln had banished Ohio Democrat Clement Laird Vallandigham from the Union and delivered him to the Confederacy in retaliation for seditious speech.) At a second meeting the following day, the cabinet agreed unanimously that Lincoln should use the power Congress granted to him in the Conscription Act to suspend habeas corpus in all cases whatsoever, but he should do so for military cases only. The proclamation was issued the same day.[38]

Two months later, buoyed by the victories at Gettysburg and Vicksburg during the summer, Republicans gained political ground in state and local elections. In Pennsylvania, the election tipped the scales in its supreme court, giving Republicans a three-to-two majority, which led to a reversal of the *Kneedler* decision. Republican judges upheld the constitutionality of the draft law by affirming the power of Congress to raise armies and by asserting that the nation's right to defend itself was an essential "attribute of sovereignty."[39]

By insisting that the conscription law be enforced, Lincoln had weathered the test of federal authority that the draft riots had thrust on his administration. But equally pivotal, in the opposite sense, was his decision not to impose martial law, not to pursue a federal investigation of the riots, and not to prosecute the Copperheads among the city's Democratic leadership—in short, not to reconstruct New York politically. By leaving the Democratic power structure in place and essentially letting the rioters and their political patrons go unpunished, Lincoln opened the door for the Democratic resurgence that unfolded over the next decade and a half. Not that he had much choice. He had already stretched his executive powers to the limit—far beyond the limit, according to his opponents—through censorship, suspension of habeas corpus, the arrest of dissenters, and his unilateral decrees, especially the Emancipation Proclamation. Had he chosen to oust elected officials in New York at the point of a bayonet, he might have given credence to Democrats' cries that he was indeed a military dictator who had destroyed the free government he had sworn to preserve.

Herein lay the tragedy of the draft riots and their aftermath. Emboldened by the compromise that allowed the draft to resume while making them heroes with their constituents, the city's Democratic leaders, particularly Tweed, consolidated and increased their political power dramatically, extending it to the state and national levels. In 1868, New York City hosted the Democratic National Convention at Tammany Hall and set the tone for the party—a white-supremacist platform that condoned the Ku Klux Klan violence then emerging in the South. Lincoln had opened the floodgates of Reconstruction with the Emancipation Proclamation, and the New York City draft riots had been the first outcry against this Republican program of freedom and equality for African Americans. The riots proved to be a harbinger of things to come. They set the pattern for a campaign of reactionary racial violence—aimed at suppressing the rights of freed black persons through murder and intimidation—that would last for decades. By 1876, the Democratic resurgence and Klan violence had put Samuel Tilden within a hairbreadth of winning the White House. Only the Compromise of 1877 took it from him, placing Republican Rutherford B. Hayes in the Oval Office, in exchange for removing the last federal troops from the defeated Confederacy. This ended Reconstruction and condemned African Americans to ninety more years of Jim Crow discrimination—until the Second Reconstruction of the 1950s and 1960s dismantled the nation's racial caste system.

Could this bleak, torturous course in the nation's history have been avoided? What if Lincoln had defied his critics and risked the potential dangers of opting for martial law and a federal investigation in New York after the riots? A recent experience abroad of occupation and purging the former elites in Iraq suggests that Lincoln's fears about New York may have been well grounded: Punishing the former ruling party can fuel an insurgency and sectarian violence. A wary compromise, giving party members a stake in the new order that is emerging, on the condition that they cooperate constructively, may be more effective in the long run. Lincoln chose the resumption of the draft, the vigorous prosecution of the war—the unity of the nation—at the expense of a just and satisfying retribution in New York. In the end, only victory on the battlefield would enable Lincoln and Congress to secure the Emancipation Proclamation, with the Thirteenth Amendment, creating a bedrock for the next struggle—to make African Americans not only free but equal.

Notes

1. Lincoln to Horatio Seymour, August 7, 1863, in Roy P. Basler, ed., *The Collected Works of Abraham Lincoln*, 9 vols. (New Brunswick, NJ: Rutgers University Press, 1953–55), 6:369–70, hereafter cited as *Collected Works*; Carl Sandburg, *Abraham Lincoln: The War Years*, 4 vols. (New York: Harcourt, Brace World, 1939), 2:369.

2. Alexander J. Wall, *A Sketch of the Life of Horatio Seymour* (New York: Self-published, 1929), 27.

3. *New York World*, July 13, 1863.

4. *New York Daily News*, July 13, 1863.

5. *The War of the Rebellion: A Compilation of the Official Records of the Union and Confederate Armies*, 128 vols. (Washington, DC: GPO, 1880–1901), ser. 3, 3:467. Hereafter cited as *OR*.

6. *New York Daily News*, July 11, 1863; *New-York Daily Tribune*, July 11 and 13, 1863; *New York Herald*, July 12, 1863.

7. News of the draft in other cities reprinted in the *New York Herald*, July 12, 1863.

8. Joel Tyler Headley, *The Great Riots of New York, 1712–1873* (New York: Dover, 1971), 149; *New York World*, July 14, 1863; *New York Herald*, July 13, 1863.

9. Headley, *Great Riots*, 153.

10. William Osborn Stoddard, *The Volcano under the City* (New York: Fords, Howard, and Hulbert, 1887), 33.

11. *OR*, ser. 1, 27: pt. 2:905–6; *New York Times*, July 14, 1863; Stoddard, *Volcano*, 41.

12. *New York World*, July 14, 1863; David Quigley, *Second Founding: New York City, Reconstruction, and the Making of American Democracy* (New York: Hill and Wang, 2004), 12; *Christian Recorder*, August 1, 1863.

13. Quoted in Richard C. Schneide, comp., *African-American History in the Press, 1851–1899* (New York: Gale, 1996), 1:302; Edward K. Spann, *Gotham at War* (Wilmington, DE: Scholarly Resources, 2002), 100.

14. Association for the Benefit of Colored Orphans, *Seventh Annual Report* (New York: New York Public Library, 1837–83), 6; Leslie Harris, *In the Shadow of Slavery* (Chicago: University of Chicago Press, 2003), 157; Martin B. Pasternak, "Rise Now and Fly to Arms: The Life of Henry Highland Garnet" (PhD diss., University of Massachusetts, 1981, 198–99; New York: Garland, 1995); Joel Schor, *Henry Highland Garnet: A Voice of Black Radicalism in the Nineteenth Century* (Westport, CT: Greenwood Press, 1977), 38–43, 47–48; Quigley, *Second Founding*, 20–21.

15. Iver Bernstein, *The New York City Draft Riots* (New York: Oxford University Press, 1990), 48–49; George Templeton Strong, *Diary of the Civil War, 1860–1865* (New York: Macmillan, 1962), 336–37.

16. Bernstein, *New York City Draft Riots*, 49.

17. Ibid., 49; Adrian Cook, *The Armies of the Streets: The New York City Draft Riots of 1863* (Lexington: University Press of Kentucky, 1974), 94–95; Strong, *Diary*, 337.

18. *New York World*, July 14, 1863.

19. *OR*, ser. 3, 3:488–94.

20. Edmund Ruffin, *The Diary of Edmund Ruffin*, 3 vols. (Baton Rouge: Louisiana State University Press, 1989), 3:70.

21. Joseph E. Stevens, *1863: The Rebirth of a Nation* (New York: Bantam Books, 1999), 293; George Opdyke, *Official Documents, Addresses, Etc.* (New York: Hurd and Houghton, 1866), 274; *OR*, ser. 1, 27, pt. 2:916; Stoddard, *Volcano*, 257, 265.

22. Abraham Lincoln to Robert T. Lincoln, July 14, 1863, *Collected Works*, 6:327.

23. Kenneth Ackerman, *Boss Tweed* (New York: Carroll and Graf, 2005), 13, 15–17, 20; *New York World*, July 15, 1863; *New York World*, July 16, 1863.

24. *New York World*, July 15, 1863; Bernstein, *New York City Draft Riots*, 50–52, 54; Ackerman, *Boss Tweed*, 20–21; Cook, *Armies of the Streets*, 106.

25. *New York Times*, July 16, 1863; Cook, *Armies of the Streets*, 139; James McCague, *The Second Rebellion: The Story of the New York City Draft Riots of 1863* (New York: Dial Press, 1968), 135–36; Herbert Asbury, *The Gangs of New York* (New York: Thunder's Mouth Press, 2001), 148; Headley, *Great Riots of New York*, 206–8, 210.

26. Bernstein, *New York City Draft Riots*, 54–55, 306nn77, 78.

27. Ibid., 55–56.

28. Robert A. Maxwell to Abraham Lincoln [undated], *Collected Works*, 6:331.

29. Bernstein, *New York City Draft Riots*, 60–61.

30. Clarence Eytinge to "My dear Admiral," July 16, 1863, Manuscripts, New-York Historical Society; Bernstein, *New York City Draft Riots*, 62–63; Maria Lydig Daly, *Diary of a Union Lady, 1861–1865* (Lincoln: University of Nebraska Press, 2000), 251–52; Joseph Hodges Choate, *The Life of Joseph Hodges Choate* (New York: Scribner's, 1921), 258.

31. James R. Gilmore, *Personal Recollections of Abraham Lincoln and the Civil War* (Boston: Page, 1898), 198–99.

32. John Whiteclay Chambers II, *To Raise an Army: The Draft Comes to Modern America* (New York: Free Press, 1987), 55–56.

33. "Opinion on the Draft," (September 14? 1863), *Collected Works*, 6:446.

34. Ibid., 6:447.

35. Ibid.

36. Ibid., 6:448.

37. "Opinion on the Draft," *Collected Works*, 6:448. This undated document is analyzed in Sandburg, *Abraham Lincoln*, 375–77, and Chambers, *To Raise an Army*, 56.

38. "Opinion on the Draft," *Collected Works*, 6:449n1; "Proclamation Suspending Writ of Habeas Corpus," September 15, 1863, *Collected Works*, 6:452.

39. Chambers, *To Raise an Army*, 56–57.

5

THE FIERY FURNACE OF AFFLICTION

CATHERINE CLINTON

*T*he Lincolns felt well rid of the past twelve months when the year's end approached in December 1862. On Christmas Day, Mary and her husband had toured hospitals in the District of Columbia and a week later faced the New Year with quivering anticipation. So much of 1862 had been characterized by losses, defeats, and setbacks—most severely the death of their son Willie in February and the ghastly bloodbath from December 11 through December 15 at the Battle of Fredericksburg, Virginia, which prompted the president to claim: "If there is a worse place than hell, I'm in it!" Although September 17 at Antietam in Maryland had been the single bloodiest day in American history, with roughly twenty-three thousand casualties, it was also the opportunity for the president to launch his most memorable wartime campaign: issuing the preliminary Emancipation Proclamation. So the advent of the New Year might signal the dawn of a new age.

Finally, on New Year's Day, with the cabinet assembled, with throngs circling the White House, Lincoln steadied his hand to make sure his signature was firm, knowing the import of this document to his reputation. He allowed the moment to be commemorated by Francis Bicknell Carpenter's later painting of the president reading the preliminary proclamation to his cabinet—setting the scene for future commentators. It was a great public celebration, but it was also a Lincoln family triumph.

Mary was equally committed to preserving her husband's legacy, and her smallest gestures were meant to promote Lincoln's historical place, to cement his deeds into fitting memorialization. She sent along a photograph of her husband as a holiday gift to Josiah Quincy, the former president of Harvard University. This likeness of Abraham Lincoln arrived in Cambridge, Massachusetts, just when the city was overwhelmed by the momentous news of Lincoln's Emancipation Proclamation. Eliza Quincy, Josiah's daughter, wrote to Mrs. Lincoln on the second of January, following festivities in Boston where "it was a day & occasion never to be forgotten."[1]

By January 1863, Mary had begun to visit the district hospitals two or three times a week. The Washington *National Republican* reported, "The fear of contagion and the outcries of pestilence fall unheeded."[2] Hospital work had become her most zealous campaign—efforts that Lincoln's secretaries wished she would make more public by taking along a reporter, which Mrs. Lincoln disdained. She was known as Madame President by this point in her husband's administration, and she had to be careful of her tarnished public image—which had been besmirched even before Lincoln took office. The First Lady's crusade for the soldiers was second only to protecting her husband from those she perceived to be his enemies. Even the snappy young male secretaries of the White House were impressed by the "Hellcat's" nine lives.

As the anniversary of Willie's death (February 20) approached, Mary became more involved in White House social obligations. She anticipated putting her bombazine—a silk fabric in twill weave—back into tissue-lined trunks, packing up her mourning garb, if not her grief, for the good of her household and her country. During the early weeks of 1863, Lincoln remained under great pressure yet continued therapeutic theatergoing and attending the last levee of the season on March 2, where Mrs. Lincoln looked particularly regal in black satin and jewels. Mary Lincoln threw herself into a crowded social schedule after her year of suspended activities. She continued her hospital work and dabbled in patronage, increasing her struggles to secure positions for friends.

She resumed her Saturday visiting hours, but guests might hear a litany of complaints. She confessed to Elizabeth Lee, sister of Lincoln's cabinet member Montgomery Blair, that except for Lee's brother, "there was not a member of the Cabinet who did not stab her husband and the Country daily."[3]

During 1863, she still sought comfort in the parlors of spiritualists, who promised to put her in touch with departed loved ones. The number of séances that Mrs. Lincoln attended following Willie's death (with or without her husband), the number of séances held at the summer cottage or in the White House, the president's attitudes toward spiritualism, and the depth of his wife's feelings continue to be a source of debate, unresolved by the evidence, which is verifiable.

The memoirs of spiritualist Nellie Colburn assert that she knew both the Lincolns from spiritualist circles in wartime Washington and that the president, too, was a spiritualist. Colburn and her fellow believers derived their claims from Lincoln's willingness to attend séances to appease his wife in the months after Willie's death. The allegations that Lincoln proposed the Emancipation Proclamation at the behest of the spirit world or that he climbed on a piano and was levitated by spirits demonstrate how confabulation can mushroom into an overblown assertion from thin threads of speculation.

Lincoln's presence in Cranston and Margret Laurie's Georgetown parlor (well known for their society séances) does not indicate much beyond his indulgence of his wife while they mourned their child. Lincoln did take meetings with spiritualists—even without Mrs. Lincoln present—but this may have reflected his extreme curiosity and courtesy rather than any affinity. By contrast, Mrs. Lincoln acknowledged her participation in spirit circles and confided that these sessions allowed her to communicate directly with Willie. She even confessed to contact with her other late son, Eddie, as well. Her belief that her dead boys appeared to her brought Mary great comfort—a comfort sought by thousands of mothers across the nation, especially mothers of soldiers during the dark days when death lists were published.

It was suggested that it might be good publicity to entertain a popular couple, and, thus, the Lincolns hosted a wedding reception in the White House for P. T. Barnum's famous "celebrity" General Tom Thumb and his bride, Lavinia Warren—who had become the subject of tabloid coverage. In the midst of a war, this folly was viewed as diverting and shows Mrs. Lincoln's willingness to be dragged from her gloom. Despite the disapproval of her son Robert, who was home from his studies at Harvard and annoyed by what he felt was his mother's lack of decorum, the First Lady invited nearly fifty guests on February 13 to meet the newlyweds—much to the delight of her other son, Tad. Mrs. Lincoln wore a rose-colored dress with a low neck and flowers bedecking her hair, marking the end to her official mourning. Both Lincolns were renewing their energies in the spring of 1863 and keeping a close watch on their remaining sons.

Going to the theater and to Stuntz's toyshop on New York Avenue were favorite pastimes for father and son Tad. Ironically, Lincoln was especially fond of taking Tad to Ford's Theatre as Mr. Ford had a son near the same age who proved a distracting playmate. Lincoln confided, "I want to give him all the toys I did not have and all the toys that I would have given the boy who went away."[4]

On February 21, Mary wrote a friend who had sent along comforting correspondence: "My dear Mrs. Welles: Allow me to thank you for your sympathizing & kindly remembrance, of yesterday, when I felt so broken hearted. Only those, who have passed through such bereavements, can realize, how the heart bleeds at the return, of these anniversaries."[5] That same day, Mary greeted guests at a reception with "the affability for which she is distinguished" and hosted Dr. Anson Henry at a White House dinner. The Springfield family friend and long-time medical adviser might have been pleased at how far his former patient had come: Lincoln had been in his care during his suicidal depression following the falling out with Mary Lincoln in 1841. Now, more than twenty years later, Lincoln was in the White House with his wife by his side, carrying the cares of the nation upon his capable shoulders.

As president, transforming the nation from a slaveholders' republic to a country rededicated to the principle that all men should be free—and (perhaps) equal—Lincoln had launched a major revolution. By enlisting African Americans in the Union army, he proffered them the status of soldier-citizens in this brave new world.

In April 1863, Jane Swisshelm attended a White House reception. As a radical abolitionist and correspondent for Greeley's *New York Herald*, she had been the first woman to report on politics from the U.S. Senate gallery. She remained an indefatigable champion of slave emancipation, Indian rights, and the rights of women. Previous to her first personal encounter with the Lincolns on April 2, she categorically had *not* wanted to meet Lincoln and most especially his wife. She had credited the rumors that Mrs. Lincoln was a Confederate spy and therefore claimed to despise her. Imagine Swisshelm's surprise when she bonded with the First Lady in their earliest introduction. When she shook hands with her, Mary Lincoln told Swisshelm not to worry that her glove might soil the First Lady's. She suggested that if it did, she would "preserve the glove to remember a great pleasure for long have I wished to see you." This was the beginning of a mutual admiration society, as Swisshelm heaped on lavish compliments: "I recognized Mrs. L as a loyal, liberty loving woman."[6] The two women found common interests, and the unlikely pair became admirers.

Swisshelm later explained to her readers that not only had Mary Lincoln become radically opposed to slavery but that it was she who urged the president "to Emancipation, as a matter of right, long before he saw it a matter of necessity." Furthermore, "whatever aid or counsel she gave him, in her eyes, his acts were his own, and she never sought any of the credit due them."[7] Her notion of Mrs. Lincoln's astuteness rings true, but her reticence to claim influence does not seem supported by other contemporaries. Further, Swisshelm is one of a handful of sources who credited Mary Lincoln with swaying her husband's policies towards emancipation, but there seems to be little evidence at the time—as opposed to posthumous speculation—that this was the case.

The First Lady's close friendship with Elizabeth Keckly, who was first her seamstress, then her confidante during her time in the White House, hints at her unusual perspective. Her sympathetic relationship with Keckly revived memories of slavery's brutalities during her own impressionable Kentucky youth. Her deepening friendship with radicals, such as Massachusetts U.S. Senator Charles Sumner, had a powerful effect. Mary Lincoln's opposition to slavery reflected a shift undertaken to court favor. Emancipation, rather than simple antislavery, developed into a litmus test for Washington's abolitionist elite, and Mrs. Lincoln managed to pass with flying colors and won over former critics.

Mary Lincoln was flattered by Sumner's White House appearances, as he would stop by the presidential manse to draw Mary out. The two exchanged floral tributes, traded visiting cards, and during Sumner's frequent chats with Mary "often late in the evening—My darling husband would join us & they would laugh together, like two school boys."[8] Sumner's courtly attentions to Mrs. Lincoln allowed the president to warm to this statesman and made him a particular friend.

Both the president and his wife enjoyed taking Tad on a water excursion on the steamer *Carrie Martin* and presenting him with a pony on April 4 in honor of his tenth birthday. The family camped in tents at General Joseph Hooker's headquarters near Fredericksburg, where the mood was light. While on an excursion with General Daniel Sickles, Lincoln was bestowed with kisses by the infamous Princess Agnes Salm-Salm.

The princess was born Agnes Joy, the daughter of a respected Vermont general (distantly related to the president himself) and was living with her sister and brother-in-law in wartime Washington. Joy married a titled European soldier of fortune, against her family's wishes. The flame-haired princess had attracted the attentions of many soldiers, especially during her rides along Pennsylvania Avenue astride her mustang, Minnehaha. The equestrian beauty at times eschewed a saddle (claiming an Indian foremother) and rebelled against Washington's conventional behavior. Her notorious reputation was somewhat redeemed by her marriage to titled nobility.

But after her marriage to the prince, the bride followed her husband to the battlefield, further defying social convention. The princess redeemed herself as she nursed wounded soldiers in campsites. Presumably, Lincoln found her spirit and patriotism refreshing. Nevertheless, he was taken aback when she entered the military tent near Aquia and "kissed him three times—once right, once left and once on the mouth—amid considerable gaiety."[9] The gaiety became ribald on the road back to headquarters, and Mrs. Lincoln learned details of the incident. General Daniel Butterfield's wife reported that Lincoln made a joke over dinner the next day to melt Mrs. Lincoln's frostiness toward General Sickles, who had been his escort. Lincoln turned to Sickles and said, "I never knew until last night you were a very pious man. . . . Mother says you are the greatest Psalmist in the army. She says you are a Salm-Salmist."[10] This mischievous remark broke the ice, as Mrs. Lincoln joined in the laughter.

The press had a field day painting pictures of the younger Mr. Lincoln by his father's side. Journalists were uncharacteristically low-key about the First Lady. One reporter noted, "Mrs. Lincoln's attire was exceedingly simple—of that particular style of simplicity which creates at the time no impression upon the mind, and prevents one from remembering any article of dress."[11] This successful family outing was a media triumph.

A very different atmosphere pervaded when Lincoln visited Hooker's headquarters a month later. Mrs. Lincoln found it impossible to keep her husband diverted, as the drumbeat of war pounded away. The Battle of Chancellorsville began on April 30 and ended on May 6. The reports from the front hammered away at fraying nerves in the White House. In one instance, Mrs. Lincoln, wearing just her wrapper and with her hair down, received women friends and, agitated as she walked the floor, exclaimed, "They are fighting at the front; such terrible slaughter; and all our generals are killed, and our army is in full retreat; such is the latest news."[12]

As in summers past, Mrs. Lincoln became restless and made several excursions northward. She found comfort in visits with intimate friends like Sally Orne, the wife of a Philadelphia carpet merchant. The president remained anchored in D.C., but on June 9, the day after she left the capital with her younger son, Mary received a telegraph from her husband with a frantic message: "Think you better put Tad's pistol away. I had an ugly dream about him." Mary sent Abraham reassurances, and after three updates from her, he finally confessed, "I am very well, and am glad to know that you and Tad are so." Days later, he suggested he was "tolerably well," putting the best face on his situation, under considerable duress. The Lincolns always exchanged confidences about dreams and premonitions, and Mary seemed to be one of the few to whom he could turn when bleakness overtook him.

Lincoln was often up early and rarely took time to sit down for breakfast, unless guests were invited. Lincoln's practice of chomping only an apple for dinner (as the midday meal was known) was legendary. Mary would often have to call him several times to supper and worried about his diet and lack of appetite. The First Lady might resort to cajolery. She even enlisted Tad's help to keep her husband from skipping meals. The president was especially fond of stewed chicken with hot biscuits and cream gravy. Mary would delegate one of the kitchen staff to cook the meal just the way the president liked it. After these delicacies were prepared, she then asked Tad to bring his father along to a room—where the table would be laden with his favorite foods. Ambushed by his wife and son, the president might clean his plate and even ask for extra helpings. Mary used whatever means she could to implement good health—insisting upon drives and excursions to take her husband's careworn mind off the constant demands of his office.

The hollows in Lincoln's cheeks were increasingly visible. And the president was dealing with political fallout, as Mary's relatives back in Springfield were accused of using the commissary to line their own pockets. As if that was not enough, bulletins warned of Confederate incursions into the North by the late spring of 1863. Mary returned home on June 13 in preparation for the family's annual summer retreat to the Soldiers' Home outside of Washington. Sadly, the retreat to their summer house a week later did not bring the halcyon relief for which Mary had hoped, and Lincoln became consumed with personal, political, and military anxieties in the early days of July.

During his daily journey from the Soldiers' Home to the White House on July 2, Lincoln decided not to take his own carriage but to ride horse-back—escorted by mounted bodyguards. The plan called for Mrs. Lincoln to follow in the carriage alone. When she did, serious mishap befell. Mary was thrown from the vehicle and landed badly, when her skull connected with a rock. The papers reported, "The driver's seat became detached from the carriage in some way, precipitating the driver to the ground. . . . [Mary] jumped and received severe bruises, the most severe was on the back of her head."[13] Reports of vehicles going awry or horses bolting had appeared in the press before in connection with the First Lady, so there was no specific alarm beyond the general concern the public felt. At first, the detachment of the seat from the carriage did not seem menacing—until investigators discovered that the "accident" was no accident at all.

When it was later discovered the carriage had been tampered with, fears over the president's safety multiplied. Lincoln was disturbed that Mary's injury was the collateral damage of sabotage. Particularly upsetting, this news unfolded over a matter of days, with some of the war's most dramatic events as backdrop—as news from a small town in Pennsylvania called Gettysburg filtered back to Washington.

After her fall, Mrs. Lincoln was taken to an army hospital, where a surgeon suggested her cuts were superficial and sent her home. Nevertheless, Lincoln believed his wife would need assistance, and he called on Rebecca Pomeroy (who had attended Mary following Willie's death) to watch over the First Lady once again. In those first days after her fall, Mrs. Lincoln seemed to be moving toward full recovery. Lincoln initially sent son Robert news to not be disturbed by press reports, as his mother was fine.

William O. Stoddard, one of the president's secretaries, had been consulting with the First Lady about plans for a spectacular Fourth of July celebration, although, after Lee's invasion of Pennsylvania, some Washington dignitaries wanted to call off elaborate celebration plans. The parade was designed to bolster patriotism in the wake of Congress's new measures for a military draft, and many feared any military setbacks might cause a backlash. When Stoddard shared the Fourth of July organizing committee's fears with the First Lady, Mary confided, "Mr. Lincoln is positive Lee will be defeated. . . . Don't you stop."[14] Stoddard promised to push ahead, and indeed, prayers were answered.

But by the time firecrackers and patriotic fervor filled the air—with news of Confederate retreat from Gettysburg and defeat at Vicksburg—the shades had to be drawn at the White House. Mary Lincoln's condition had taken a turn for the worse. Pomeroy detected infection. Mary's wound required reopening, and the First Lady was ordered to bed following her surgical procedure. With his wife's situation precarious, Lincoln summoned his oldest boy to Washington with a telegraph on July 11. When he failed to respond and hadn't shown up for two days, Lincoln became even more distressed. The Draft Riots had broken out in New York, where he had last had contact with Robert.

With the Conscription Act, a draftee could either provide a substitute or pay a fee of $300, a feature that Lincoln had opposed, but Congress allowed. This infuriated those who felt it was a "rich man's war, but a poor man's fight." Angry mobs responded by attacking a draft office in New York City on Monday, July 13. One of the first places to be looted during the Manhattan rampage was a Brooks Brothers store. Soon, rioters erupted throughout the city. Diarist George Templeton Strong suggested that irate crowds were Irish immigrants—"every brute in the drove was pure Celtic"—and anarchy reigned.[15]

The draft riots had severe consequences for African Americans, trapped in the melee during these ghastly four days. Princess Salm-Salm described in her memoir, "Wherever Negroes were discovered, they were hung or either barbarously murdered."[16] The beleaguered president was forced to send in troops to restore order.

By July 14, the president was overwhelmed with worry and wrote to his absent son, "Why do I hear no more of you?" For Lincoln, surely this anxiety was extreme. While the nation rejoiced in the victories at Gettysburg and Vicksburg, while angry mobs roamed Manhattan—his wife was fading, felled by a plot against him. Robert Lincoln, when he finally did show up, recalled his father's deep gloom, especially upset over this military blunder of Lee's escape: Lincoln broke down "in tears with his head bowed upon his arms."[17]

Mary needed a healthier environment, as a heat wave broke out in the capital. By July 28, Mrs. Lincoln headed to New England, joined by both Tad and Robert. She could not suffer the tropical summer weather in Washington, especially with the malaria scare in the city. Stoddard described the problem at length: "We are not above the tide-water here, and there is no current to speak of at high tide. . . . [A]n ooze has been developed which can testify its peculiar qualities to best advantage when the river is low and the tide is out."[18]

The paper reported both men and horses dropping dead in the streets. Stoddard and the other young men of the White House staff fell ill. The best advice physicians could offer was to flee, which is exactly what Mary and her sons did. The First Lady had selected for her convalescence a resort in Manchester, Vermont—the Equinox, nestled in the magnificent Green Mountains. This spot began as a popular tavern during the American Revolution, frequented by the legendary Green Mountain Boys. In 1853, Franklin Orvis opened the Equinox Hotel and billed it as a premier summer resort, with its natural mountain mineral water advertised for its "health maintaining properties." The air, the waters, and the well-heeled clientele recommended the place to Mrs. Lincoln.

The president was left behind, but his letters were full of charm and news, as when he wrote on August 8, "Tell dear Tad, poor 'Nanny Goat' is lost; and Mrs. Cuthbert & all are in distress about it." (Unfortunately, this letter never actually reached Mary but was returned to the president after having gone astray and landing in the possession of a soldier.) Lincoln was in better spirits, as he hoped there had been a turning point in the war, and Union victory appeared more and more a certainty; one of the president's personal secretaries wrote, "The Tycoon is in fine whack. I have rarely seen him more serene and busy."[19]

By the seventh week of Mary's absence, Lincoln's entreaties for her to return home become more wheedling: on September 20—"I neither see nor hear anything of sickness here now," and on September 21—"The air is so clear and cool, and apparently healthy that I would be glad for you to come." He also used go-betweens to try to get his family back to Washington, writing on the twenty-second: "Mrs. Cuthbert did not correctly understand me. I directed her to tell you to use your own pleasure whether to stay or come; and I did not say it is sickly and that you should on no account come. . . . I really wish to see you. Answer this on receipt." Mary responded that she had called for transportation to return from New York and that she was anxious to return home.

Before Mary arrived back in Washington, the president sent along news of a great Yankee triumph in Tennessee, where Union General William S. Rosecrans bested Confederate General Braxton Bragg at the Battle of Chickamauga. The president was jubilant over military successes and pleased at Mary's imminent return. Yet, he was devastated when black-bordered news arrived: the death of Confederate General Ben Helm,

Mary's brother-in-law, the husband of the Lincolns' beloved "Little Sister" Emilie. Ben Helm had turned down Lincoln's generous offer for a high commission in the federal army and returned South to enlist with the Confederates. Promoted to brigadier general after Shiloh, he was commanding the famed Orphan Brigade (the volunteer unit from Kentucky that fought for the Confederacy) when he was killed at Chickamauga on September 20, 1863. When Illinois friend David Davis arrived at the White House on the very day Lincoln heard the news, he found the president in a state of personal despair: "I feel as David of old did when he was told of the death of Absalom." When Mary arrived four days later, she and Lincoln mourned in private because, as her niece confided, "she knew that a single tear shed for a dead enemy would bring torrents of scorn and bitter abuse on both her husband and herself."[20] Mary hid her grief not *from* her husband but *to protect* her husband.

In September, Sarah Josepha Hale penned an editorial in which she asked, "Would it not be better that the proclamation that appoints Thursday the 26th of November (1863) as the day of Thanksgiving for the people of the United State of America, should, in the first instance, emanate from the President of the Republic?"[21] Hale appealed directly to President Lincoln, yet even when Secretary of State William Henry Seward replied on September 29 that her letter was receiving personal attention, Hale did not hold out hope. She had, after all, thus far written similarly to six presidents to no avail. But with hundreds of thousands of soldiers away from home and with Lincoln keenly attuned to the mood of the nation, he issued a proclamation in 1863 that Thanksgiving would be celebrated on the "last Thursday of November next." In a nod to historic precedent, he made the proclamation on the very same October 3 date on which Washington had proffered his own thanksgiving proclamation more than seventy years before. Lincoln put on his bravest face when he suggested in the middle of a war "of unequaled magnitude and severity" that "harmony has prevailed everywhere, except in the theater of military conflict."[22] The president's invocation of memories of holidays past struck a chord with the war-torn Union.

The Lincolns still sought diversions from worries at the theater. On October 17, Charlotte Cushman played Lady Macbeth to James Wallack's Macbeth in a benefit for the Sanitary Commission that netted over $2,000. The gala not only entertained the President and First Lady but was attended by "Master Thaddy." On November 9, the president enjoyed *The Marble Heart* at Ford's Theatre, a play starring John Wilkes Booth, the heir apparent to his father Junius's throne as the greatest actor in America and a serious rival to his brother Edwin's premiere status. But even these nights at the theater could not distract Mrs. Lincoln from the tangle of debt and duplicity she had woven for herself, a web in which she had now become entrapped.

The First Lady pleaded illness when her husband suggested they both attend the wedding of Kate Chase to Senator William Sprague on November 12, the social event of the season. Mary deeply distrusted Kate Chase and her father, Salmon P. Chase, former Ohio senator and governor, who lost his bid for the White House in 1860 when Lincoln became the Republican candidate. Lincoln appointed Chase as his secretary of the treasury, and he and his twenty-year-old daughter, Kate, attracted the crème de la crème to their home. Tales of Mary's jealousy abounded.

Kate Chase was charming, attractive, formidable, and ambitious, and her engagement to the wealthy Senator Sprague attracted widespread attention. A notice in the *Savannah News* described the extravagant engagement ring as a solitaire worth $4,000. At the wedding, the new Mrs. Sprague was resplendent in a white, velvet bridal dress with a point-lace veil. Lincoln knew his wife's boycott of the occasion would stimulate talk, so he spent over two hours at the reception to "take the cuss off the meagerness of the presidential party."[23] But it was Tad, not Mrs. Lincoln, who genuinely took ill a few days later—causing another White House crisis.

A national cemetery had been scheduled to open at the great battlefield in Pennsylvania to relieve the burdens placed upon Gettysburg, and Lincoln had been invited to speak. More than 170,000 soldiers the previous July had overrun the little town of roughly 2,500. The armies suffered over 50,000 casualties. A festival of death on such a scale was relatively new for the Union. The burial work that began in July 1863 was not completed until March 1864, nearly four months after the president journeyed to Gettysburg to deliver his famous address. The reburial of dead federal soldiers in the new cemetery was one of the costs of this war, one the nation needed to pay.

Mary Lincoln, hysterical over Tad's ill health, had begged her husband not to go. Tad's decline echoed the fatal stupor into which Willie had fallen nearly eighteen months before. As Lincoln prepared to depart for Gettysburg, both Seward and Blair agreed to accompany him on the noon train on November 18, but other cabinet secretaries begged off. The annual message to Congress was due soon, another year of war to explain, and politicians were seeking cover.

The morning Lincoln was scheduled to leave, his boy was too ill to eat his breakfast. Lincoln was torn between his fears for his son and his need to bolster spirits in Pennsylvania. Lincoln left the capital with a heavy heart. After a long day, he received a message from Stanton: "Mrs. Lincoln informs me that your son is better this evening." The president was up past midnight working on his speech. The next day, Stanton telegraphed again:

"Mrs. Lincoln reports your son's health is a great deal better and he will be out today."[24] This bolstered Lincoln's outlook even more. On the platform, he sat serenely through Edward Everett's two-hour oration, which the former president of Harvard delivered from memory. Then, the sixteenth U.S. president rose to the podium, put on his glasses, and read out what has become the most famous speech in American history—the Gettysburg Address. Spontaneous applause following the speech was, by all accounts, warm and enthusiastic. However, no one in the crowd, least of all Lincoln, could have imagined his words would become a national gospel, a creed that transcended its context and gave him lasting and international fame.

Nevertheless, Lincoln's speech was an immediate revelation to noted orator Edward Everett, who wrote to the president the next day, "I should be glad if I could flatter myself that I came as near to the central idea of the occasion, in two hours, as you did in two minutes." Even more telling, Everett lavished praise on the president after dining with him the night before. Mary would have loved Everett's estimation that the polish that Abraham Lincoln had acquired "may be credited to the influence of his wife."[25] As the crisis over her son's health passed, her husband had triumphed at Gettysburg, and Mary might have looked forward to the arrival of December with some anticipation, but events again intervened.

The strain of a divided house, which had been a metaphor for most of the war, became quite literal when the Lincolns welcomed Mary's half-sister Emilie Todd Helm to visit them in December. She arrived in Washington under presidential protection, but her brief stay stirred up a tempest and underscored fissures within the Lincoln White House. This Confederate widow's visit unbalanced the high-wire act Mrs. Lincoln had struggled to maintain. Emilie was making her way home to Kentucky to be with her mother when she was stopped at the Union border for refusing to take the oath of allegiance to the United States. The loyal wife complained that she could not dishonor her dead husband's memory. Military authorities detained her at Fort Monroe, at the tip of the Virginia Peninsula, and sent a telegram to the president, asking what they should do. His direction was simple "Send her to me, A. Lincoln."

When Emilie Helm arrived at the White House, a "pathetic little figure" with "pallid cheeks, tragic eyes," swaddled in black crepe, both Lincolns embraced her. The first night, Mary and Emilie had dinner alone together, avoiding inflammatory subjects, fearing to "open a fresh and bleeding wound." Emilie appreciated tours of the grand salons, noting that the Red Room contained the portrait of George Washington that Dolley Madison, a Todd kinswoman, had saved. Emilie settled in to guest quarters, the "Prince of Wales room," with its gloomy purple hangings brightened only by yellow cords. A fire kept her comfortable despite the December chill.

The strains of White House life were extreme. Republican Orville Hickman Browning suggested that Lincoln wanted Mrs. Helm's presence in the house kept secret. Yet, both Lincolns hoped Emilie might remain with them. Lincoln hoped the two sisters could comfort one another, as he feared his wife's nerves were still "gone to pieces." After Emilie had spent some time with Mary, she understood the intensity of her brother-in-law's concerns, as the First Lady's agitation was disturbing. She was alarmed by her older sister's "wide and shining" eyes during rapturous descriptions of visitations from the dead. To Emilie, this confirmed her sister's "abnormal" state. The First Lady confessed she might commune with her dead son Willie—not just in spirit circles but when he came to her chamber at bedtime. Mrs. Lincoln confided, "He lives, Emilie! . . . Little Eddie is sometimes with him and twice he has come with our brother Alec. He tells me he loves his Uncle Alec and is with him most of the time. You cannot dream of the comfort this gives me." Emilie's heart was wrenched seeing that her sister's bereavement had destroyed her peace of mind and hearing Mary's weepy confessions, such as, "When I thought my little son in immensity alone without his mother to direct him, no one to hold his little hand in loving guidance it nearly broke my heart."[26] A belief in an afterlife did not so much ease her suffering as demonstrate her precarious state of mind.

Emilie Helm, like most of her countrywomen North and South during the Civil War, was buoyed by faith in Christian redemption. She embraced tenets of spiritual salvation promised by Christian faith but feared the effects of Mary's preoccupation with the dead. The First Lady's embrace of the afterworld, Emilie recognized, was causing an increasing imbalance—a withdrawal from the "real world." Instead of being tempted herself by these escapes, Emilie recoiled. Abraham Lincoln hoped that Emilie would stay as long as she could because "it is good for her [Mary] to have you with her."[27] Perhaps as an antidote for both spiritualists and spirits, Lincoln invited Emilie at least to spend the summer with them at the Soldiers' Home.

When she first lost her son Willie, the First Lady was able to lean on sympathetic friends—Mary Jane Welles (wife of Secretary of the Navy Gideon Welles), Pomeroy, and Keckly. However, she had a limited number of fellow mourners, and many urged her to pack away her grief and get on with taking care of her family. As she struggled to do so, Mary's prolonged imbalance was a devastating hardship on Tad as well as her husband. Mary's situation worsened during her permanent expulsion from her "old Kentucky home" and Southern relatives allied with the Confederacy. This sense of exile was reinforced and her isolation accentuated by her Springfield relations deserting her.

To compound matters, Mary knew she was suspected of Confederate sympathies and criticized for the company of her sister Emilie in the flesh or her stepbrother Alec in spirit. She was unbalanced on the subject of her sons, and keeping Robert out of the army was one of her most passionate campaigns.

One of the sorest points among Washington Republicans was that Robert was not in the army. During December 1863, New York Senator Ira Harris was visiting the president's home and suggested that Robert should be in uniform: Harris had only one son, who had already enlisted. At the thought of Robert in the army, Mary's "face turned white as death." Senator Harris and General Sickles had come to quiz Emilie about conditions in the South, inquiring at first about mutual friends, then widening the dialogue. When Harris boasted about "whipping the rebels at Chattanooga"—particularly insensitive considering Emilie Helm had only been widowed a matter of weeks—she tartly countered by bringing up the fact that Yankees had fled Confederate troops at the Battle of Bull Run. This was particularly discourteous to General Sickles, who had recently lost his leg at the Battle of Gettysburg. Such slights were sure to provoke and did. Mrs. Lincoln tried to change the subject, but Harris turned to Helm to insist, "If I had twenty sons they should all be fighting the rebels." Whereupon, Emilie blurted out, "If I had twenty sons, General Harris, they should all be opposing yours," and ran crying from the room. Mary Lincoln followed to comfort her, and the two wept together once alone. When Lincoln gave him an audience, Sickles repeated the verbal fireworks. The president seemed amused: "The child has a tongue like the rest of the Todds." But Sickles did not see the humor, thundering that the president should not have a Rebel in the White House. Whereupon Lincoln replied, "My wife and I are in the habit of choosing our guests. We do not need from our friends either advice or assistance."[28]

When Emile's daughter Katherine and her cousin Tad were playing one day, the little girl insisted that Jefferson Davis was the president, and a shouting match between the cousins ensued. Lincoln intervened, keeping the peace. But Emilie knew her days with the Lincolns were numbered and confessed, "My being here is more or less an embarrassment to all of us."[29]

The breach remained an impasse. Emilie described it: "Sister and I cannot open our hearts to each other as freely as we would like. This frightful war comes between us like a barrier of granite."[30] Emilie left to return South, but she was not the only troublesome Todd in Washington, as one of Mary's other half-sisters, Martha Todd White, created a scandal of her own during her visit to Washington. At the end of 1863, Mrs. White had come to the capital to try to purchase things not available in her home in Selma, Alabama. When she arrived, she sent her card to her sister—indicating her interest in paying a call. The First Lady declined to receive or see Martha, ignoring overtures on more than one occasion. Despite this rebuff, Martha was granted a pass by the president to return to her home.

Rumors circulated that Martha had transported home to the South three large trunks, allegedly filled with medicines the federal embargo prohibited. She had also reputedly brought back a Confederate uniform decorated with gold buttons—and the value of these buttons was reported from $4,000 to $40,000 in various press reports. In the wake of these reports, scandal erupted. Many papers abused the president for granting his Confederate sister-in-law special treatment, presuming that she smuggled goods with his connivance. Horace Greeley, editor of the *New York Tribune*, affirmed these rumors by reprinting them: "Mrs. J. Todd White, the sister of Mrs. Lincoln, did pass through our lines for Richmond via Fortress Monroe with three large trunks containing merchandise and medicine, so that the chuckling of the Rebel press over her safe transit with Rebel uniforms and buttons of gold was founded in truth."[31]

Later evidence demonstrated that Lincoln not only denied White favors but warned her that she would be imprisoned if she did not leave without further fuss. His cabinet heard details from the president when the incident blew up in the press. Whatever the truth of the matter, these rumors were extremely damaging, especially Mrs. White's later intimations that she had outwitted her brother-in-law. (Indeed, she was invited to the Confederate White House in Richmond as a celebrity once the scandal appeared in the headlines.) Relatives boasted that, at a minimum, she had brought back her weight in quinine, defying the blockade. The White House tried to remain above the fray, but this was a source of grievous embarrassment to both Lincoln and his wife.

Both the Lincolns dreaded charges of Confederate sympathizing, and did all they could to quell such rumors. Emilie Helm sent a letter to Lincoln on December 20 after she arrived back in Kentucky, requesting that the president waive the prohibition against prisoners receiving clothing and other goods. Her request was ignored. Abraham Lincoln had many more worries on his mind. His own health was precarious—he was just recovering from varioloid, a mild form of smallpox. Lincoln's doctors confined him to bed rest, which gave him more time to work on his annual message to Congress.

Lincoln loved to tell the tale of "Jack the turkey." Tad had been delighted when a friend sent a live turkey to the Lincolns in December 1863. Their son befriended the bird—the boy was a magnet for creatures great and small. Tad became apoplectic when he discovered the bird, whom he had named "Jack," was slated for Christmas dinner. He begged his father to provide a stay of execution, and Lincoln wrote out an actual reprieve to spare him. (In homage, every president since Harry S. Truman has issued a pardon for a turkey in a ceremony shortly before Thanksgiving—both Thanksgiving and pardoning a turkey being associated with the Lincoln White House.)

By Christmas, Lincoln felt fully recovered and the next day proposed an outing with Tad and Mary down the river. But this third December in the White House was perhaps even more dispiriting than the year before. It was the second holiday season without Willie, and his birthday had always been a highlight, falling four days before Christmas. So it was a rather subdued holiday, another year without him, as Mary struggled to embrace the New Year.

When 1864 finally rolled around, both the Lincolns realized that in addition to their regular and exhausting round of duties, the president would soon enter the race for his party's nomination—and confront another election. On New Year's Day, the Lincolns faced their public at the traditional White House reception. The president seemed "brighter and less woebegone," according to several observers, while Mary Lincoln had abandoned her mourning garb. Both hoped that other families might avoid the trials and travails that they had faced and soon peace might be restored, as the Lincolns braced for yet another year of uncertainty.[32]

Notes

1. Eliza S. Quincy to Mary Lincoln, January 2, 1863, Abraham Lincoln Papers, Library of Congress, Washington, DC.

2. *Washington National Republican*, January 26, 1863.

3. Virginia Jeans Laas, ed., *Wartime Washington: The Civil War Letters of Elizabeth Blair Lee* (Urbana: University of Illinois Press, 1999), 231.

4. Ruth Painter Randall, *Lincoln's Sons* (Boston: Little, Brown, 1955), 180.

5. Justin G. Turner and Linda Levitt Turner, *Mary Todd Lincoln: Her Life and Letters* (New York: Knopf, 1972), 147.

6. Ruth Painter Randall, *Mary Lincoln: Biography of a Marriage* (Boston: Little, Brown, 1953), 321–22.

7. Ibid., 323.

8. Ibid., 319.

9. Michael Burlingame, *Lincoln Observed* (Baltimore: Johns Hopkins University Press, 1998), 35.

10. Julia L. Butterfield, *A Biographical Memorial of General Daniel Butterfield* (New York: Grafton Press, 1904), 162.

11. *New York Herald*, April 10, 1863.

12. Nettie Coburn Maynard, *Was Abraham Lincoln a Spiritualist or Curious Revelations from the Life of a Trance Medium?* (Whitefish, MT: Kessinger, 2003), 100.

13. *New York Herald*, July 4, 1863.

14. William O. Stoddard, *Inside the White House in Wartime: Memoirs and Reports of Lincoln's Secretary*, ed. Michael Burlingame (Lincoln: University of Nebraska Press, 2000), 117–18.

15. J. Matthew Gallman, *The Civil War Chronicle* (New York: Gramercy Books, 2003), 334.

16. Princess Felix Salm-Salm, *Ten Years of My Life* (Detroit: Belford Brothers, 1877), 56.

17. John S. Goff, *Robert Todd Lincoln* (Manchester, VT: Friends of Hildene, 1969), 52.

18. Stoddard, *Inside the White House*, 123–24.

19. John Hay, *At Lincoln's Side: John Hay's Civil War Correspondence and Selected Writing*, ed. Michael Burlingame (Carbondale: Southern Illinois University Press, 2000), 49.

20. Katherine Helm, *The Story of Mary: Wife of Lincoln* (New York: Harper, 1923), 217.

21. Catherine Clinton, "A History of the Thanksgiving Holiday," Gilder Lehrman Institute of American History, http://www.gilderlehrman.org/history-by-era/government-and-civics/essays/history-thanksgiving-holiday (accessed December 29, 2011).

22. Ruth E. Finely, *The Lady of Godey's: Sarah Josepha Hale* (Philadelphia: Lippincott, 1931), 202.

23. Burlingame, *Lincoln Observed*, 90.

24. Edwin M. Stanton to Abraham Lincoln, telegram reporting military developments in Tennessee, November 19, 1863, Abraham Lincoln Papers, Library of Congress.

25. Catherine Clinton, *Mrs. Lincoln: A Life* (New York: Harper Collins, 2009), 209–10.

26. Helm, *Story of Mary*, 227.

27. Ibid., 225.

28. Clinton, *Mrs. Lincoln*, 213–14.

29. Helm, *Story of Mary*, 231.

30. Ibid., 224.

31. Stephan J. Berry, *House of Abraham: Lincoln and the Todds, A Family Divided by War* (Boston: Houghton Mifflin Harcourt, 2007), 159.

32. Noah Brooks, *Mr. Lincoln's Washington: Selections from the Writings of Noah Brooks, Civil War Correspondent*, ed. P. J. Staurdenraus (South Brunswick, NJ: Yoseloff, 1967), 273.

6

And the War Goes On

John F. Marszalek and Michael B. Ballard

$\mathcal{I}$t was an event unlike any other in American history. The tall, gaunt president, tired from shaking hands at the New Year's Day reception, pulled the official paper before him. He made ready to sign the document that would begin the final end to the institution of slavery in the United States. He hesitated, noting that there was a tremor in his fingers from all the hands he had shaken that day. He waited for the shaking to stop; he did not want his signature to indicate any hesitancy about signing the final Emancipation Proclamation. When he finally signed this document, his signature was sure.[1]

It was one thing to declare the end of slavery in those areas of the Confederacy still in opposition to the United States, but it was another to accomplish that feat. Many in the North were outraged at Abraham Lincoln's action, and in Richmond, Virginia, an issue of the *Southern Illustrated News* showed Lincoln unmasked as the devil himself.[2] The Emancipation Proclamation was a dramatic statement that the American Civil War had moved from a conflict between two armies on the battlefield to a conflagration between two entire societies. The war had begun because the states of the Confederacy were determined to protect their "peculiar institution," and now the United States showed beyond doubt that slavery's days were numbered.

Lincoln's cabinet had convinced him not to issue the proclamation until he could claim an important military victory. Antietam (Sharpsburg), Maryland, was that success; it was actually a drawn battle, but that was good enough for Lincoln. Soon after Robert E. Lee's troops withdrew from Maryland and hurried back to Virginia, thus giving Union General

George Brinton McClellan possession of the battlefield, Lincoln made public his statement on September 22, 1862. He gave the slaveholding regions in rebellion until January 1, 1863, to eliminate slavery before he would abolish it himself. On January 1, 1863, Lincoln followed through on the threat of his preliminary statement. He abolished slavery in disloyal areas.

There had been concern among African Americans and other antislavery people that Lincoln would not follow through on his September 22, 1862, pronouncement. He would back away and not emancipate anyone, antislavery activists worried. Despite the victory in Maryland, those who supported the Union grew increasingly concerned over the Federal war effort. It did not seem to be moving forward. The Emancipation Proclamation might not really be a statement of victory; it might be an indication of the desperation of the United States and its president.

On the battlefields of the war, there seemed to be no end to Union military defeats. The Army of the Potomac under McClellan was hurled back by Lee during the Virginia Peninsular Campaign in the spring, John Pope was defeated at Second Bull Run in August, and the Army of the Potomac under Ambrose Everett Burnside lost again when it was bloodily repulsed at Fredericksburg in December. Antietam was hardly an unquestioned success. Ulysses S. Grant, the hero of Forts Henry and Donelson, and Shiloh, Tennessee, and second-in-command to Henry Wager Halleck during the Union capture of Corinth, Mississippi, in May, then survived the later difficult battles at Iuka and Corinth. Grant followed with the Union campaign against Vicksburg, Mississippi, in December and saw it begin miserably. He sent William Tecumseh Sherman's force down the Mississippi River to attack from the transports, while he planned to push through central Mississippi and attack Vicksburg from the east. Sherman's attacking force was driven back with heavy losses at Chickasaw Bayou, while Grant had to turn back when Confederates burned his supplies at Holly Springs, Mississippi.[3]

In another area of the war, during the final days of 1862 and the first days of 1863, William S. Rosecrans and Confederate Braxton Bragg fought to a bloody impasse at Stones River, Tennessee (Murfreesboro). The Federals withstood several attacks, and the Confederates withdrew from the battlefield. Still, casualties were high on both sides, and the Union victory was hardly conclusive.

As Lincoln signed the Emancipation Proclamation on January 1, 1863, therefore, there was no expectation that the end of the war was anywhere in sight. Even when Union forces had won on the battlefield, their victories had hardly been absolute enough to cause overwhelming confidence.

The Northern public saw little reason to feel enthusiastic. In the spring of 1862, the Confederate army had suffered what seemed to be a terrible loss at the Battle of Seven Pines in Virginia; Joseph E. Johnston was seriously wounded. His replacement, Lee, was hardly greeted as a savior, his performance in West Virginia creating little faith that he could stand up to the Army of the Potomac. In fact, he did just that. He pushed McClellan's force away from Richmond and secured the city. Then he smashed Pope's army at Second Bull Run, while McClellan stood by seemingly enjoying the spectacle. Thomas Jackson, who had won the nickname "Stonewall" at First Bull Run, played a vital role at the second battle there. James Longstreet also demonstrated leadership and improved his reputation. The Confederacy seemed to be producing the winning generals.[4]

It was hardly as encouraging on the Union side. Halleck became commanding general of all Union armies after his successes in the western theater. Lincoln looked to him to provide leadership in the eastern theater, but he demonstrated no such military talent. He suffered physically and emotionally and proved not to be the leader Lincoln had expected. McClellan had a huge ego, but he did not perform in a manner to match its size. Burnside was reluctant to take command of the Army of the Potomac, and his time in control proved disastrous. Rosecrans was competent but evoked little excitement.[5]

Two Union generals had questions surrounding them, but they were later raised up for praise. Grant had shown brilliance in many of his 1862 actions, notably Forts Henry and Donelson. He stumbled during the first day at Shiloh, but he regained his step the next day and drove the Confederates off the field. His performance at Iuka was lackluster, and his role in the Battle of Corinth in October raised eyebrows. Grant's earliest moves against Vicksburg were also disappointing. Still, he was constantly on the offensive, testing and pushing the enemy. Lincoln put it best when he commented to critics of Grant: "I can't spare this man, he fights."[6]

Sherman was a similar uncertainty. He suffered through an anxiety and depression crisis in Kentucky and Missouri at the start of the war, but he found himself and proved an able ally to Grant in the Forts Henry and Donelson campaigns, providing logistical support. He fought well at Shiloh, but he took a lot of blame for the surprise Confederate attack there. He ably led a wing of Halleck's army at Corinth when the Union army marched down from Shiloh in April and May. He helped force the Confederate evacuation of that Mississippi city. He had a controversial tenure as military governor of Memphis and then failed at Chickasaw Bayou in opening the Vicksburg campaign. At the same time, he had become controversial for destroying the town of Randolph, Tennessee, in retaliation for Confederate guerrilla sniping against Union vessels on the Mississippi River. Sherman hardly showed promise as a winner.[7]

In short, while the early months of 1862 had been encouraging to the Union war effort, the end of the year demonstrated problems on all military fronts. Even politics did not look promising. In the 1862 election, Republicans lost twenty-two seats, and Democrats picked up twenty-eight, a swing of fifty seats.[8] Certainly, Lincoln's issuance of the Emancipation Proclamation in September hurt Republican chances, but so, too, did the unhappy situation on the battlefields.

The promulgation of the Emancipation Proclamation January 1, 1863, did not change the tempo of the war. Burnside attempted to make up for his December loss at Fredericksburg by going on a winter offensive in January. All he accomplished in what derisively came to be called a "Mud March" was a further deflation of Union hope. It was bad enough to see Union troops defeated on the battlefield by the likes of Lee, but to have weather, mud, and rain do so was almost too much to bear.[9]

Once again, therefore, failure seemed to be haunting the Union war effort. Lincoln was beside himself and gave command of the Army of the Potomac to Joseph Hooker, a brash, confident commander who believed he was the one to crush Lee. Hooker restored the army's morale and then began to move against the Confederates. His plan was to shift his army westward from Fredericksburg to outflank Lee. A Union force commanded by John Sedgwick stayed behind at Fredericksburg to keep Lee's attention.[10]

Upon learning of Hooker's move, Lee left Jubal Early in Fredericksburg with a small force and turned the rest of his army west to meet Hooker. Breaking all the rules of warfare, Lee divided his army yet again, detaching Jackson's division to march in a semicircle across the front of Hooker's army, which faced south. Jackson's goal was to get beyond Hooker's right flank and attack. Lee and the remainder of the Army of Northern Virginia remained in front of the Army of the Potomac. The tactical march by Jackson could produce a devastating surprise attack if Hooker did not realize what was going on.

Lee had less than fifty thousand men on hand, having not only left Early at Fredericksburg but also going into battle without Longstreet's division detached to Suffolk, Virginia. Hooker had seventy thousand men in front of Lee. By sending Jackson's twenty-six thousand troops on the flanking march, Lee left himself with twenty-four thousand to confront Hooker.

Early on May 2, 1863, Jackson's troops crashed into Hooker's flank and destroyed it, sending Union soldiers fleeing east toward the rest of the army or northeast toward the Rappahannock River. When Lee heard the commotion, he assaulted Hooker's left flank, commanded by George Gordon Meade. This attack kept Hooker from unifying his force, but Confederate successes came at a great cost. In the evening shadows, Jackson fell seriously wounded, accidentally shot by some of his own men. Jackson would eventually lose his left arm and die of complications. Lee commented that he had lost his right arm when he lost Jackson.

On May 3, fighting continued until Hooker was struck by artillery-induced debris from the house that was his headquarters. Temporarily incapacitated, Hooker could no longer command, and one of his subordinate generals ordered a retreat across the Rappahannock and Rapidan Rivers, where the Union forces quickly reorganized. The struggle at Chancellorsville came to be called Lee's greatest victory, and, indeed, it was. The loss of Jackson, however, crippled Lee's efforts for the remainder of 1863. In truth, though, Union troops had suffered a humiliating defeat. Lincoln and the nation were driven into another state of hopelessness.

Northern fears only grew higher when Lee left Virginia and began moving his reunited army, now about seventy-five thousand men strong, toward Pennsylvania. Lee had convinced Jefferson Davis that another invasion of the North would produce positive results. Success might bring foreign recognition of the Confederacy as a separate country. Lee also believed and convinced Davis that moving north would take pressure off Confederate forces in Vicksburg. The truth was that Lee did not want to send any detachments from his army to the western theater. He had to know that Union armies had enough men to concentrate significant numbers both against him in Virginia and John C. Pemberton in Mississippi.[11]

On June 12, 1863, the lead elements of Lee's force crossed into the Shenandoah Valley, brushed aside Union resistance at Winchester, and on June 16 started crossing the Potomac River. On June 25, the commander of Lee's cavalry left the main column and led his riders on a path between the Union army and Washington. Lee's willingness to allow James Ewell Brown Stuart to make such a ride proved to be a major mistake.

On June 26, the advance troops of Early's division reached the town of Gettysburg, Pennsylvania. Hooker had trouble tracking Lee's movements, so once across the Potomac River, the Confederate army marched in a leisurely fashion. Upset and angry at Hooker's performance, Lincoln placed Meade in command of the Union army on June 27.

Unsure of Lee's location, Meade moved his army of one hundred thousand men north of the Potomac River to get in position to protect Washington. Lee reacted by ordering his three corps commanders, Longstreet, Ambrose Powell Hill, and Richard Ewell (Stonewall Jackson's replacement), to concentrate at Gettysburg and Cashtown. With his cavalry commander still roaming around east of his army, Lee had little news about Meade's location. The coming conflict at Gettysburg proved to be a case of two large armies literally bumping into each other.

On July 1, 1863, Hill's corps clashed with John Buford's Union cavalry. Reinforcements from both armies rushed to the sound of battle. By the end of the day, Confederates had pushed Meade's army through Gettysburg, but, significantly, the Army of the Potomac took possession of the heights of Cemetery Ridge, Culp's Hill, and the two Round Tops. Lee wanted to keep pressing the enemy, and his army's failure to do so left the Army of the Potomac in a strong position, a fishhook formation on high ground.

On July 2, Lee ordered Longstreet to attack the Union left and Ewell to attack the right. Ewell quickly demonstrated that he was no Stonewall Jackson, and Longstreet, who firmly believed Lee was mistaken to assault Meade's strong position, did not perform aggressively. Longstreet wanted to flank the Union army off the high ground, but Lee insisted on trying to drive forward to push the Federals into a retreat that way. Two hills, Little and Big Round Tops, on the far left of Meade's line proved too strong for the Confederates to carry. Both armies suffered significant casualties as the fighting raged up and down the battle lines all day. With his line stretched over an extended area, Lee could not coordinate his attacks, and lack of reinforcements at critical times led to a stalemate. Still, Lee persisted with his plan to defeat Meade head-on.

On July 3, Lee concentrated fifteen thousand men to attack the Federal center. Diversionary action against both ends of the Union line failed, but Lee ordered the attack anyway, preceded by a tremendous artillery bombardment that did little damage. Longstreet hesitated to give the order because he was convinced that it could not succeed. Finally, he relented, and the Confederates moved forward in what is commonly known as Pickett's Charge. Though some Rebels actually reached and penetrated the Union line, they were too few to hold the forward position, and the attack failed. Stuart finally arrived on the north end of Meade's line, but his cavalry failed to cut off Meade's possible retreat route. Lee defiantly remained in place through the night of July 3–4, 1863, but he really had no choice except to retreat into Virginia.

During this three-day struggle, Meade lost more than 23,000 men out of 80,000 engaged, 29 percent; Lee had about 65,000 men participating in the fighting and lost 20,500, 32 percent. The Confederate assault at Gettysburg is referred to as the "high tide of the Confederacy," and, certainly, Lee's army was never the same after this bloodbath. At this point, however, the situation was not all that clear, and it ignored what was going on in the western theater of the war.

As the embarrassment of the Mud March, the crushing defeat at Chancellorsville, and the significant Union victory at Gettysburg were taking place, one of the still unproven Union generals began a series of even more important military actions along the Mississippi River. In the spring of

1862, the Union navy had failed in its solo effort to force the surrender of Vicksburg, one of the South's major cities. It became obvious that a joint navy-army effort would be required, and Grant undertook it. First, he resurrected a failed effort from the previous year: the canal project. He did not believe in it, but Lincoln did, so Grant had his men start digging a ditch across a neck of land protruding into the Mississippi River in front of Vicksburg. The river made a hairpin turn there, and if the water could be diverted away from the point of the peninsula, Union boats could bypass the heavy guns perched along several levels of the high bluffs on which Vicksburg sat.[12]

The canal failed again as it had earlier. Grant then tried to find ways south via several canals in Louisiana, but all failed. He also tried to approach Vicksburg from the north via inland rivers in Mississippi, but Union forces got only as far as Fort Pemberton at Greenwood before they were forced to back out. An attempt by David Dixon Porter to lead his navy through narrow waterways to bypass Confederate guns on the Yazoo River also failed. Thus, Grant's attempts to gain footholds along the bluffs north of Vicksburg came to nothing. The failures of the previous year seemed manifested again.

In April 1863, Grant came up with another idea, this time of moving his army down the western side of the Mississippi River and using Porter's navy to cross his men into the state of Mississippi below Vicksburg. To go south to provide the transportation Grant needed, Porter had to run his gunboats and transports past the feared Vicksburg batteries. He did so with the loss of only one boat. By maneuvering his fleet from one side of the river to the other, he kept Confederate gunners from producing effective fire. Pleased with the results, Porter successfully ran more vessels past the guns. Meanwhile, Grant had cavalry, led by Benjamin Grierson, conduct a raid through eastern Mississippi from La Grange, Tennessee, to Baton Rouge, Louisiana, to confuse the Confederates. It worked.

Grant wanted to cross his troops at Grand Gulf, a heavily fortified position on the east bank of the Mississippi. Porter found that getting past these gunners would not be easy, however. After a lengthy battle in which the navy fleet suffered severe damage, Grant decided to continue south to find another crossing. Thanks to a slave, he found a landing called Bruinsburg, and on the evening of April 30, his army began steaming across the Mississippi in Porter's transports.

On May 1, 1863, with only one of his three corps and part of another on Mississippi soil, Grant ran into a small Confederate force west of the town of Port Gibson. After an all-day battle in rugged terrain, Grant's soldiers drove the Confederates away. Grant decided to move north by northeast toward the Southern Railroad of Mississippi, which connected

Vicksburg with Jackson, the capital of Mississippi, and with Meridian near the Mississippi-Alabama state line. Theoretically, the line, disconnected in some areas, connected with the Confederate east coast from where Rebel reinforcements were already en route to reinforce Pemberton, commander of the Confederate army at Vicksburg.

After he received word of the Confederate defeat at Port Gibson, Pemberton made no effort to challenge Grant. Grant moved inland with one corps on his right, commanded by James McPherson, and one on the left, led by John A. McClernand. Sherman's corps eventually arrived after staging a feint along the Yazoo River to the north.

McPherson ran into a Confederate brigade near Raymond, Mississippi, but his superior numbers forced the Rebels to retreat toward Jackson, Mississippi. By this time, Confederate General Johnston had arrived in Mississippi's capital to take command, but he immediately sent word to Davis, "I am too late." Johnston despised Davis and vice versa, and his heart was never in the Vicksburg campaign. The Confederate general proved to be little more than a spectator.[13]

Grant, aware of Johnston's presence, decided to attack the city of Jackson and try to disperse the Confederate troops gathered there. On May 14, 1863, with McPherson attacking from west to east, and the newly arrived Sherman assaulting the city from the south, Grant soon had possession of the capital. Johnston had retreated north to Canton, Mississippi, and left only a token force in Jackson.

Leaving Sherman behind to destroy Confederate military supplies and installations, Grant turned McPherson's corps to the west, where McClernand's unit joined it. The two corps moved toward Edwards, Mississippi, and en route ran into Pemberton's army in a countryside dominated by high ridges. The result was the May 16, 1863, battle at Champion Hill. Pemberton's army was not in position to fight, and Grant used his forces wisely. Surviving a deadly counterattack by John Bowen's Confederate division, Grant won the day in the key battle of his inland campaign. The next day, McClernand chased away Confederates at the Big Black River.

Pemberton retreated into the Vicksburg fortifications, and his men then beat back two attacks by all three corps of Grant's army. Grant settled in for a siege that lasted forty-seven days. With Porter dominating the river and thousands of reinforcements coming to his aid, Grant forced Pemberton's surrender on July 4. The North cheered, and Grant's reputation was made. He had captured a city, an army, and thousands of munitions. With the Federal capture of Port Hudson, Louisiana, a few days later, the Mississippi River was open to Federal forces from its source in Minnesota to the Gulf of Mexico.

Now the Union cause seemed much more positive. The victories at Gettysburg and Vicksburg had an enormous impact on the Union psyche. The capture of the army and the city of Vicksburg in such dramatic fashion demonstrated that the Federals had found the general to lead their armies to victory.

In the Tullahoma campaign in Tennessee between June 23 and July 1, 1863, another Union general, Rosecrans, was also demonstrating masterly military skill. He maneuvered Bragg's army out of Tennessee into the northwest corner of Georgia. By mid-September, the two armies had been jockeying for several more months. Then Rosecrans captured Chattanooga. He created a line of battle stretching southwest along a mountainous ridge that culminated at Lookout Mountain overlooking the city. Bragg had the advantage of gaining Longstreet's corps, sent from Virginia, but Rosecrans soon received Hooker's troops, which also arrived from the east. However, Bragg had negative relationships with all his other generals, and eventually Longstreet joined this dissident group.

Bragg's army was unable to cut off Rosecrans's forces, which kept roads open into Chattanooga. The first day of battle along Chickamauga Creek was a stalemate. That evening in mid-September 1863, Rosecrans concentrated his troops, and the Union army hurriedly dug breastworks for the expected continuation of the fight the next day. On the Confederate side, the remainder of Longstreet's corps, earlier hampered by transportation problems, arrived on the scene. Bragg gave Longstreet command of the left wing of the army and Leonidas Polk the right.[14]

Midday of September 20, 1863, Longstreet found a section of Rosecrans's line wide open. Confusion in Union orders had caused this gap in the Federal line, and Longstreet sent his corps pouring through it. Rosecrans had no choice but to retreat. George H. Thomas's stubborn resistance (earning him the sobriquet "Rock of Chickamauga") saved the Union army from disaster. Bragg's hesitancy to press the attack also allowed the Union army to escape into Chattanooga. During the two-day fight, Rosecrans lost over 16,000 men, and Bragg 18,500.

Bragg contented himself with setting up a quasi-siege of Chattanooga, posting his men along the slopes of Lookout Mountain and on the heights of Missionary Ridge overlooking the city. A stalemate ensued until Rosecrans was removed from command.

The military circumstances quickly changed. Rosecrans's replacement, the victor of Vicksburg, arrived soon, followed by Sherman's corps from Mississippi. Grant opened a supply route for the Union army, and after organizing it, he began launching attacks on Bragg's line, initiating the November 23–25, 1863, Battle of Chattanooga. Sherman had expertly rushed his troops to the scene, and although he could not dislodge Confederate

General Patrick Cleburne's force during the battle, his very presence was crucial to Grant and his effort. Hooker had been defeated severely at Chancellorsville, but now his troops drove Confederates off Lookout Mountain (called the "battle above the clouds"), forcing those Rebels onto Missionary Ridge, too. At the same time, Thomas's division fought its way to the foot of the ridge where they were supposed to stop. On their own initiative, however, these troops surged forward and began scaling the heights in front of them. Confederates panicked, and Bragg's army fell into disorganized retreat. Grant, Sherman, and Thomas had led the Federals to a year-ending victory of enormous significance.[15]

The early part of 1864 did not produce anything as dramatic as the January 1, 1863, Emancipation Proclamation. But these months did indicate that the war effort had changed momentum. In 1863, Union troops had won major victories at Vicksburg, Gettysburg, and Chattanooga. The seemingly invincible Lee had blundered by attacking frontally at Gettysburg, and then he had to limp back to Virginia. Had Union commander Meade followed him and trapped Lee's army against the Potomac River, he might have annihilated the Confederate force. But Meade did not press Lee, so the war in the western theater would continue in stalemate for another eighteen months. Lee may have bled his army at Gettysburg, but there he was back in Virginia, blocking the Army of the Potomac from the capital city of Richmond.

In the western theater, 1863 had seen an even greater change in the military situation. The Union army had won an important victory at Vicksburg, thus opening the Mississippi River to commerce and sealing the Trans-Mississippi region from connection to the eastern Confederacy. The capture of Chattanooga pointed a dagger into the very vitals of the South and opened the way for later Federal successes—Sherman's victory at Atlanta and his destructive march to the sea.

Even more important, 1863 produced the two military men who would conclusively lead the Union forces to military success. Grant and Sherman worked together successfully in numerous military campaigns that year and developed a bond of cooperation that would only grow in the months ahead and lead the Union troops to total victory.

It was also in 1863 that Lincoln's January Emancipation Proclamation began to be implemented. In April 1863, in the midst of Grant's Vicksburg campaign, Secretary of War Edwin M. Stanton sent General Lorenzo Thomas to organize into military units the many African American males who had fled slavery. Grant cooperated and encouraged slaves to enter Union lines and gain their freedom, and the young males then became part of the United States Colored Troops (USCT).[16] Try as the slaveholders might, they could not keep such news from their chattels. Consequently, slaves left plantations in even greater droves and attached themselves to the Union army, not knowing or caring whether they resided in areas still in rebellion. As the Confederacy lost on the battlefield, it also lost its plantation labor force that supported its armies, and the Federals gained nearly two hundred thousand more soldiers.

It was the Emancipation Proclamation that authorized the recruitment and use of African Americans as soldiers. The USCT became a part of the Federal forces. It was at Milliken's Bend and Port Hudson along the Mississippi River that black troops demonstrated their courage and their effectiveness as combatants. It was in 1863, then, that African Americans began their essential contributions to the Union war effort and showed conclusively that their contentment with slavery was simply a Confederate self-deception. The Emancipation Proclamation not only freed many slaves but it also empowered them and made them an essential part of the Union military effort.[17]

After the results of the events of 1863, the Confederacy really had no hope of military survival. When Lee surrendered to Grant at Appomattox and Johnston surrendered to Sherman at Durham Station, both in April 1865, the Union army could trace its victory and the Confederacy its defeat to 1863. Yet, the fighting did go on for another two years. Confederate armies remained in the field despite the crushing losses of 1863. Southern honor could not tolerate stopping the war, short of annihilation. Grant and Sherman, with Lincoln's approval, provided such a final result in 1864–65. The war went on until then.

Notes

1. For a recent account of the Emancipation Proclamation and its impact on the Civil War, see Harold Holzer, Edna Greene Medford, and Frank J. Williams, *The Emancipation Proclamation, Three Views* (Baton Rouge: Louisiana State University Press, 2006). See also John Hope Franklin, *Emancipation Proclamation* (New York: Anchor Books, 1965); Allen Guelzo, *Lincoln's Emancipation Proclamation: The End of Slavery in America* (New York: Simon and Schuster, 2006).

2. Adalbert J. Volck, "Writing the Emancipation Proclamation," cartoon, Library of Congress, www.loc.gov.

3. There are many books on the military history of the Civil War, far too many to mention or even sample. An excellent study is James M. McPherson, *Tried by War: Abraham Lincoln as Commander-in-Chief* (New York: Penguin Press, 2006).

4. Emory Thomas, *Robert E. Lee, A Biography* (New York: Norton, 1995); James I. Robertson Jr., *Stonewall Jackson: The Man, the Soldier, the Legend* (New York: Macmillan, 1997); Jeffrey D. West, *James Longstreet, The Confederacy's Most Controversial Soldier* (New York: Simon and Schuster, 1993).

5. John F. Marszalek, *Commander of All Lincoln's Armies, a Life of General Henry W. Halleck* (Cambridge, MA: Harvard University Press, 2004); Stephen W. Sears, *George McClellan, the Young Napoleon* (New York: Ticknor and Fields, 1988); William

Marvel, *Burnside* (Chapel Hill: University of North Carolina Press, 1991); William M. Lamers, *The Edge of Glory, A Biography of General William S. Rosecrans* (Baton Rouge: Louisiana State University Press, 1961).

6. Jean Edward Smith, *Grant* (New York: Simon and Schuster, 2001); Josiah Bunting III, *Ulysses S. Grant* (New York: Holt, 2004); Alexander K. McClure, *Lincoln's Yarns and Stories* (Philadelphia: Neil, 1901), 108.

7. John F. Marszalek, *Sherman, a Soldier's Passion for Order* (New York: Free Press, 1993).

8. Thomas Rice, "Burnside's Mud March: Wading to Glory," *Civil War Times Illustrated* 20, February 1981, 16–27.

9. Bruce Tap, "Election of 1862," in David S. and Jeanne T. Heidler, eds., *Encyclopedia of the American Civil War* (New York: Norton, 2000), 639–40.

10. Stephen W. Sears, *Chancellorsville* (New York: Houghton Mifflin, 2001).

11. Gettysburg is the most written-about battle of the Civil War. A good recent overview of the campaign is Steven E. Woodworth, *Beneath a Northern Sky: A Short History of the Gettysburg Campaign* (Lanham, MD: Rowman and Littlefield, 2008).

12. Michael B. Ballard, *Vicksburg: The Campaign That Opened the Mississippi* (Chapel Hill: University of North Carolina Press, 2004).

13. Joseph E. Johnston, *Narrative of Military Operations, Directed, during the Late War between the States* (New York: Appleton, 1874), 175–76; Craig Symonds, *Joseph E. Johnston, a Civil War Biography* (New York: Norton, 1992).

14. Peter Cozzens, *This Terrible Ground: The Battle of Chickamauga* (Urbana: University of Illinois Press, 1996).

15. Peter Cozzens, *The Shipwreck of Their Hopes: The Battles for Chattanooga* (Urbana: University of Illinois Press, 1996).

16. John Y. Simon, ed., *The Papers of Ulysses S. Grant* (Carbondale: University of Southern Illinois Press, 1979), vol. 8.

17. An excellent example of the revealing modern research on black soldiers is David Slay, "Abraham Lincoln and the United States Colored Troops of Mississippi," *Journal of Mississippi History* 70, no. 1 (2008): 67–86. See also John F. Marszalek, "Marching to Freedom: The U.S. Colored Troops," in Harold Holzer and Sara Vaughn Gabbard, *Lincoln and Freedom: Slavery, Emancipation, and the Thirteenth Amendment* (Carbondale: Southern Illinois University Press, 2007), 113–29.

7

PICTURING THE WAR

BOB ZELLER

*P*osing for the camera was no routine thing in 1863. The latest technology back then—the wet-plate negative—was an improvement on earlier methods but still required the sitter to remain rigid during an exposure that would take from three to twenty or more seconds.

"To prevent a tremulous motion of your head, which the bewildered state of your feelings renders only too probable, [the photographer] wedges it into a horrible instrument called a 'head-rest,' which gives you exactly the appearance as if somebody was holding onto your hair behind," wrote the *American Journal of Photography* that year in an essay "Having Your Photograph Taken."[1]

Being forced to use such a device seemed only slightly more daunting than trying to decide what expression to give to the camera: "You have a vague expression that to look smiling is ridiculous, and to look solemn is still more so. You desire to look intelligent, but you are hampered by a fear of looking sly. You wish to look as if you were not sitting for your picture; but the effort to do so fills your mind more completely with the melancholy consciousness that you are."[2]

If anyone was used to it, though, it was Abraham Lincoln, who by then was one of the most frequently photographed human beings on the face of the earth, having already been captured by the camera almost a hundred times in sittings for several dozen photographers (see fig. 7.1).[3]

One of those images, a full-length portrait of Lincoln that Mathew B. Brady took in New York City on the morning of Lincoln's address at the Cooper Union Institute on February 20, 1860, was reproduced thousands of times and sold to eager customers. It provided a face to the name of the

Fig. 7.1. Abraham Lincoln had become one of the most photographed men on the planet by the time this majestic portrait was taken by Washington photographer Alexander Gardner on Sunday, November 8, 1863. (Library of Congress)

western politician everyone had heard so much about and helped popularize Lincoln during his presidential campaign. Years later, Brady would recall Lincoln saying, "Brady and the Cooper Institute made me president."[4]

So it was no surprise that President Lincoln would agree to a visit on Sunday, August 9, 1863, to photographer Alexander Gardner's new gallery at Seventh and D Streets NW (see fig. 7.2). The president "was in good spirits," wrote secretary John Hay in his diary, as Lincoln sat for four carte de visite photos (CDV) and three larger images. And as would any typical customer at Gardner's Gallery, Lincoln offered his critique when the prints arrived at the White House nine days later. "I think they are generally very successful," Lincoln wrote in a note of thanks. "The Imperial [camera] photograph in which the head leans upon the hand I regard as the best that I have yet seen."[5]

That year, millions of Americans would go through the same routine at the thousands of photo galleries in cities and small towns across the nation. Other photographers flocked to the army camps to ply the lucrative trade of photographing soldiers, who would sometimes argue among themselves whether or not to pose with their muskets. Common soldiers would most often have their photograph taken as a ferrotype or tintype—an inexpensive, one-of-a-kind image on a thin sheet of metal usually housed

Fig. 7.2. Some of the best-known photographs of Abraham Lincoln were taken in Alexander Gardner's sign-festooned Washington gallery, which opened around May 1863 at the corner of Seventh and D Streets NW. (Library of Congress)

in a small, wooden case. Officers and commanders were more likely to have their photographs taken as glass-plate negatives so, as with Lincoln, multiple copies of card photographs could be reproduced and handed out to their men or others. A soldier might discard many personal items on a hard march, but he would always keep close to him his photographs of loved ones at home. Likewise, on the home front, the photograph of a family's man in arms was one of the most cherished keepsakes in the house. Nearly every soldier had his photograph taken during the war, and millions were produced. The soldier portrait was, by far, the most common and popular form of picturing the Civil War.

Almost immediately after taking the photographs of Lincoln that August, Gardner would put these new images of the president on display at his gallery and offer them for sale to the public. It was a mutually beneficial arrangement; Gardner made money from Lincoln's photos while the president gained fresh fame and publicity while satisfying the public's demand for new images of him. Two months later, in November 1863, Lincoln would return to Gardner's Gallery to have more photographs taken, and he would come back a third time in February 1865.

Although the vast majority of American photographers devoted their business to making portraits of people in their studios, a handful of the bigger operators, including Brady and Gardner, also produced scenic and landscape photographs on paper that they mass marketed as stereo views, card photographs, folio (5 × 7 inch) prints, and Imperial camera (11 × 14 inch) prints.

Photography had been introduced to the world in Paris, France, in 1839 as the daguerreotype, a photograph on the mirror-like, polished surface of a silver-plated copper sheet invented by Louis Jacques Mande Daguerre. America quickly adopted this amazing invention as its own, and improvements and new methods came quickly. In much the same manner that the phonograph record was replaced by the cassette tape and then the CD in the span of about twenty years in the twentieth century, the daguerreotype was obsolete by the mid-1850s, having been replaced by tintypes, ambrotypes (a one-of-a-kind, positive photo on glass), and the wet-plate, glass negative, which was invented by an Englishman, Frederick Scott Archer, in 1851.

Around 1859, E. & H. T. Anthony & Co., the country's largest seller of photographic supplies, began mass marketing both carte de visite photographs of notable people and stereo-view cards of scenic wonders, such as Niagara Falls and the Hudson River Valley. The Anthony Company printed separate mail-order catalogs—both updated regularly—of the hundreds of stereo views or CDV card photographs they offered for sale. Both formats became immensely popular and sold by the thousands in 1859 and 1860.

The CDVs were photographic keepsakes, usually depicting family members or notable people and kept in elaborate photograph albums with slotted pages for the images. Stereo cards served a different purpose. They provided a 3-D photographic viewing experience that allowed the viewer to slip under the hood of a stereo viewer and peer into the depths of uncannily lifelike scenes. In an age without electricity, long before the movies or television, the stereo viewer provided a wondrous experience. It was one of the first forms of mass-marketed home entertainment, and the numbered stereo-view cards were among the earliest examples of collectible cards.

No written record is known to exist of Lincoln's visit to Gardner's Gallery in August 1863 beyond Hay's few words and the president's note to Gardner. But there can be little doubt that the president paused at some point during his visit to look at the graphic, new, battlefield images that Gardner and his associates made at Gettysburg just a month earlier, in the aftermath of the three-day battle there.

Lincoln was well familiar with the stereo view and its magical illusion of 3-D, since he had a stereoscopic viewer and stereo-view cards in the parlor of his own home in Springfield, Illinois. So it is likely that while at Gardner's Gallery on that August day in 1863, he took a stereo viewer in hand to gaze in 3-D at the shocking scenes of the dead at Gettysburg. Gardner and his associates shot a majority of their photographs at Gettysburg in the stereoscopic format for 3-D viewing, and of the fifty-three stereo views they produced, thirty-two showed the carnage of battle. Images looked upon today as pure history were breaking-news photographs back then, as fresh and startling back in 1863 as the latest viral video is in today's virtual world (see fig. 7.3).

On the eve of the Civil War, a vast new market had suddenly opened up for photographs of both people and places, especially documentary photographs from the battlefields. This provided tremendous incentive for the biggest men in the business, such as Anthony, Gardner, and Brady, to send photographers into the field—or go themselves—to take photographs of war scenes.

In the 1850s, with the advent of professional photographic associations and the creation of the first periodicals devoted to the craft, such as *The Daguerreian Journal* and the *American Journal of Photography*, the American photographic community had become a fraternity. The latest doings of far-flung photographers, such as Alexander Hesler, who photographed Lincoln at least twice in his Springfield, Illinois, studio, were reported in these journals. George S. Cook of Charleston, South Carolina, destined to become perhaps the greatest of the Southern photographers during the Civil War, often visited the North before the war and for a time ran Brady's New York gallery while Brady was in Europe.

Entered according to Act of Congress, in the year 1863, by Alex. Gardner, in the Clerk's Office of the District Court of the District of Columbia.

Fig. 7.3. Alexander Gardner's photographs of the dead at Gettysburg were produced and sold as twin-image stereoscopic views, and Lincoln almost certainly saw them through the lenses of a 3-D viewer. (Robin Stanford collection)

As the conflict loomed, Cook kept up a lively correspondence with Northern photographers, some of whom had worked for him. In January 1861, as business steadily improved at Cook's gallery on King Street, he was obviously upbeat, as evidenced in a January 19, 1861, letter from New York, that a former assistant, J. B. Van der Weyde, wrote to him: "I must confess that although you do not seem to be at all alarmed at the present state of affairs, I cannot share so hopeful a sentiment. . . . Even should everything go smooth for a month or so, Lincoln's inauguration will upset all. Like the witches in Macbeth I say, 'Beware the Ides of March!' With all our troubles I am glad you do feel sanguine for with you it is not (as with me) a matter of mere inconvenience but a question of safety or ruin."[6]

It was a prophetic statement, considering Cook's eventual woeful fate. But what better job could Cook have in Charleston on the eve of war than that of a photographer? In this time of crisis and looming danger, nearly everyone wanted a photograph to remember someone else by. In fact, during the same month, Cook began receiving letters from Northern photographers asking him if he could secure a photograph of Major Robert Anderson, the Union commander who occupied Fort Sumter in Charleston Harbor and was refusing Confederate demands to give it up. "A Major Anderson is quite popular [in the] North," said Philadelphia photographer Walter Dinmore to Cook on January 11, 1861. "I think that we might make considerable money if we had his picture."[7]

It took some doing for Cook to gain permission to go to the fort, including the intervention of South Carolina Governor Francis Wilkinson Pickens's attractive, young wife, Lucy Holcombe Pickens. But on February

8, 1861, Cook was rowed out to the brick bastion, where he made a series of images of Anderson and his staff.

In the days following, with little else to do, Anderson and his staff critiqued the proof prints that Cook sent back out to the fort and placed their personal orders. At the same time, Cook sold copy negatives in the North for $25 each. Soon, the Anthony Company and others were selling CDVs of Anderson by the thousands.

One of the first things president-elect Lincoln did after his arrival in Washington on February 23, 1861, was to pay a visit to Brady's Gallery on Pennsylvania Avenue (see fig. 7.4). There, Gardner, who was then Brady's Washington gallery manager, took five CDV portraits of a pensive Lincoln at the request of the illustrated newspaper *Harper's Weekly*, which reproduced one of the images as a woodcut engraving in its April 27 issue. "When I entered the room, the President was seated in a chair wholly absorbed in deep thought," remembered George H. Story, an artist and friend of Brady, who was asked to help pose the president. "Lincoln seemed

Fig. 7.4. This was Pennsylvania Avenue in early 1863 as Lincoln knew it, with the unfinished dome of the U.S. Capitol in the hazy distance. Before the year was out, the dome would be finished. (Bob Zeller collection)

absolutely indifferent to all that was going on about him, and he gave the impression that he was a man who was overwhelmed with anxiety and fatigue and care. I said in an undertone to the operator [Gardner], 'Bring your instrument here and take the picture.'"[8]

On March 4, when Lincoln took the oath of office as the sixteenth president of the United States in front of an unfinished Capitol dome, photographers captured the scene from at least two different vantage points and with both stereoscopic and single-lens cameras.

After the war started with the bombardment of Fort Sumter on April 12, 1861, Confederate photographers became the first to photograph the Civil War. In the days following Anderson's surrender on April 13, photographers from two different Charleston galleries (but not Cook) photographed the battle-damaged forts, Sumter and Moultrie, as well as other sites in Charleston Harbor. Alma A. Pelot—the first photographer of the Civil War—took large-plate images on April 15 for Jesse H. Bolles's Temple of Art gallery on King Street. These images were mounted on large, stiff, board mounts that were hand inscribed at first and later produced with printed titles. They were immediately advertised for sale in the *Charleston Mercury* newspaper. Within a few days, photographer James M. Osborn of Osborn and Durbec's Southern Stereoscopic and Photographic Depot at 223 King Street had also visited Fort Sumter and other sites in the harbor and returned with at least forty-three photographs—all taken in stereo. This is the largest group of Confederate outdoor images known to exist, stereoscopic or otherwise, and it is also one of the most complete photographic records of any Civil War battle or engagement.

In the North, Brady and other photographers spent the first months of the war taking photographs in army camps. But when the Union army marched out to Bull Run, Virginia, to meet the Confederates in the war's first major land battle on July 21, 1861, Brady followed with two wagons. William A. Croffut, a young correspondent for the *New York Tribune*, recalled seeing the photographer near Sudley Ford (see fig. 7.5):

> Shortly another civilian came up and joined us. Like myself, he wore a long linen duster, and strapped to his shoulders was a box as large as a beehive. I asked him if he was the Commissary.
>
> "No," he laughed; "I am a photographer, and I am going to take pictures of the battle."
>
> I asked him if he could get the fellows who were fighting to stand still and look pleasant. With a very serious face he said he supposed not, but he could probably get some scenes that would be worthwhile. His name was Brady, he added, and the protuberance on his back was a camera. . . . I saw him afterwards dodging shells on the battlefield.[9]

Photo taken
July 22ᵈ
1861

BRADY
The Photographe
returned from
Bull Run

Fig. 7.5. The only photograph Mathew B. Brady secured in his effort to photograph the First Battle of Bull Run was this self-portrait taken in his Washington studio after his retreat from the battlefield. (Library of Congress)

Brady was caught up in the Union rout and forced to retreat back to Washington with no photographs. Undaunted, he sent his photographers back to Bull Run in March 1862 when Confederates withdrew from the area. He also sent them on the Peninsula Campaign with the Army of the Potomac in the spring of 1862 and to South Carolina to cover the Federal occupation of the coastal low country around Beaufort.

When the Army of the Potomac marched out of Washington and into the Maryland countryside in September 1862 in pursuit of Robert E. Lee's Confederate army, it was Brady's Washington gallery manager, Gardner, who went along (see fig. 7.6). On September 19, 1862, two days after the battle of Antietam at Sharpsburg, Maryland, on September 17, Gardner stepped onto the battlefield with his cameras as the burial crews labored at the gruesome task of burying dead Confederate soldiers in mass graves. Gardner's Antietam photographs include twenty images of the dead—all taken in stereo. These are the first photographs of American dead on a field of battle. When they were put on display at Brady's New York gallery, the images shocked New Yorkers like no photographs ever had.

"Mr. Brady has done something to bring home to us the terrible reality and earnestness of war," reported the *New York Times* on October 20, 1862.

Fig. 7.6. After the battle of Antietam in September 1862, photographer Alexander Gardner, Brady's Washington gallery manager, photographed Lincoln's visit to the battlefield. (Courtesy of the Center for Civil War Photography)

"If he has not brought bodies and laid them in our dooryards and along streets, he has done something very like it. At the door of his gallery hangs a little placard, 'The Dead of Antietam.' Crowds of people are constantly going up the stairs; follow them, and you will find them bending over photographic views of that fearful battlefield, taken immediately after the action. . . . There is a terrible fascination about it that draws one near these pictures, and makes him loath to leave them. You will see hushed, reverend groups standing around these weird copies of carnage, bending down to look in the pale faces of the dead, chained by the strange spell that dwells in dead men's eyes."

Oliver Wendell Holmes, who had gone to Antietam in search of his son, who was wounded in the battle, commented on the photographs: "Let him who wishes to know what war is look at this series of illustrations. . . . It was so nearly like visiting the battle-field to look over these views, that all the emotions excited by the actual sight of the stained and sordid scene, strewed with rags and wrecks, came back to us, and we buried them in the recesses of our cabinet as we would have buried the mutilated remains of the dead they too vividly represented."[10]

The war raged on, and in December 1862, Washington became a sea of gloom and mangled soldiers as thousands of wounded from the Battle of Fredericksburg were brought back to the capital. Around that time, Gardner decided to leave Brady's employ and start his own photographic gallery in Washington, which opened in May 1863.

The war was not going well for the Union at the beginning of 1863, and for the army's foot soldiers, fighting the bloodiest war in American history, the prospects were gloomy at best. It might not have been the safest time to be an infantryman, but it was a good time to be a photographer (see fig. 7.7). In fact, so many photographers had flocked to the Army of the Potomac's winter quarters in Falmouth, Virginia, that the army in early 1863 began keeping a register of approved "photographists" and other civilians granted access to the army. Each division of the army had its own approved photographer, along with one or more assistants. The 1863 register lists the names of twenty-nine different photographers and forty-one assistants or clerks approved to shoot photographs in camp. No similar records exist for Confederate armies, but there is little doubt that photographers plied their trade in Southern camps, too, although lack of supplies and lack of access meant there were far fewer photographers working on a much more limited basis than in Northern camps.[11]

North or South, soldiers wanted photographs to send to their loved ones, and vice versa. "This has given unwonted employment to photographers throughout the country, and the profession was never before so prosperous as it has been during the past year," the *American Journal of Photography*

Fig. 7.7. Mathew B. Brady brought his cameras to the White House conservatory on March 27, 1863, to photograph a visiting American Indian delegation and, possibly, Mary Lincoln (standing at right). (Library of Congress)

commented in an essay on New Year's Day 1863. "A new year has commenced, big also with the promise of momentous events. What these events may be—what the coming months have in store for our country, for our race, or even for our wonderful art, no human prescience can tell. Shall our country be torn asunder, and the broken fragments be given a perpetual prey to internecine wars with each other, or shall it come forth from its baptism of blood bound together in bonds stronger than ever?" (see fig. 7.8).[12]

As the printing press inked the paper of that issue of the journal, no one could answer that question. Indeed, though, it would be a momentous year, both for the country and for the craft of photography, as cameramen edged ever closer to the action at the front.

In early 1863 came the initiative to create the first official U.S. Army photographer when Andrew J. Russell, a captain in the 141st New York Volunteers, was detached from his unit in February 1863 to learn wet-plate photography and take photographs for Brigadier General Herman Haupt, chief of the U.S. Military Railroads (USMRR).

Haupt, a brilliant engineer and inventor, had decided that in detailing and describing his innovations and other railroad engineering projects to his peers and superiors, he needed more than words, and only photographs could do justice to the subjects at hand. Russell spent most of his

Fig. 7.8. In this circa 1863 photograph by Lewis E. Walker, Lincoln is wearing a watch chain of braided California gold. (Courtesy of the Center for Civil War Photography)

time taking technical photographs of bridges or other construction and engineering projects. But as a captain in the Union army—the only official army photographer on either side—Russell had unprecedented access, which gave him the opportunity to take some remarkable photographs.

In April 1863, Russell or an assistant took a camera up to Stafford Heights, overlooking the Rappahannock River and, on the other side, Confederate-held Fredericksburg. His assignment was to take pictures of the destroyed railroad bridge so engineers could figure out what they needed to do to rebuild or replace it in advance of a Union assault. On the other side of the river, Confederates warily watched the man on Stafford Heights set up a tripod, but when they were satisfied it was just a photographer, a handful of them came out on their side of the ruined bridge to pose for the enemy cameraman in what are now considered some of the most unusual and compelling images of the war.

A month later, as Joseph Hooker launched his ill-fated advance at Chancellorsville, Russell photographed troops at the ready for an assault as they waited in trenches outside Fredericksburg. And as Union troops stormed the Stone Wall on Marye's Heights in the much more successful, so-called Second Battle of Fredericksburg, Russell took photographs of the distant battle with a huge Imperial camera, creating massive 14 × 17 inch glass-plate negatives that for the first time showed the progression of a distant land battle.

As soon as Marye's Heights was taken, Russell folded up his tripod and packed his camera in his wagon, crossed the Rappahannock on the Union pontoon bridge, and proceeded directly through the deserted city to the Stone Wall. Here, he took his most famous war photograph of the war—a view that looks down the length of the wall, with several dead Confederates and the litter of a battle that had raged perhaps as soon as only thirty minutes earlier (see fig. 7.9).

A few weeks later, Haupt began distributing Russell's photographs to key members of the administration, and on May 18, 1863, President Lincoln and cabinet members were each presented with a set of 33 small, mounted, albumen-print photographs, possibly stereo views. On July 23 and 24, 1863, Lincoln received more images—25 large photographs and 24 small ones. In February 1864, he was presented with 46 more large photos and 67 small ones. In all, Lincoln received 195 photos from the USMRR in 1863 and 1864. Alas, the register that documents this does not tell what the photographs depict, but it is likely that some or all of the 124 "small" photographs were stereo views and that one of the large views was the graphic scene after the battle at the Stone Wall.[13]

Although Russell managed to bring photography closer than ever to the action on the battlefield, his lens did not actually see the enemy, nor

Fig. 7.9. Lincoln received dozens of photographs taken in the field by U.S. Army photographer Andrew J. Russell, probably including this one of the Stone Wall at Fredericksburg taken almost immediately after the Second Battle of Fredericksburg on May 3, 1863. (Library of Congress)

was he himself under fire as he exposed his glass-plate negatives to the sunlight, covered with the still-wet, light-sensitive collodion. But the feat of taking the world's first combat-action photograph was not far off. And when it happened in September 1863, it was a Confederate photographer—Cook—who accomplished the feat. And it happened by accident.

For Cook, the premier photographer in Charleston, 1863 started off well. The first customer through the door of his photographic gallery at 235 King Street on that New Year's Day, a Sergeant Robinson, bought a framed whole-plate image of himself, paying $12.50. January 1 that year was a Thursday—a "fine day"—Cook wrote in the left margin of his account book, where he usually jotted a word or two about the day's weather. By day's end, the names of nine customers would be written in the book, their purchases totaling $67.00.[14]

But that New Year's Day was for Cook a particularly strong business day for another reason. On that day, he also recorded the sale of more than $170 worth of photographic supplies to at least three other Southern photographers. Although the Union blockade of Southern ports had put a stranglehold on commerce in the South and shuttered more than a few photographic galleries, some photographers still managed to ply their trade, and they could thank Cook for that. Cook invested in blockade runners during the war, and it was on these ships that he received his photographic supplies from Europe—supplies that not only kept him in business in 1863 but also at least a dozen other Southern photographers as well. That day, J. W. Perkins of Augusta, Georgia, bought $12 worth of ether, a quart of alcohol for $6, and another $6 worth of photographic paper. Other photographers bought collodion, glass, cyanide, and additional supplies.[15]

As winter gave way to early spring in Charleston, Cook's business boomed. In January, he had 217 customers; by May, it was up to 549, with gross receipts exceeding $4,700. But he was already fighting a losing battle against the spiraling inflation of the Confederate paper dollar. At the beginning of 1863, it took $2.50 in Confederate paper to equal $1 in gold. The $1,670 that Cook grossed that month was actually worth only $668. By the end of the year, however, it was far worse. Despite nearly tripling prices and taking in $4,915 in the month of December from 314 customers, Cook was pummeled by an inflation rate that had ballooned to 17 to 1, rendering the actual value of Cook's receipts that month to a mere $275.[16]

But he labored on, and the usual summer slump (only 259 customers in July) was followed in late August by a terrifying new development. The Union forces that occupied Morris Island at the south end of the mouth of Charleston Harbor, after incessantly shelling Fort Sumter but failing to gain its surrender, now began shelling the city of Charleston itself. On August 22, 1863, less than two weeks after Lincoln's visit to Gardner's Gallery in Washington, Cook wrote in the left margin of his account book: "Shelled the city, from 2 to 4 A.M. 14 shells."[17]

On September 6, the Confederates abandoned Battery Wagner, their last toehold on Morris Island. The following day, Rear Admiral John A. Dahlgren, commander of the Union Naval forces, told his diary, "I send a flag demanding surrender of Sumter. Answer: 'Come and take it.'"[18]

Fort Sumter was, in a fashion, the Civil War's ultimate prize, given that the dispute over its possession had triggered the war itself. Beginning on August 17, 1863, and continuing for seventeen days, Union gunners fired 6,878 shots into the fort, killing two men, wounding fifty, and silencing its guns for good. The fort was gradually reduced to rubble, but that just made it stronger against the shelling, and the bastion remained in Confederate hands, as it would until nearly the end of the war.[19]

In Charleston, Confederate commanders considered Sumter's resilience a point of pride, and the commanding general, Thomas Jordan, approached Cook about making a trip out into the harbor with his cameras "to preserve a faithful delineation of the ruins of Fort Sumter, and to show to future generals what Southern troops can endure in battle," the *Charleston Daily*

Courier reported on September 12, 1863. For Cook, who spent most of the days of the war—six days a week—in his King Street gallery busy with the lucrative trade of taking portrait photographs, the trip out into the field was a rare exception. But this was business, too, and copies of 1863 receipts from the Confederate States Engineering Department to Cook show that the Confederate government was a good customer, including a $468 order on July 31 for more than two hundred photographs.[20]

On September 8, 1863, as Cook and Osborn, his assistant formerly of the Osborn and Durbec gallery, set up their cameras and took photographs of the destruction inside the fort, Dahlgren sent the Union monitor USS *Weehawken* on a reconnaissance mission past Sumter. The ironclad promptly ran aground on a sandbar. Although Sumter's guns were now silent, the Confederate batteries in Fort Moultrie began shelling the stuck warship. The *Weehawken* was hardly defenseless, as the second shell it fired in its own defense hit an ammunition cache in Fort Moultrie, killing sixteen Confederates, wounding twelve more, and silencing Moultrie's guns for more than a few minutes. Nevertheless, the full force of the Union navy came to the *Weehawken*'s defense and that "led to what was probably the severest naval engagement in American history up to that time," reported John Johnson, a Confederate major of engineers. For four hours, Fort Moultrie's guns engaged the fleet, including at least five monitor-class ironclads and the boxy, lumbering USS *New Ironsides*, the largest battleship in existence.[21]

At Fort Sumter, the Confederate commander, Major Stephen Elliott Jr., watched the spectacle. "The engagement this morning was one of the most beautiful sites you can imagine," he related that afternoon in a letter to a friend. "All the ironclads were within a mile of us and not firing on us at the time, which improved the view considerably."[22]

In telegrams to headquarters, Elliott provided a blow-by-blow account of the action. "Ironsides was heavily hit just now, throwing great deal sand off her deck," he telegraphed at 11:15 A.M. "Enemy very busy at their old works on Morris Island. One Parrott gun from there opened on fort just now."[23]

As the battle raged, Cook crawled up onto the northeast section of the parapet, mounted his camera on a broken gun carriage, and exposed two small wet-plate negatives, one right after the other, as the *New Ironsides*, its guns blazing, led two other Union monitor-class warships on a battle pass of Fort Moultrie. Cook moved his camera a couple of inches to the right between exposures, thus ensuring that the two negatives together would work as a stereo photo, allowed viewers to see the scene in 3-D.

If the definition of a combat photographer is one who takes photographs of battle while under fire himself, Cook became the world's first combat photographer that day. The *Weehawken* alone fired forty-six shells into Fort Sumter that day. Cook's photographs not only showed battle, they showed the enemy in action. Although Cook's accomplishment has remained relatively obscure and only in recent years has been fully recognized for what it is, it is perhaps the only photographic event during the Civil War to make news in both Northern and Southern newspapers.

"The Ironsides and Two Monitors Taken—A Bold Feat," said the headline in the *Charleston Daily Courier* on September 12, 1863. "The artists . . . had the good fortune to secure, amid the smoke of battle in which they were earthed, a faithful likeness of the Ironsides and two Monitors." The paper called the photograph "one of the most remarkable acts . . . ever recorded in the history of war."

On October 20, 1863, in Rhode Island, the Providence, Rhode Island, *Daily Journal* reprinted a story from the Mobile, Alabama, *Advertiser* that its Charleston correspondent had filed on September 11: "Subsequently, an admirable battle scene was taken, representing the Ironsides and two monitors, wreathed in their own smoke, while delivering their fire on Fort Moultrie. I learned it is intended after a time, to make these pictures public, and to reduce them to stereoscopic dimensions."

By September 12, Cook had produced thirty-six copies of his larger photographs and seventy-two stereo views for the Confederate general headquarters. Over the next five months, he would sell at least forty-five more sets of views in more than twenty different transactions.[24]

Cook was not the only photographer to capture the *New Ironsides* in action in Charleston Harbor. On the beach on Morris Island, quite possibly on that same day, September 8, 1863, Union photographers Philip Haas and Washington Peale set up a camera on the sand and made a magnificent glass-plate negative of the *New Ironsides* in battle, with a plume of smoke spreading away from the ship and arching high into the air (see fig. 7.10) The profiles of five monitor-class ironclads are visible on the waterline. Several dozen soldiers and civilians stand on the beach—all of them facing away from the camera, riveted by the action in the harbor. This negative, which is even more obscure than Cook's images, is labeled "Unidentified Camp" at the Library of Congress. It was first recognized as a battle-action photograph by historian Jack Thomson in the 1990s.

For Cook, business would continue to be strong through the end of 1863 and into the early months of 1864, even as the continued existence of his Charleston gallery and his own safety became chancy. In November 1863, Union guns began bombarding the city of Charleston in earnest. For 545 days, shells rained down on Charleston, and Cook continued taking note of the fact in the margins of his account book.

"Shelling," he simply wrote on November 20, 1863.

"Shelling—one in Beaufain," he wrote the next day. Beaufain Street met King Street a half block south of Cook's gallery.

Fig. 7.10. One of history's first photographs of battle action is this Philip Haas and Washington Peale photograph taken on the beach on Morris Island, South Carolina, in 1863, showing smoke from the shell fire of the USS *New Ironsides* drifting over Charleston Harbor. (Library of Congress)

"Shelling. Hart's building struck." December 11.

December 31: "Shells thick. Dibble's and Marisso."

Eventually, he began to note everything that came out of the sky, both natural and man-made.

January 12 (1864): "Rain & shells."

January 13: "Rain & shelling."

January 14: "Rainy & shelling."[25]

Customers continued to flock to the King Street gallery despite the bombardment. Cook had 350 customers and grossed more than $5,000 (in inflated Confederate dollars) in February 1864, the last full month recorded in his known account books. The records of his business are lost for the rest of 1864, but sometime late in the year, he closed his gallery and moved it to Columbia, just in time to lose everything when the Union army burned the city on February 17, 1865. After the war, he moved back to Charleston and reopened his King Street gallery in August 1865.

As the war dragged on through 1864 and into 1865, the camera became a routine fixture at major events, and some news events began to be photographed literally as they happened. At Gettysburg on November 19, 1863, Lincoln was captured by cameras at least four times as he made his way to Cemetery Hill and spoke at the dedication of the Soldiers' National Cemetery, where he gave what is now known as the Gettysburg Address. In March 1865, photographers captured several images as he stood at the podium in front of the Capitol and delivered his famous address at his second inauguration. After his assassination the following month, countless images were taken of the twenty-day funeral procession back to Springfield, Illinois.

And when four conspirators in his murder were hanged in July in Washington, Gardner was there, exposing both stereo and large plates as fast as he and his assistants could, chronicling one of the final events related to the Civil War, almost second by second. It was a final triumph for photography, which had grown and matured during the war and laid the groundwork for photojournalism as it is known today.

Notes

1. "Having Your Picture Taken," *American Journal of Photography* 5, no. 13, January 1, 1863, 312.

2. Ibid.

3. Charles Hamilton and Lloyd Ostendorf, *Lincoln in Photographs—An Album of Every Known Pose* (Dayton, OH: Morningside, 1985), 369–89.

4. *New York World*, April 12, 1891, 26.

5. D. Mark Katz, *Witness to an Era—The Life and Photographs of Alexander Gardner* (New York: Viking, 1991), 112.

6. J. B. Van der Weyde to George S. Cook, January 19, 1861, George Smith Cook Collection, Manuscript Division, Library of Congress, Washington, DC.

7. Walter Dinmore to George S. Cook, January 11, 1861, Cook Collection.

8. Hamilton and Ostendorf, *Lincoln in Photographs*, 77.

9. William A. Croffut, *An American Procession 1855–1914: A Personal Chronicle of Famous Men* (Boston: Little, Brown, 1931), 49–50.

10. Oliver Wendell Holmes, "Doings of the Sunbeam," *Atlantic Monthly*, July 1863, 11–12.

11. "Prisoners, Agents, Sutlers," entry 4075, part 1, vol. 3, record group 393, Army of the Potomac Register No. 77, U.S. National Archives and Records Administration (NARA), Washington, DC.

12. "Editorial Department," *American Journal of Photography* 5, no. 13 (1863): 312.

13. "Distribution of Photographs of Construction and Transportation Departments," "Photography" subfiles, Quartermaster General's Consolidated Correspondence File, box 815, record group 92, NARA.

14. George S. Cook, daily account book. December 1862–June 1863, George S. Cook Collection, Valentine Richmond History Center, Richmond, Virginia.

15. Ibid.

16. Ibid.

17. Ibid.

18. Madeleine Vinton Dahlgren, *Memoir of John A. Dahlgren, Rear-Admiral U.S. Navy* (Boston: James R. Osgood, 1882), 413.

19. John Johnson, *The Defense of Charleston Harbor* (1890; repr., Germantown, TN: Guild Bindery Press, 1994), 143.

20. "Confederate Papers Relating to Citizens or Business Firms," also known as the "Rebel Archives," George S. Cook, microfilm, NARA.

21. Johnson, *Defense of Charleston Harbor*, 158.

22. Stephen Elliott Jr. to "Hal," September 8, 1863, copy in author's files, private collection.

23. *Official Records of the Union and Confederate the Navies in the War of the Rebellion*, 30 vols. (Washington, DC: GPO, 1894–1922), ser. 1, 14:1, 575.

24. George S. Cook, daily account book of, June 1863–March 1864, Cook Collection, Library of Congress.

25. Ibid.

8

THE GENERAL TIDE

WILLIAM C. DAVIS

*I*f President Abraham Lincoln felt buoyed at noon on January 1, 1863, when he signed the final Emancipation Proclamation, thus redeeming the promise of ultimate freedom from slavery always implicit in the Republican Party platform, he had little else to lift his spirits that day. By this time, the president had learned what some of his generals had still to divine, that the Confederacy lived in its armies. Remove them from the field, and the rebellion died with them. While there was no risk of a similar disappearance of his own legions, still he well knew that if they did not perform better than they had during the past eighteen months, then his hopes of reunifying the riven nation would evaporate, and the Union would be perhaps permanently cut in two. Given that, the epochal document he signed that noon would be pointless, one of history's cruel and embarrassing jokes.

The problem came down to the men in command. Lincoln knew that his soldiers were every bit the equals of their foemen. Moreover, they were better clothed, better fed, better trained, better equipped, and better paid. With only a few exceptions, however, what they had not been for the past year and one-half was better led. Army commanders had come and gone like a cruel surf, too often leaving defeat and demoralization in their ebb. Worse, some real successes went largely unappreciated because they came in far-flung theaters of the contest, while the most spectacular failures had beset Lincoln's largest legion, the mighty Army of the Potomac, almost in Washington's shadow and right under the eyes of most of the nation's press, whose reports spread the word of defeat after defeat all across the nation and around the world.

Now on this first day of 1863, if Lincoln hoped for new resolution and a new vigor from his commanders, he saw little to give him encouragement. Several hundred miles west at Murfreesboro, Tennessee, his major army in that region was locked in battle with the Confederate Army of Tennessee and had been driven to the defensive, its commander struggling with the decision to stay on the field and await more enemy attacks or withdraw and leave the Rebels with another victory to their account. On the Mississippi, a once-promising movement aimed at taking the critical stronghold at Vicksburg from its rear, landward side had foundered at Chickasaw Bayou, its commander preparing now to retreat. Though Lincoln did not know it yet, this very day Confederates attacked and captured a Federal outpost at Galveston, Texas, opening an important port for blockade runners.

Meanwhile in the capital, the president spent what should have been a pleasant holiday at his traditional White House reception contending with depressing manifestations of his problem commanders right in his Executive Mansion office. Major General Ambrose Everett Burnside, in command of the Union's premier force the Army of the Potomac, had already led it to humiliating defeat less than three weeks earlier at Fredericksburg, Virginia, after only five weeks in command. Now he called on Lincoln with a plan for a new thrust at Confederate General Robert E. Lee's Army of Northern Virginia in its positions south of the Rappahannock River. But Burnside also burdened the president with the disconcerting news that none of the general's senior commanders had confidence in his plan. Worse, he informed the commander in chief that he believed that the rank and file of his own army had lost confidence in Secretary of War Edwin M. Stanton, in General-in-Chief Henry Wager Halleck, and worst of all in Burnside himself. "Old Burn" had always been a reluctant army commander, lacking confidence in himself. Lincoln had had to persuade him to take the command in November, and now Burnside suggested that he should resign.

So now the commander of Lincoln's principal army gave him a plan of campaign in which no one seemed to feel confidence and capped that with saying he wanted to resign. On top of that, Halleck resigned his position when Lincoln insisted on the general in chief taking a position on the Burnside plan. Both generals agreed to stay on, but the events of that day scarcely made a combination to sweeten the president's expectations that the year ahead might see a turning of the tide in his favor in his armies' leadership.

Yet, signs there were, albeit modest, and as had been the case in the war thus far, virtually all distant from his immediate vision. Far away in Arkansas, one of Lincoln's least-known yet most successful department commanders was Major General Samuel Curtis, in charge of the Department of Missouri. His forces had already taken much of northeastern Arkansas and had won an important small battle at Prairie Grove in December 1862. Through all of 1863, as a result, Missouri and most of Arkansas would remain essentially secure in Union hands despite continual guerilla activity. While holding the state contributed little to Union fortunes, its loss was a serious blow in manpower and matériel to the Confederacy, as Jefferson Davis acknowledged on November 19, even as Lincoln was speaking at Gettysburg, Pennsylvania, when Davis spoke of the loss of Arkansas as a "source of disappointment and sorrow" and urged his own department commander west of the Mississippi to expend every effort to retake the state.[1]

Unfortunately for the Union, Curtis compromised his own further usefulness. At first, rumors, and then testimony before a court of inquiry, suggested that he was involved in speculating in confiscated Confederate cotton seized in Arkansas.[2] Then Curtis, an avowed abolitionist, got into what Lincoln himself termed "a pestilential factional quarrel" with fellow Unionists led by Missouri's proslavery Governor Hamilton Rowan Gamble. The feud was damaging the Union cause in the state. Lincoln could not remove the governor, so he removed the general on May 24, replacing Curtis with his troublesome subordinate Major General John M. Schofield.[3] Still, Curtis left the Union a secure Arkansas for the balance of the war, and his successor Schofield would launch his own rise from that base to take command of the Army of the Ohio in 1864.

Virtually next door to Curtis's command lay another often overlooked region whose commander would send even better tidings to Lincoln in the months following that New Year's Day of 1863. After the fall of New Orleans in April 1862, the troublesome politician Major General Benjamin F. Butler had commanded the Department of the Gulf, chiefly constituted of that portion of Louisiana then in Federal hands. Just two weeks before the end of the year, a new commander came to take over, Major General Nathaniel Banks. He lacked any qualifications whatever for high rank but had been himself a prominent politician before the war. He failed at almost every assignment given him during the Civil War, but his one high point would be 1863, when he actually succeeded at something, and something important at that, though in a bumbling and politically self-serving manner typical of the man.

By the dawn of 1863, the Confederacy had lost the southern end of the Mississippi at New Orleans and all of its upper reaches north of Vicksburg. The South controlled only that stretch between Baton Rouge, Louisiana, and Vicksburg, which became vital as a corridor for moving men and supplies to the eastern side of the river from western Louisiana, Texas, and what remained of Confederate-held Arkansas. Two bastions protected that corridor: the cannon-laden bluffs above Vicksburg and a similar river fortress erected on the east bank a few miles above Baton Rouge at Port Hudson. If the North took both of them, then Union gunboats would have full sway the entire length of the Mississippi, the Confederacy would be cut in two, and the third of it west of the Mississippi would be hopelessly isolated.

The plan that unfolded called for Major General Ulysses S. Grant to move against Vicksburg from above with a combined force of infantry and gunboats, while Banks was to make a similar campaign against Port Hudson from his base in New Orleans. Indeed, Halleck told Banks when he left to take his new command that Lincoln regarded the opening of the Mississippi River "as the first and most important of all our military and naval operations, and it is hoped that you will not lose a moment in accomplishing it."[4] Instead, Banks delayed and detoured into what was for him the more comfortable realm of politics as he concentrated on the civil administration of New Orleans and opening its markets to friendly Northern cotton speculators.

Not until March 7 did Banks finally push north to take Baton Rouge, by which time Admiral David G. Farragut, commanding the fleet of gunboats intended to cooperate with Banks in taking Port Hudson, became so frustrated at the army's delays that he was ready to move against the Confederate batteries without Banks. When finally the attack came on March 14, half of Farragut's squadron safely passed the batteries while the rest were turned back, and Banks launched only a half-hearted demonstration against the fort's land side that did little to aid the naval forces. That would be the story for Banks for the rest of the campaign, moving slowly and often diverted by self-interest. Ironically, had he moved quickly to take Port Hudson in March, April, May, or even June, then taking his victorious forces upriver to join in the operations against Vicksburg would have made him senior commander on the scene, since his commission predated Grant's. Had he been in command when Vicksburg fell, the consequences for the Union during the war and afterward might have been dramatic indeed. The capture of Vicksburg put Grant on the road to ultimate command of all Northern forces and, a few years later, to the presidency. The result of Banks being in those positions instead cannot be divined, but it likely would not have been good.

Still, Banks did take Port Hudson on July 9. It did not make him a hero in the North—that honor went to Grant—but he had accomplished his task and helped divide the Confederacy. For the rest of the year, if he did nothing more, at least he did no harm militarily, devoting himself instead to helping Northern friends capitalize on Louisiana cotton and building the political base for his postwar career. Unfortunately, his performance was just good enough that he kept his command and thus would be in place to revert to form, and failure, in 1864.

Banks would be the only Union department commander to hold his position throughout the entire year 1863. All the others lost their commands, being replaced for failure in the field or for political reasons like Curtis. Only one man commanding an army or a department on January 1, 1863, left his department command during the year as a result of promotion to higher position, but he was the one who would prove to be the essential commander for Lincoln and the Union.

On July 13, 1863, the president sent a letter to Grant, a letter that began wide circulation throughout the nation's press on August 31. "I do not remember that you and I ever met personally," Lincoln began. He went on to confess that he originally disagreed with Grant's plans for the campaign to take Vicksburg, but now he was happy to concede that "you were right and I was wrong."[5] It was the beginning of a relationship that, though never intimate, would have a profound impact on the course of the war.

Grant had been the source of most of what good news Lincoln received in 1862. Rising from obscurity in 1861, Grant achieved a series of victories of far-reaching significance in the following year. His capture of Forts Henry and Donelson in February had opened the Tennessee and Cumberland Rivers to Union gunboats, at a stroke taking virtually all of west Tennessee from the Confederates and forcing the evacuation of Nashville and much of the middle part of the state. Despite being surprised at Shiloh in April, he recovered, for the first time revealing his imperturbable calm and clear thinking in a crisis, and won the battle.

For a time, Grant was almost eclipsed by the jealousy of his then-immediate superior Halleck, but in July, Lincoln brought Halleck east to become general in chief, and Grant assumed command of the District of Mississippi, which included the Army of the Mississippi and the Army of the Tennessee. Three months later, he was shifted to command of the new Department of the Tennessee. By that time, forces under his command had already added to his victories in a small engagement at Iuka, Mississippi, and then the repulse of a substantial Confederate attack at Corinth, Mississippi. All that fall, Grant himself concentrated on efforts to take Vicksburg, for the first time having to deal with serious setbacks in his conquest of the Mississippi Valley. He sent his chief subordinate Major General William Tecumseh Sherman with more than thirty thousand soldiers on transports down the Mississippi and up the Yazoo River to land and commence a march on Vicksburg from its rear. In coordination with Sherman, Grant intended to lead his main army south to hit Vicksburg from the east, but a Confederate raid destroyed his supply base at Holly Springs, Mississippi, on December 20, forcing Grant to cancel his plan. Meanwhile, Sherman went on unaware that Grant would not be coming, and as the year drew to a close, he met bloody repulses at

Chickasaw Bayou. By January 2, 1863, he had given up and commenced a withdrawal.

Still, as the New Year dawned, Lincoln had good cause to expect good things from Grant in the coming months. As he had shown at Shiloh when taken by surprise, Grant could not be rattled, and he would not retreat as so many of the president's commanders had done in the east. There was a relentlessness about the man. During the year past, he had moved unwaveringly south along the line of the great river, taking more than thirty thousand square miles of Confederate territory in Tennessee and Mississippi. Lincoln's army in Virginia had taken barely 5 percent of that. And unlike the eastern commanders, Grant stayed out of politics and kept his eyes fixed on his military goals. He had steadily risen in responsibility from command of a single volunteer regiment at the war's outset to supervision of the Union's second largest army, and he showed every indication of being competent to handle even more in the days ahead.

Consequently, when Grant began rebuilding his supply base and planning another move downriver against Vicksburg, Lincoln had every reason to sustain him—even if he did disagree with the general's plan of campaign. Of course, Grant vindicated that trust. Undeterred by multiple setbacks along the way, he took Vicksburg in July, which with the fall of Port Hudson five days later opened the Mississippi to unimpeded Union control all the way to the Gulf of Mexico. More than that, however, Grant showed an insightful grasp of the multiple layers of the kind of war the Union was fighting. After he took Fort Donelson, he sent all of the surrendered Confederates to Northern prison camps, where they were a burden on the Union. Now, however, he passed that burden on to the Confederacy by paroling the thirty thousand men in the Vicksburg garrison, sending them home under penalty of death if they took arms again before being properly exchanged for captured Union soldiers. That saved the Union the considerable money and manpower necessary to house and subsist them in prisons and, instead, made them a burden on the Confederacy's already strained infrastructure, which would have to feed and house them without being able to use them. Moreover, Grant realized that even after exchange, many of these disheartened men would never return to their regiments, putting them essentially out of the war.

Grant was also bringing something else to the table. This war was still expanding in scope and ferocity. That meant additional strains on the command cadre. Battlefield losses and creation of new divisions, corps, and even armies meant that Lincoln needed capable men to fill senior positions. As he had already discovered in the Virginia army, depending on seniority to fill vacancies was no guarantee of capable army commanders. All across the Union military, good men were rising through the ranks, marked by performance and ability for higher command, but senior positions commanding corps and armies were still largely locked in the Old Army system of filling vacancies with men whose commissions predated others of the same rank.

Fortunately, Grant showed a good eye for talent in his subordinates and had an equally good sense of those who were going to be trouble. He had his favorites and his prejudices like any other person, but he seldom let personal feelings get in the way of advancing talented men. Early in 1862, he put James B. McPherson on his staff as chief of engineers and watched as the young officer performed well through that summer. Grant was among those recommending him for promotion to brigadier and a division command, and as 1863 dawned, McPherson had risen to major general and command of the XVII Corps. Throughout 1863 and the Vicksburg campaign, McPherson rewarded Grant's confidence and would be on his way to an army command of his own by year's end.

Grant could also spot problem generals, especially the politicians who gained rank not for their military experience but for their influence on the home front in persuading their constituencies to enlist. Early on he spotted trouble in John A. McClernand, a career Democratic politician whom Lincoln made a brigadier on May 17, 1861, and a major general on March 21, 1862. That made him senior to virtually all of Grant's generals and put him in line to take Grant's place should something happen to him. McClernand lost no opportunity to intrigue against Grant while publicly aggrandizing himself, even to taking credit for the successes of others, all the while expecting his close ties with Lincoln to shield him from the consequences of his acts and insubordination. In June 1863, Grant showed his political courage by relieving McClernand of his command and sending him home to Illinois. In his place, Grant put Major General E. O. C. Ord, whom he had personally seen perform well in the Iuka and Corinth campaign and who would also rise to an army command by war's end.

Of course, his greatest subordinate was and would be William Tecumseh Sherman. Grant could take no credit for Sherman's early rise, for he became a brigadier in August 1861, actually several days senior to Grant's own commission. In November, he suffered what may have been a nervous breakdown and was relieved of his command. After three months' rest, he was given a division and sent to reinforce Grant and was with him at Shiloh, where his performance won him his second star. Grant and Sherman worked well together, though each was something of a mystery to the other. It is largely due to Grant's tolerance for a subordinate whose intellect outmatched his own and whose volatile and sometimes erratic nature made him difficult to get along with that the two became the greatest partnership in the Union army. Sherman reputedly quipped once, "Grant stood by me when I was crazy and I stood by him when he was drunk. And now we stand by each other always."[6]

Sherman began 1863 in severe frustration at his inability to get beyond the Rebel defenses at Chickasaw Bayou to take Vicksburg. That frustration only mounted when he withdrew and immediately encountered his senior McClernand, who attached Sherman's forces to his own and led them on an unauthorized campaign into the Arkansas interior. He obeyed dutifully but was no doubt delighted when Grant ordered them all back to join his forces moving again on Vicksburg and soon put McClernand out of the picture. Sherman assumed command of the XV Corps and performed ably in the subsequent campaign, and Grant soon trusted him to operate independently from the main army in taking Jackson, Mississippi.

By weeding out the liabilities like McClernand and promoting others for demonstrated ability, Grant steadily improved the command structure of his army. At the same time, he was also evolving a more comprehensive and efficient staff than any other yet seen in the war. Grant had failed at comparatively simple things like farming and selling real estate, but he had a natural instinct for executive management. He found fine officers to perform specific tasks and allowed them to do their jobs. It is no accident that by war's end, many of the officers serving on his staff in 1863 became general officers in their own right and a couple of them leaders of distinction, most notably his engineer Lieutenant Colonel James H. Wilson, who would finish the war as a major general and one of the Union's top cavalry commanders.

On October 16, the War Department in Washington created the Military Division of the Mississippi and assigned Grant to take charge of the new supercommand, the largest territorial responsibility yet handed to a Union general. This put Grant in charge of all Union forces between the Appalachians and the great river, including the Army of the Tennessee, the Army of the Cumberland, and the Army of the Ohio. Lincoln had found his most successful general to be many things—Grant the Strategist, Grant the Conqueror, Grant the Army Builder—and now he turned to him to be yet something else, Grant the Fixer.

Sadly, another general of once-great promise had become a disappointment. The army locked in battle at Murfreesboro, Tennessee, when the year began actually emerged from the fight with a tentative claim to success, for the Confederates attacking it withdrew from the field. Though Grant himself disagreed, Lincoln insisted on regarding the result as a victory. The man in charge had been Major General William S. Rosecrans commanding the Army of the Cumberland. He had fine credentials for the position. Back in July 1861 when Union successes were agonizingly elusive, he won a small action in western Virginia that helped boost his senior commander George Brinton McClellan into the national spotlight. Again, at Iuka and Corinth, he commanded the forces on the field that gained two victories for his commander Grant. This time, in addition to helping advance the careers of his commanders, Rosecrans got a reward himself, command of the Army of the Cumberland.

During the ensuing winter and spring, Rosecrans remained in place at Murfreesboro, rebuilding his army after the heavy losses incurred in the recent battle. Washington chaffed at his inactivity and urged him to move against the Confederate Army of Tennessee, then arrayed to protect Chattanooga. The president himself implored the general, "I would not push you to any rashness, but I am very anxious that you do your utmost, short of rashness."[7] Still the general delayed, until Halleck virtually gave him an ultimatum to move. Finally, Rosecrans launched his campaign in late June and early July of 1863, and what he did stunned his opponents. Using his army as deftly as any commander in history and without fighting a single battle or more than a few minor engagements of note, he employed maneuver and strategy to completely baffle the Confederates out of their positions and force them back into Chattanooga itself and then out of the city and into northern Georgia. With his army poised to take Chattanooga, Rosecrans had good claim to the kind of celebrity that had been accorded to McClellan and Grant.

Then came a humiliating defeat at Chickamauga in September. Rosecrans lost his composure, and perhaps his nerve, and rode away from his army, which soon followed him into defenses around Chattanooga. Capitalizing on their initiative, the Confederates quickly all but surrounded the Federals and began a siege to starve them out. Hence, Grant's new supercommand and instructions for Grant the Fixer to go to Chattanooga with discretion to relieve Rosecrans of his command instilled new spirit into the defeated army and lifted the siege.

That is exactly what Grant did. He replaced Rosecrans with Major General George H. Thomas, one of Rosecrans's subordinates whose initial overreaction to enemy attacks at Chickamauga had helped set up the defeat but who afterward held his ground to buy the army time to retreat, gaining him the sobriquet "Rock of Chickamauga." Grant and Thomas did not much like each other, but Thomas would command the Army of the Cumberland for the rest of the war and deliver crushing victories a year from now. Meanwhile, Grant put Sherman in command of the Army of the Tennessee and ordered him to come aid in the relief of Chattanooga. Thereafter, Grant's armies lifted the siege and drove the demoralized Confederates back into north Georgia.

In the process, Grant spotted yet another talented officer from whom he would extract much in the year ahead. Prior to November 25, 1863, Major

General Philip H. Sheridan had been an obscure division commander, but that day his men spearheaded the taking of what were presumed to be impregnable Confederate positions atop Missionary Ridge, in the offing dividing the Rebel army and precipitating a retreat that soon turned into a rout. Thereafter, Grant took Sheridan into his intimate circle of generals, and the next year, Sheridan would be winning fame and glory in Virginia. He, like Sherman, would one day rise to become commanding general of the U.S. Army.

Thus the year came to an end in Tennessee in a turnaround from January 1 that could only have given Lincoln joy. Now he had two seasoned commanders at the head of armies in that theater. Thomas may have been a plodding and none-too-imaginative fellow, and he did unwisely let his lack of enthusiasm for Grant and Sherman show, but still he would reward Grant's standing by him. Despite his feet of clay early at Chickamauga, he would genuinely be solid as a rock and a source of inspiration and loyalty for his soldiers in the campaigns ahead. For his part, Sherman immediately led part of his army to Knoxville, Tennessee, in December to relieve a Union command being besieged there and finished the year formulating plans for a campaign to strike at Confederate communications and munitions centers at Meridian, Mississippi, and Selma, Alabama. He was using good weather in the Deep South to keep his army fit and accomplish some good, but he was already eyeing something bigger, a strike through Georgia to Atlanta, a real nerve center of the Confederacy. Though he would continue to be controversial and occasionally prickly with the public and politicians, Sherman never ceased to think and act in perfect concert with Grant. The days ahead would establish him as unquestionably the premier commander of the Union, save only Grant himself.

And Grant had shown once again that he was the man for any job and that no responsibility seemed to stretch him beyond his capacity for growth. On December 8, looking back on the relief of Chattanooga and Knoxville, Lincoln sent Grant a brief personal note offering "you, and all under your command, my more than thanks—my profoundest gratitude—for the skill, courage, and perseverance, with which you and they, over so great difficulties, have effected that important object."[8] It is probable that even then, as 1863 was on the verge of winking out, the president had in mind something more than thanks for his general. In his wake, Grant had left a divided Confederacy, Union domination of the Mississippi and its tributaries, and virtual hegemony in the war west of the Appalachians. Yet, there was one place Grant had not been yet, one place where Lincoln, despite one great success, needed more action, more victories. Perhaps what he needed was Grant.

The year 1863 began as a qualified nightmare for the Union in Virginia. Major General Burnside had been reluctant to take command of the Army of the Potomac the previous fall after Lincoln finally relieved the glacially slow McClellan. Burnside frankly expressed his doubts in his ability to handle the command and proceeded to demonstrate that his doubts were well founded. He had planned a fine campaign to drive the Confederates from their defenses along the Rappahannock River, but his own logistical support system let him down, delaying and compromising his plans. Stubborn, and unable like Grant to modify a tactical plan in response to the unexpected, Burnside went ahead and launched his army in futile attacks at Fredericksburg in December and suffered horrible losses for no gain. On New Year's Day, he wrote to Lincoln, outlining his commanders' lack of faith in him and suggested that he resign, but the president persuaded him to stay. On January 19, Burnside launched another campaign to get across the Rappahannock and in the next few days became so bogged down by heavy rains that he called off the effort, ever-after dubbed the "Mud March."

In frustration, Burnside tried to dismiss three of his senior generals. Instead, Lincoln faced the fact that the general's self-doubts had been well justified, and he relieved Burnside as well as two corps commanders who had sown dissension. Lincoln now realized that the command culture in his major army was poisoned by in-fighting, conflicting ambitions, and Burnside's ineptitude, all compounded by yet another costly and humiliating defeat. In Burnside's place, the president unfortunately placed one of the chief malcontents, Major General Joseph Hooker. Lincoln knew the risk he took. Hooker was boastful, egotistical, and had politicked against Burnside openly. Yet, he was also known as a fighter, a man of supreme confidence that contrasted with Burnside's diffidence and lack of mettle. In giving Hooker the assignment, Lincoln frankly told him, "[T]here are some things in regard to which, I am not quite satisfied with you." Acknowledging Hooker's confidence and ambition, he said he was aware of how the general had worked against his superior to advance himself and even that Hooker had said the country needed a dictator. "Only those generals who gain successes, can set up dictators," the president told him. "What I now ask of you is military success, and I will risk the dictatorship."[9]

Hooker reinvigorated the army rank and file, but he could not entirely put down the acrimonious culture among its high command that he had himself helped to create. He planned a brilliant campaign to push around the Confederates on the Rappahannock and cut them off from Richmond and even took them by surprise at first when his army moved at the end of April. But then the weight of his responsibility apparently overwhelmed him, and as he put it, he lost confidence in himself. The foe quickly reacted, and when the Battle of Chancellorsville was done, the Army of the Potomac had suffered its most embarrassing defeat to date.

Between them, Burnside and Hooker had cost the rank and file of the Army of the Potomac most of the pride and spirit it had won in its first victory at Antietam the previous September. Lincoln, faced with the nation's loss of confidence in Hooker, began looking for a replacement and offered the command to Major General John F. Reynolds, who declined it, not wanting to have to contend with the headquarters politics he had seen work against both previous commanders. Then the Confederates moved out of Virginia and into the North on a massive raid, and Hooker and his army followed; Hooker confessed to the president, "I don't know whether I am standing on my head or feet."[10] Three days later, on June 27, Lincoln decided to relieve the general and replace him with the only senior commander in the Army of the Potomac who seemed solid, capable, and free from the taint of army politics, Major General George Gordon Meade.

Less than a week later, Meade gave Lincoln the biggest victory of the war in the east at Gettysburg. At last, it seemed, the president had a general. The disillusionment set in within days, for Meade, whose army was almost as badly battered as the enemy's, did not pursue his retreating foe or follow up on the victory. On July 14, a distraught Lincoln wrote to Meade, "Your golden opportunity is gone, and I am distressed immeasureably [*sic*] because of it."[11] Prudently, he did not send that letter, and Meade retained his command and at least some of the president's confidence. In October, Meade reacted well to a Confederate offensive aimed at Washington, and though he was driven back on defenses near the old Bull Run battleground, still he stopped the Rebel advance.

A month later, Meade responded with an offensive of his own along the line of Mine Run that able Confederate defense, in turn, stopped. Still, at year's end, the Army of the Potomac seemed stabilized, well placed a little farther into Virginia than it had been at the beginning of 1863, with a major victory under its belt to give it the confidence that it could beat Robert E. Lee and with a commander in Meade, who, though not flamboyant or personally inspiring, was still capable, cool under pressure, and able to foster a more positive atmosphere at headquarters despite his irascibility. It was the most dramatic turnaround in any of Lincoln's armies that year. Combined with Grant's success and that of his rising subordinates like Sherman and Sheridan in the western theater, the modest gains in Arkansas, and Banks's success in Louisiana, the prospect looked rosy. Even Hooker, after recovering his composure, had performed well when reassigned to a corps under Sherman at Chattanooga in November, though Burnside failed yet again when placed in command of northeastern Tennessee that fall, and Sherman had to save him when he was besieged at Knoxville. Still Lincoln could not bring himself to accept Burnside's multiple offers to resign, and he would be around in a subordinate capacity to present a problem in 1864.

By January 1, 1864, the unrelenting months of failures and changes in command were at an end. Every department and army was in the hands of a better commander than when the year began, except for Banks. Every one of those commanders, including Banks, had made a positive contribution to the war effort in 1863, and all but Banks were in place to make even greater contributions in the year ahead. He would soon disappear from command, and Meade, Sherman, Thomas, Schofield, and soon Sheridan would be fixed as the team that would give Lincoln and the Union real cause to celebrate when New Year's Day 1865 rolled around. Most of all, Grant was now the indisputable premier commander of the Union, and already as the shadows closed on 1863, Lincoln must have been thinking of one change more.

With Sherman and Thomas in place with their armies looking toward Atlanta and the Deep South, Banks being pressed to move up Louisiana's Red River in the spring, and a steady Meade now facing Lee in Virginia, it needed only one guiding hand to bring it all together. Halleck had been general in chief for eighteen months now, but he had demonstrated that he was not the man for that job. Grant, and only Grant, had shown the imagination and the capacity to wage war on a macro scale. Perhaps already the president contemplated reviving the old rank of lieutenant general in the New Year and giving it to Grant, which would make him senior to everyone in the entire army and virtually general in chief even without a formal appointment.

On January 1, 1864, Lincoln actually felt able to begin stating his policy of universal amnesty for Confederates after the war and universal suffrage for the men serving in his black regiments. The ebb in the Union's fortunes seemed replaced by a rising tide thanks to Grant and the rest of the team who rose through the adversity of the past two years to assume leadership of his legions. Now this day, Lincoln could look ahead with some confidence to what he termed "our complete success in the field."[12]

Notes

1. Jefferson Davis to Theophilus H. Holmes, November 19, 1863, in Jefferson Davis, *The Papers of Jefferson Davis*, ed. Lynda Lasswell Crist, Kenneth H. Williams, and Peggy L. Dillard (Baton Rouge: Louisiana State University Press, 1999), 10:79, Davis to E. Kirby Smith, November 19, 1863, Davis, *Papers of Jefferson Davis*, 10:80–81.

2. *Columbus (OH) Crisis*, June 3, 1863; *Illustrated New Age* (Philadelphia, PA), August 15, 1863.

3. Lincoln to John M. Schofield, May 27, 1863, in Roy P. Basler, ed., *The Collected Works of Abraham Lincoln*, 9 vols. (New Brunswick, NJ: Rutgers University Press, 1953–55), 6: 234, hereafter cited as *Collected Works*; *Boston Daily Advertiser*, July 3, 1863.

4. Ludwell H. Johnson, *Red River Campaign, Politics & Cotton in the Civil War* (Kent, OH: Kent State University Press, 1993), 23.

5. *Daily National Intelligencer* (Washington, DC), September 1, 1863.

6. L. P. Brockett, *Our Great Captains: Grant, Sherman, Thomas, Sheridan, and Farragut* (New York: Charles B. Richardson, 1866), 175.

7. Lincoln to William S. Rosecrans, May 28, 1863, *Collected Works*, 6:236.

8. Lincoln to Ulysses S. Grant, December 8, 1863, *Collected Works*, 7:53.

9. Lincoln to Joseph Hooker January 26, 1863, *Collected Works*, 6:78–79.

10. Joseph Hooker to Henry Halleck, June 24, 1863, U.S. War Department, *War of the Rebellion: Official Records of the Union and Confederate Armies*, 128 vols. (Washington, DC: GPO, 1880–1901), ser. 1, 27:1:56.

11. Lincoln to George Gordon Meade, July 14, 1863, *Collected Works*, 6:328.

12. Lincoln to James S. Wadsworth, January 1864 (?), *Collected Works*, 7:101.

9

THE GETTYSBURG ADDRESS REVISITED
ORVILLE VERNON BURTON

In Frank Capra's classic 1939 film, *Mr. Smith Goes to Washington*, a disgraced and defeated Senator Jefferson Smith (Jimmy Stewart) is quitting. His optimistic outlook dims when his idol, Senator Paine (Claude Rains), tries to include him in a corrupt scheme, and it shatters completely when the bad guys finger Smith himself as the guilty party. With two suitcases in tow, he hightails it out of town, thoroughly disenchanted with politics, and maybe no longer so naïve. Before leaving, he makes his second visit to the Lincoln Memorial. As Smith stares, we also see emblazoned across the large screen familiar words: "that this nation under God shall have a new birth of freedom—and that government of the people, by the people, and for the people shall not perish from the earth." Reading that address, a teary-eyed Smith finds the will to persevere and take on government corruption.

In making the film, Capra, who was born in Sicily in 1897, moved to America in 1903, and was naturalized in 1920, stated that the soul of the film would be Abraham Lincoln: "Our Jefferson Smith would be a young Abe Lincoln, tailored to the rail-splitter's simplicity, compassion, ideals, humor, and unswerving moral courage under pressure." Capra set up the above scene earlier in the film when Jimmy Stewart as the new junior senator tours D.C. and admires monuments and statues of the founding fathers. As he climbs the steps of the Lincoln Memorial, "The Battle Hymn of the Republic" playing in the background, he notes the second inaugural address, but more compelling is the Gettysburg Address. A young lad of about eight reads the address aloud with the help of an elderly man, presumably his grandfather. A stately, dignified-looking African American enters the Lincoln Memorial. He doffs his hat and stands reverently before the words to the Gettysburg Address. Capra honored these words, and Americans continue to hold them dear.[1]

The bloodiest war in American history, the Civil War posed in a crucial way what clearly became persistent themes in American history: the character of the nation and the fate of African Americans (read large, the place of minorities). Consequently, scholars have been vitally interested in the Civil War, searching out clues for the identity of America. Lincoln articulated that identity and meaning in the Gettysburg Address.

After the Battle of Gettysburg, called by historian Eric Foner "the greatest battle ever fought on the North American continent," and the siege of Vicksburg, called by James M. McPherson, dean of Civil War historians, "the most important northern strategic victory of the war," it remained an open question as to whether the Northern public would continue to give political support to Lincoln and the Republican Party. Now, when victory might be a matter of time and determination, the politically astute Lincoln knew that the public could still withhold its support of the army so necessary to grind down Confederate opposition. Lincoln, therefore, welcomed the invitation of David Wills, a Gettysburg banker, to attend the ceremony at Gettysburg battlefield and make "a few appropriate remarks" as an opportunity to address the nation. Wills had been appointed an agent of Governor Andrew Curtin of Pennsylvania and in that role had provided order to a chaotic environment in which souvenir hunters had been looting the battlefield for prized mementos. He also tried to coordinate the effort of various states to memorialize the honored dead at Gettysburg. As a resident of Gettysburg, Wills was aware of the tourism possibilities of the battlefield and also recognized the benefits of national attention that the dedication would receive with Lincoln present. Lincoln's address was meant to provide a fitting summary to other remarks that would address the battle in more detail. The heavy lifting would be the lengthy oration by Edward Everett of Massachusetts, widely considered America's preeminent orator.[2]

The Gettysburg Address was situated within a political environment in which Lincoln sought to defend the Civil War, and he did so by linking the current struggle to the revolutionary tradition. America had been created by the Declaration of Independence, Lincoln suggested, and whether the country could live up to the promise of that document was the central question of the entire war. Moreover, the purpose of the war had expanded from simply preserving the Union, because, in order to save the union, it was necessary to end American slavery and move toward the incorporation of African Americans into the body politic. Lincoln also sought to acknowledge the real sacrifices soldiers and their families made, as part of an ongoing effort to convince the Northern public to stay the course. He held aloft the promise that victory would mean the creation of a better world and fulfill the hopes of America's founding fathers.

For Lincoln, the hopes of the founding fathers included the United States as the example of popular government for the rest of the world: "that government of the people, by the people, and for the people shall not perish from the earth." Lincoln was reinforcing his July 4, 1861, message to Congress that secession "embraces more than the fate of these United States. It presents to the whole family of man, the question whether a constitutional republic, or a democracy—a government of the people, by the same people—can or cannot, maintain its territorial integrity against its own domestic foes." Lincoln believed that freedom and the right of people to govern themselves had a global context, because he knew what was happening to democracy in the rest of the world. The American Revolution had unleashed the forces of democracy and constitutional government and began to change the world. Following the French Revolution, however, Napoleon did away with the Consulate of the French Republic and crowned himself emperor in 1804. The European revolutions of 1848 failed. The republics in South America were failing because of a strong authoritarianism among the military forces, and monarchists were gaining power in Mexico. And even though democracy-loving Garibaldi reunited Italy, it became a monarchy, not a republic. Thus, the forces of history were with the Confederacy, moving away from democracy and self-government. And European powers wanted the Confederacy to win and thus to lessen the power and influence of the United States. Lincoln was aware that the preservation of the Union was "the last best hope of earth." Lincoln was therefore very much aware of the need to speak honestly and directly with the American people about the struggle that remained.[3]

It was on November 19, 1863, in the military cemetery at Gettysburg that was still hardly half finished, now four and a half months after the Battle of Gettysburg, that standing in the autumn chill, Lincoln awaited his turn to speak while the twenty-thousand-strong crowd anticipated the words of another man, silver-tongued Everett. Everett, they knew, would speak of valor and values and victory, the stuff of melodrama that they so loved. Everett, former congressman, senator, governor of Massachusetts, secretary of state, minister to England, and president of Harvard University, was also the vice presidential nominee with John Bell in 1860 on the ticket of the Constitutional Union Party (conservative Whigs who wanted to maintain the Union and not break up over slavery). After Lincoln's election in 1860, Everett paid attention to Lincoln's speeches and was not impressed. On February 15, 1861, he wrote in his diary, "These speeches thus far have been of the most ordinary kind, destitute of everything, not merely of felicity and grace, but of common pertinence." Everett concluded that Lincoln "is evidentially a person of very inferior cast of character wholly unequal to the crisis." At Gettysburg, Everett and Lincoln had very different purposes. Everett had the responsibility to place the battle within context, Lincoln to offer a brief summation. Both men were impressed by what the other had to offer. A day after Gettysburg, Everett wrote Lincoln to express his appreciation and admiration: "[T]he thoughts expressed by you, with such eloquent simplicity & appropriateness, at the consecration of the Cemetery . . . I should be glad, if I could flatter myself that I came as near to the central idea of the occasion in two hours, as you did in two minutes." It was more than lip service. Everett campaigned hard for Lincoln's reelection in 1864. Lincoln similarly was impressed by Everett's speech, particularly Everett's remarks on a state-centered understanding of the constitution. That part of Everett's speech, Lincoln suggested, was new to him and "one of the best arguments for the national supremacy." That Lincoln would pick out that element in a long speech suggests the importance that he attached to the nationalist interpretation of the constitution and why it was one of the central themes of the war itself.[4]

Historian David Donald notes, "Lincoln's address assumed an hourglass form: an opening account of the events of the past that had led up to the battle of Gettysburg; three brief sentences on the present occasion; and a final, more expansive view of the nation's future." The opening of the Gettysburg Address must rank as one of the more famous lines in all of American history. It weaves together themes that had long dominated Lincoln's thought: the revolutionary tradition the founding fathers wrought, the nationalist interpretation of the American government, and the guiding principles of the Declaration of Independence: "Four score and seven years ago our fathers brought forth on this continent a new nation, conceived in Liberty, and dedicated to the proposition that all men are created equal." This sentence carries with it principles that Lincoln had defended throughout the antebellum period. With precision, Lincoln links the audience with the patriots of 1776.[5]

In his Gettysburg Address, President Lincoln articulated the meaning of the war. Constructing and consecrating military graveyards were—and are—far from what the Revolutionary founders aimed at with their words and deeds. Lincoln implied that the dedication of the new cemetery was a waste of time and effort if that was all it accomplished: "The brave men, living and dead, who struggled here, have consecrated it, far above our poor power to add or detract." But they had left their work "unfinished." A "great task" lay ahead. Human liberty and democracy themselves were at stake. There would be overflowing cemeteries, vacant chairs at family tables, and men broken bodily and spiritually, but "government of the people, by the people, for the people shall not perish from the earth." Lincoln here spoke a language of love, patriotism, and piety to his listeners: Honor, dedication, increased devotion, and high resolution needed to be brought to the labor. More than simply preserving the liberty of the fathers, the nation, Lincoln's new nation "under God" would have "a new birth of freedom."[6]

Lincoln began his remarks at Gettysburg with a grand, overreaching claim, declaring that "our fathers" had brought forth "a new nation." Yet, from the start, thirteen separate political entities had divergent cultural traditions and economic interests. They had been lashed together by the rebellious acts of a strident minority in the mid-1770s, and even after the British had been expelled, even after the federal Constitution supplanted the Articles of Confederation in 1787, state power and regional differences remained stronger than national unity. Most citizens considered themselves New Englanders, or Virginians, or derived their identities from smaller localities still. Others used occupation, religion, or ethnicity to explain who they were.

The population of the country eighty-seven years earlier was about 2.5 million women and men; the population in 1863 was about 32 million and rising. It now included other settlers, women and men from Ireland, Germany, China, and more. They had played no part in shaping the country's fortunes initially but were now making their presence felt on the battlefield, the home front, and the broader culture, bringing forth a myriad of contested views over the meaning of freedom. In Chicago in 1858, Lincoln included these newcomers in the American dream. He pointed out that they could not trace American ancestors back to July 1776, but they could join because of a belief in the Declaration of Independence. They could believe in the "moral sentiment" of those founding fathers: "We hold these truths to be self-evident, that all men are created equal." Lincoln averred, "They have a right to claim it as though they were blood of the blood, and flesh of the flesh of the men who wrote that Declaration, and so they are." Lincoln had made just this connection in his Lyceum speech in Springfield, Illinois, in 1838 when he declared that the founding fathers were pillars in the temple of liberty and that the whole edifice would collapse unless "we, their descendants, supply their places with other pillars, hewn from the solid quarry of sober reason."[7]

Lincoln's intellectual trajectory can be traced from this first public speech at the Young Men's Lyceum in Springfield to its full explanation in the Gettysburg Address. In all, Lincoln relied on the Declaration of Independence for America's highest ideals. In 1838, he spoke of how "the patriots of seventy-six" supported the Declaration of Independence. In Peoria in 1854, discussing the Kansas-Nebraska Act, he gave many reasons he opposed "the monstrous injustice of slavery" but most of all, "because it forces so many really good men amongst ourselves into an open war with the very fundamental principles of civil liberty—criticising the Declaration of Independence." He stated that consent of the governed was "the sheet anchor of American republicanism, Our Declaration of Independence."[8]

In December 1856 after the Democrat James Buchanan had defeated the Republican John Charles Frémont for president, Lincoln advised his fellow Republicans, "Our government rests in public opinion." Lincoln argued that public opinion favored equality: "And although it was always submitted patiently to whatever of inequality there seemed to be as matter of actual necessity, its constant working has been a steady progress towards the practical equality of all men." Lincoln called for a renewal of "the broader better declaration . . . that 'all *men* are created equal.'"[9]

When one of the most accomplished politician of the age, Stephen Arnold Douglas, learned that Lincoln was his opponent in the Illinois Senate race, he used his considerable talents to discredit Lincoln, calling into question Lincoln's House Divided speech in remarks of his own at Chicago on July 9, 1858. On the very next evening from the same balcony in Chicago, Lincoln responded. He defended himself by clarifying the House Divided statement, but he became more animated when refuting Douglas's assertion that the U.S. government was "founded on the white basis. It was made by the white man, for the benefit of the white man, to be administered by white men." Possibly keyed up in the argument, Lincoln threw caution to the wind and claimed remarkable privilege for the Declaration of Independence and its implications about race and equality: "I should like to know if taking this old Declaration of Independence, which declares that all men are equal upon principle and making exceptions to it where will it stop. If one man says it does not mean a negro, why not another say it does not mean some other man? If that declaration is not the truth, let us get the Statute book, in which we find it and tear it out!" He called upon the audience, "My friends . . . let us discard all this quibbling about this man and the other man—this race and that race and the other race being inferior, and therefore they must be placed in an inferior position. . . . Let us discard all these things, and unite as one people throughout this land, until we shall once more stand up declaring that all men are created equal."[10]

In February 1861, on his way to Washington for his March inauguration, Lincoln spoke at Independence Hall, Philadelphia: "[A]ll the political sentiments I entertain have been drawn, so far as I have been able to draw them, from the sentiments which originated and were given to the world from this hall. I have never had a feeling politically that did not spring from the sentiments embodied in the Declaration of Independence." He felt so strongly that if the country could not be saved on the principles of the Declaration, "I would rather be assassinated on this spot than surrender it."[11]

Douglas was not the only white to contest the idea that the Declaration of Independence meant equality among all races. Race divided the founding fathers in 1776 just as it divided the nation in 1863. Moreover, the constitutional framers in 1787, with no hope of achieving unity to legislate its uprooting, had written racial division (though studiously avoiding the word "slavery" itself) into the fundamental law of the land. Enslaved blacks, asserted the wisest of white minds, were only three-fifths human when it came to reckoning taxation and political representation. Statute law and simple racism ranked both free and enslaved African Americans lower still. Freedom-seeking fugitives from slavery were to be captured and reenslaved. In the early republic, political unity and freedom of commerce were the more fundamental values. Jefferson's self-evident "truth" about human equality had become to Lincoln's generation a very debatable "proposition."

Under the incredible pressures of the Civil War, Lincoln's confidence in the equality of mankind deepened, and his understanding of a new nation built upon liberty broadened. The Gettysburg Address announced that the Declaration of Independence was no longer a proposition. The new birth of freedom, though still a task unfinished, would bring the proposed ideal to fulfillment.

The Gettysburg Address has become part of American civic religion. I have argued that Lincoln was not only the greatest president but also the greatest theologian of the nineteenth century, and the Gettysburg Address is his benediction. As the terrible devastation, deaths, and horrors of war weighed on the commander in chief, Lincoln turned more toward God and grew in his faith. It was Lincoln's belief that God was using him to do His work in history that enabled Lincoln to find the esteem he had so desired and that was so much a part of his southern honor's cultural heritage. The Address contains but a single reference to God, but Lincoln used the rich language and phrasing of the Old Testament. Psalm 90 declares, "The days of our years are threescore years and ten; and if by reason of strength they be fourscore years, yet is their strength labour and sorrow." Lincoln had referred before to the founding of the nation and the declaration, as in his Peoria speech in 1854, "Near eighty years ago we began by declaring that all men are created equal; but now from that beginning we have run down to the other declaration that for some men to enslave others is a 'sacred right of self government.'" And in his remarks from the White House balcony after the victory at Gettysburg: "Eighty-odd years, since upon the Fourth of July, for the first time in the world, a union body of representatives was assembled to declare as a self-evident truth that all men were created equal." But by November 1863, Lincoln changed "eighty-odd" into "four score and seven" in one example of uplifting the Gettysburg Address with an infusion of biblical cadence and religious significance. Lincoln's words and references held symbolic significance for many of that millennial generation: dedicate, fitting and proper, consecrate, devotion, in vain, perish, and new birth.[12]

The effect of the Gettysburg Address is more than heart-throbbing patriotism. Lincoln used words to make a difference, articulating how the war changed all. It made a squabbling set of profoundly disunited states into what he called—five times in some 270 words—a nation. And how could this be when the land was torn asunder and rivers of American blood continued to flow in battle? President Lincoln's answer was an articulation of the meaning of the battle, of the war, of the American dream. Jesus had once told Nicodemus, "Unless you are born again, you cannot see the Kingdom of God." Likewise, America had to be born again, and at Gettysburg Lincoln called for a "new birth of freedom."

And that birth was begotten of death. At Gettysburg in July 1863, twenty-three thousand Northern soldiers fell in three days of fighting, one-fourth of Meade's force. Robert E. Lee lost a shattering twenty-eight thousand men, fully one-third of his army. Sophronia Bucklin, one of the first Union nurses to reach Gettysburg, reported, "It seemed impossible to tread the streets without walking over maimed men. . . . [T]hey lay on the bloody ground, sick with the poisons of wounds, grim with the dust of long marches and the smoke and powder of battle, looking up with wild haggard faces imploringly for succor." Births are often bloody.[13]

Battles had not been going well for the Union prior to mid-1863, and great fear had gripped the Northern public in the summer of 1863 when the Confederate army moved into the Northern state of Pennsylvania. Moreover, to the west, the Union's campaign against Vicksburg dragged on so long that a prospect of victory seemed increasingly remote. Within days of one another, however, both campaigns ended with momentous triumphs for the Union army. The victories inflicted a crippling blow on the military fortunes of the Confederacy. Commander in chief Lincoln wanted more in the aftermath of Gettysburg. On July 7, 1863, he telegraphed General Henry Wager Halleck, that if General George Gordon Meade could complete the destruction of Lee's army, then "the rebellion will be over." Meade, however, failed to prevent Lee's retreat into Virginia, a subject of considerable dispute between the White House and generals in the field. Nevertheless, the victory, which nearly coincided with the birthday of the nation on July 4, the day Lincoln's beloved Declaration had been signed, provided ample evidence that the military situation was improving for the Union. Such at least was the judgment of most Northern voters who cast their ballots in the 1863 state elections, labeled by historian Peter Parish a "political watershed" and pronounced "one of the important turning points in the political history of the nation" by historian Allen Nevins. Unlike the previous year's congressional midterm election, so damaging to Lincoln, these state contests won Republican majorities. Even so, the 1863 margins for winning Republicans had been slim, especially in the critical states of Ohio and Pennsylvania. Even when most Northerners would give the Lincoln administration and his party the benefit of the doubt, the political environment remained toxic, and many Democrats decried vigorous prosecution of the war. In particular, they railed against one particular war measure—the Emancipation Proclamation, written in 1862, effective January 1, 1863.[14]

As suggested by the Gettysburg Address, Lincoln's understanding of liberty became the greatest legacy of the Civil War and the age of Lincoln. Lincoln, however, believed that the Emancipation Proclamation was "the central act of my administration and the great event of the nineteenth century." The Emancipation Proclamation was, like the Gettysburg Address, a document of freedom. While the Gettysburg Address called for a new birth of freedom, the Proclamation actually produced freedom, at least for those slaves of owners not loyal to the federal government in areas still in rebellion. Like the Gettysburg Address, the Emancipation Proclamation is tied to a battle. On advice from Secretary of State William Henry Seward, Lincoln awaited a victory before announcing his proclamation, and the battle at Antietam provided that opportunity. In early September 1862, the Confederate army invaded Union territory in Maryland (reminding many a working person in the North that the extremist proslavery position, such as that of South Carolina politician James Henry Hammond and social theorist George Fitzhugh, maintained in their mudsill view of society that Northern wage workers would be better off as slaves). Union forces went on the attack and launched a series of three piecemeal attacks against the rebel line. Properly coordinated, the Union army might have cracked Southern resolve and perhaps put in motion Confederate collapse itself. Lee, however, had caught wind of General George Brinton McClellan's drive to intercept his divided forces. He regrouped and built defensive positions along Antietam Creek. McClellan waffled once more, and the battle proved a saw-off, disastrous to both sides. Antietam ended in a military draw with both armies retreating from the field under a flag of truce, but because Lee then retreated from Maryland, the battle created an enormous political victory for Union forces.

Though he winced at the awful cost—twenty-three thousand more Northern and Southern boys killed or wounded in a single day—Lincoln used this victory to announce in his preliminary Emancipation

Proclamation to go into effect on January 1, 1863, that "all persons held as slaves within any State or designated part of a State, the people whereof shall then be in rebellion against the United States, shall be then, thence-forward, and forever free." It also encouraged African Americans to serve in the Union armed services at a time when manpower needs were critical. Almost two hundred thousand African American men mustered into Federal service over the next two years.[15]

Arming and deploying African American soldiers had been politically risky for Lincoln. Some conservative and moderate Republicans, including his Illinois confidantes Orville Hickman Browning and David Davis, tried to convince him to revoke the Emancipation Proclamation, and the Indiana legislature called for its withdrawal. Some Union officers resigned because of it, and a few elected political leaders switched allegiance to the Confederacy. In July, soon after Gettysburg, the New York draft riots turned into a race riot where African Americans were "literally hunted down like wild beasts." Soon thereafter, however, the Union army had proof of the value of the new recruits. African American soldiers proved their mettle in Louisiana at Port Hudson (March–July 1863) and Milliken's Bend (June 7, 1863). Two weeks after the momentous Confederate defeat at Gettysburg and months before the Gettysburg Address, African Americans proved their determination to fight and die for freedom. On the evening of July 18, 1863, the African American 54th Massachusetts Regiment took on the frontal assault on a Rebel fort near Charleston, South Carolina. Although unsuccessful in its assault, the Massachusetts 54th fought bravely and earned laurels and commendations for its actions. The heroic efforts by African American troops in these and other battles showed skeptics that black troops would make an important contribution to the Union war effort.[16]

Lincoln accepted the proof. Some of the logic for the Gettysburg Address began in a letter of August 26, 1863, to his old-time friend James C. Conkling, who had invited him to speak back home in Springfield, Illinois. Lincoln saw this as an opportunity to speak to "unconditional union men" about a policy many opposed—emancipation and the arming of black troops. Lincoln could not leave D.C. and asked Conkling to read his letter at the public meeting. Lincoln eloquently defended the importance of freedom and of judging men by their actions rather than the color of their skin. He minced no words: "But, to be plain, you are dissatisfied with me about the Negro. Quite likely there is a difference of opinion between you and myself upon that subject. I certainly wish that all men could be free, while I suppose you do not. . . . You dislike the Emancipation Proclamation and, perhaps would have it retracted. You say it is unconstitutional—I think differently." Lincoln used the successes on the battlefield as part of his argument for black troops: "[S]ome of the commanders of our armies . . . who have given us our most important successes believe the emancipation policy and the use of colored troops constitute the heaviest blow yet dealt to the rebellion, and that at least one of those important successes could not have been achieved when it was but for the aid of black soldiers." Lincoln alluded to the golden rule, "You say you will not fight to free Negroes. Some of them seem willing to fight for you, but no matter." He wrote logically for the audience, "But Negroes, like other people, act upon motives. Why should they do anything for us if we will do nothing for them? If they stake their lives for us they must be prompted by the strongest motive—even the promise of freedom. And the promise being made, must be kept." Lincoln reminded the people of Illinois, whose soldiers fought heroically at the siege of Vicksburg and whose citizens benefitted immensely from navigation of the Mississippi River, that "Father of Waters again goes unvexed to the sea." In listing who accomplished this feat, he included, "The sunny South too, in more colors than one, also lent a hand. On the spot, their part of the history was jotted down in black and white. The job was a great national one, and let none be banned who bore an honorable part in it." In concluding, Lincoln thanked all in a three-way account he would use in the Gettysburg Address, past creation of the republic, present freedom-loving people, future better than ever: "For the great republic—for the principles it lives by and keeps alive—for man's vast future—thanks to all."[17]

Freedom had to be kept alive. Even as he hoped the military course would proceed to the Union advantage and end in victory, Lincoln knew it was possible that some form of slavery could be reinstated after the war. So Lincoln wanted to solidify the notion of equality, certified in the Declaration of Independence, the mission statement of the United States, by making it part of the working government, the Constitution. The first step was the Thirteenth Amendment, which the Senate passed on April 8, 1864, and the House on January 31, 1865, and, after Lincoln's death, ratified on December 6, 1865. Slavery was gone, but the country needed to specify citizenship and voting rights.

As early as 1834, when Lincoln was in the Illinois General Assembly, he explained to a local paper, the *Sangamo Journal*, his belief in "sharing the privileges of the government." With social responsibilities went political rights, he declared. "Consequently I go for admitting all whites to the right of suffrage, who pay taxes or bear arms (by no means excluding females)." Lincoln's views in 1834 show the limits racial prejudice imposed; Lincoln's restricting the extension of voting rights to whites alone reflected the cultural prejudices of his day. Yet, Lincoln's Whiggery was thorough-going: Whatever private prejudices he may have harbored, Lincoln loathed the artificial bonds society and government placed on an individual's ability to work hard, accumulate property, and rise upward. Lincoln's views evolved and expanded throughout his career as he pondered such questions and became acquainted with African Americans, such as Frederick Douglass, Harriet Tubman, Martin Delaney, Robert Smalls, and Sojourner Truth. His belief in freedom led him first to deny the equation of voting rights with property holding, which had rooted the political philosophy of his idol Henry Clay. That step across class lines was an enormous one, too easily overlooked in our own age when all may vote but the control of wealth so vitally determines who runs for office, who wins, and whose interests are served thereby. It led him second to deny the equation of voting rights with race. If it was government's task to promote the common good through banks, railroads, and tariffs, regardless of class, religion, or even gender, why limit that assistance along racial lines?[18]

Ultimately, a meaningful vote was necessary for citizenship, and Lincoln was killed for such an idea. On April 11, 1865, from the White House balcony, Lincoln delivered a speech to the gathering crowd about postwar efforts: "We must simply begin with, and mould from, disorganized and discordant elements." He spoke about the need for citizenship for the valiant African Americans who fought for the Union. One listener at this speech, John Wilkes Booth, read his darkest fears into Abraham Lincoln's vision and told his companion, "That means nigger citizenship. Now, by God, I'll put him through. That is the last speech he will ever make."[19] Lincoln was shot on April 14, 1865, and died the following day for advocating voting rights for African American soldiers, the logical extension of the arguments presented at Gettysburg on November 17, 1863. The Fourteenth and Fifteenth Amendments, adopted after his assassination but absolutely part of his legacy, revolutionized personal freedom in the United States by assuring that it was protected by law.[20]

The Reconstruction Amendments, this "new birth of freedom," involved a redefinition of the role of government in securing liberty. The Bill of Rights protected the people from governmental powers. The First Amendment reads: "Congress *shall make no law* respecting an establishment of religion, or prohibiting the free exercise thereof; or abridging the freedom of speech, or of the press; or the right of the people peaceably to assemble, and to petition the Government for a redress of grievances." The Thirteenth, Fourteenth, and Fifteenth Amendments state, "Congress *shall have power to enforce*" (italics mine). Lincoln, and his legacy after his assassination, institutionalized positive liberty. This was the new birth of freedom.[21]

While the language of the Emancipation Proclamation dug deep into legal, contractual, logical reasoning, the Gettysburg Address soared.

Lincoln wanted to capture the heart of the whole country, to move beyond a war measure, a legal document proclaiming that slavery was no more. He wanted to redefine the meaning of that freedom. The Gettysburg Address held the grandeur and emotion of poetry.

The historiography of the Gettysburg Address is complex and often clashing. Scholars have debunked the popular myth that Lincoln wrote the address hastily on the back of an envelope on the train to Gettysburg, although he was still tinkering with his speech and added the important "under God," phrase at the very last moment. But other issues are still contentious. Lincoln scholar Douglas Wilson notes that for "almost every issue involving the Gettysburg Address, there is contradictory testimony to be confronted and sorted out." Gabor Boritt clarifies how historians and history itself have treated the address. Still controversial among historians is the reception of Lincoln's address at that time. No one had anticipated the president's challenge, set forth in the sweep of a few sentences. Across the North, newspapers covered the cemetery dedication thoroughly, but they particularly emphasized Everett's speech, whose entire remarks were often displayed on the front page of Republican newspapers. But Everett had sent his speech to the newspapers ahead of time; Lincoln had not. Reporters could not get all the words right, and Lincoln's address was inaccurately reported in several aspects, some wrong words and some license with the text. Among many examples, one of Lincoln's hometown newspapers, the *Illinois State Journal*, reported, "Four score and seven years ago our fathers established upon this continent a Government subscribed in liberty and dedicated to the fundamental principle that all mankind are created free and equal by a good God."[22]

Newspapers dedicated twice as many editorials to Everett as to Lincoln. Boritt contends that the rarity of comments about Lincoln's address in Republican newspapers suggests that they viewed them as "routine" and that the remarks were too brief to be considered a memorable speech. The majority of Democratic papers viewed Lincoln's speech as the beginning of his presidential campaign and thus wanted to avoid it. They gave the headlines to Democratic hopefuls. If commenting on the president's Gettysburg speech at all, they criticized it as advancing black equality. Boritt believes that the recognition of the Gettysburg Address as one of Lincoln's greatest speeches did not come until years after the Civil War. Others disagree. Wilson points out that while perhaps the immediate response was not overwhelming, a number of media immediately recognized "something notable." *Harper's Weekly* reported, "The few words of the President were from the heart to the heart. They cannot be read, even, without kindling emotion. . . . It was as simple and felicitous and earnest a word as was ever spoken." Wilson argues that Lincoln knew exactly what he was doing in crafting a compact message, short enough to be reported on the front page of the newspapers. And since the event was ceremonial and his remarks nonpartisan, chances increased that it would be reported in the Democrat Party's newspapers as well. Michael Burlingame, in his massive, 2009, two-volume biography of Lincoln, contends that the Gettysburg Address was perceived as something special and received immediate attention and widespread praise. Burlingame is less excited about Everett's speech and its reception: "Everett's speech as a whole did not move everyone." However, immediately Lincoln's speech was read by Union soldiers and civilians, and it spoke to them of universal and biblical values that transformed the meaning of the Civil War as well as the meaning of democracy and liberty. It is good that historians continue to argue over every detail of the writing and the reception of the Gettysburg Address. Such arguments mean a finer tuning of the history itself and continued career paths for historians.[23]

The concepts that Lincoln addressed at Gettysburg, as well as concepts the historical profession wrote about and discussed, remain worthy topics. In this digital age, new methods can be brought to bear. The nine volumes of *The Collected Works of Abraham Lincoln* are all digitized and online, a remarkable resource for scholars and public alike, a resource that would have seemed miraculous a score of years ago. A new digital tool is a "word cloud." Although a word cloud cannot measure poetry and grandeur, it shows, in my opinion, in an interesting and artistic way (I have been informed that William Faulkner would not agree) the number of times certain words are used: The more times a word is used, the larger the size and prominence in the word cloud. It basically counts words. But, of course, words hold meaning, and so a counting can highlight the concepts emphasized in the speech or letter.[24]

A comparison of figure 9.1 for the Gettysburg Address and figure 9.2 for the Emancipation Proclamation offers some analysis of how Lincoln used particular words for the two different occasions (see figs. 9.1 and 9.2). The word most used in the Gettysburg Address is "dedicated," a word with immense religious significance and a word Lincoln heard often in the churches he attended with his wife, Mary, and one common among Presbyterians, the denomination he was most drawn to (he never joined a church). "Consecrated," "hallow," and "devotion" all share the same religious connotations in figure 9.1. "Nation" is the second most used word. From figure 9.2, the Emancipation Proclamation, there are very different kinds of words, much more legalistic. One does not see either "dedicate" or "dedicated", "devotion," or "nation." The Emancipation Proclamation highlights words like "rebellion," "necessary," "authority," and "designated," all of which are about establishing the legitimacy of Lincoln's order. From figure 9.2, the Emancipation Proclamation emphasizes "persons." "People" is the one word that is common across both documents, significant because in both instances, Lincoln is talking not for himself but instead for everyone. Overshadowing the words of the Emancipation Proclamation in figure 9.2 are the words "United" and "States," with "States" significantly larger. Whereas the Gettysburg Address uses "nation," the Emancipation Proclamation refers to the "United States"; while this could be simply a legalistic decision over a more emotive one, Lincoln word usage in the Emancipation Proclamation is more authoritative.

Figure 9.3 shows words that Lincoln used from his inauguration on March 4, 1861, up until the Gettysburg Address, and figure 9.4 shows those he used in the Gettysburg Address and afterwards until his last on April 14, 1865, a huge number of words covering five volumes, volumes 4 to 8, of *The Collected Works of Abraham Lincoln*.[25]

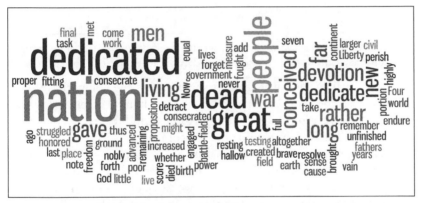

Fig. 9.1. Word cloud from the Gettysburg Address.

Fig. 9.2. Word cloud from the Emancipation Proclamation.

Fig. 9.3. Word cloud showing Lincoln's written words from the date of his inauguration, March 4, 1861, to the Gettysburg Address, November 19, 1863.

Such visualization can highlight some interesting comparisons. One would expect the word "slavery" to be used much more before the Emancipation Proclamation and Gettysburg Address, and that is clear in figures 9.3 and 9.4. The idea of nation that Lincoln stresses in the Gettysburg Address is prominent especially for Lincoln in figure 9.4. Noteworthy is Lincoln's use of the words "United" and "States." They are prominent in both word clouds, but in figure 9.3, the word "States" is much larger than "United," and in figure 9.4, after the Gettysburg Address, the two are nearly identical in size. And the word "new" takes special significance after Lincoln's announcement of his "new birth of freedom." The word clouds suggest there is a shift in emphasis for Lincoln, beginning with the Gettysburg Address.[26]

Ultimately, the Gettysburg Address is the voice of mankind dispossessed. It echoes around the globe today, causing splendid trouble everywhere it is heard. It is the linchpin of five hundred years and more. There is no statement more revolutionary and more conservative since the Bible. Lincoln said, "The world will little note, nor long remember what we say here, but it can never forget what they did here." Today more Americans remember the Gettysburg Address than the Battle of Gettysburg. The Gettysburg Address rightly deserves its hallowed place in the history of not just the United States but the world. Jean Arthur as Clarissa Saunders in *Mr. Smith Goes to Washington* had it right. As she encourages the despondent Jefferson Smith, "Remember the first day you got here? Remember

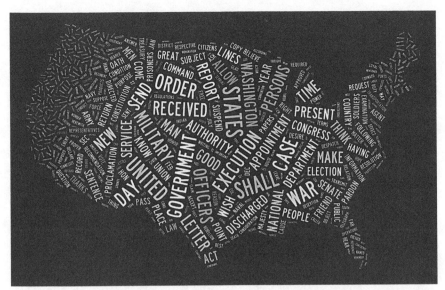

Fig. 9.4. Word cloud showing Lincoln's written words from the Gettysburg Address to April 14, 1865.

what you said about Mr. Lincoln? You said he was sitting up there, waiting for someone to come along. You were right. He was waiting for a man who could see his job and sail into it, that's what he was waiting for." The Gettysburg Address is there to inspire us all.

Notes

1. Frank Capra quoted in *The Name above the Title: An Autobiography* (New York: Macmillan, 1971), 260. The movie was based on an unpublished novel by screenwriter Lewis R. Foster, who called his story both "The Gentleman from Wyoming" and "The Gentleman from Montana." The movie was nominated for eleven Academy Awards and won for best writing, original story. It was nominated for Best Picture, but *Gone with the Wind*, which offered a very different vision of the legacy of the Civil War, won it.

2. Eric Foner, *The Fiery Trial: Abraham Lincoln and American Slavery* (New York: Norton, 2010), 263; James M. McPherson, *Battle Cry of Freedom: The Civil War Era* (New York: Oxford University Press, 1988), 637; David Wills to Abraham Lincoln, November 2, 1863, Papers of Abraham Lincoln, Library of Congress (now available as "Mr. Lincoln's Virtual Library," American Memory, Library of Congress, http://memory.loc.gov/ammem/alhtml/alhome.html). See also Orville Vernon Burton, *The Age of Lincoln* (New York: Hill and Wang, 2007), especially 3–9, 140–54, 179–84, 203–13; Benjamin Thomas and Harold Hyman, *Stanton: The Life and Times of Lincoln's Secretary of War* (New York: Knopf, 1962); James M. McPherson, *Tried by War: Abraham Lincoln as Commander in Chief* (London: Penguin Press, 2008); Jeffrey D. Wert, *The Sword of Lincoln: The Army of the Potomac* (New York: Simon and Schuster, 2005); and Harry T. Williams, *Lincoln and His Generals* (New York: Knopf, 1952).

For the arrangements and background to the Gettysburg Address, see Garry Wills, *Lincoln at Gettysburg: The Words That Remade America* (New York: Simon and Schuster, 1992), and, more recently, Gabor Boritt, *The Gettysburg Gospel: The Lincoln Speech That Nobody Knows* (New York: Simon and Schuster, 2006).

3. "Gettysburg Address," final copy, November 19, 1863, in Roy P. Basler, ed., *The Collected Works of Abraham Lincoln*, 9 vols. (New Brunswick, NJ: Rutgers University Press, 1953–55), 7:17–23 (hereafter cited as *Collected Works*); "Message to Congress in Special Session," July 4, 1861, *Collected Works*, 4:426; "Annual Message to Congress," December 1, 1862, *Collected Works*, 5:537. Lincoln's speeches and writings cited in this paper are also collected conveniently in Orville Vernon Burton, *The Essential Lincoln: Speeches and Correspondence* (New York: Hill and Wang, 2009). On the international and transnational awareness of Lincoln, see Burton, *Age of Lincoln*, and especially Richard Current, "The Civil War and the American Mission," in Cullom Davis et al., eds., *The Public and Private Lincoln* (Carbondale: Southern Illinois University Press, 1979); Phillip Shaw Paludan, *The Presidency of Abraham Lincoln* (Lawrence: University Press of Kansas, 1994), 89; Michael Burlingame, *Abraham Lincoln: A Life*, 2 vols. (Baltimore: Johns Hopkins University Press, 2008), 2:569.

4. Paul Revere Frothingham, *Edward Everett: Orator and Statesman* (Port Washington, NY: Kennikat Press, 1925), 415; Ronald C. White Jr., *A. Lincoln: A Biography* (New York: Random House, 2009), 372; Edward Everett to Abraham Lincoln, November 20, 1863, Papers of Abraham Lincoln, Library of Congress; Abraham Lincoln to Edward Everett, November 20, 1863, *Collected Works*, 7:24. In addition to Wills, *Gettysburg*, and Boritt, *Gettysburg Gospel*, David Herbert Donald, *Lincoln* (New York: Simon and Schuster, 1995), 459–66, though brief, is excellent on the background and the ceremonies.

5. Donald, *Lincoln*, 461.

6. "Gettysburg Address," final copy.

7. Burton, *Age of Lincoln*, 3–9; "Speech at Chicago Illinois," July 10, 1858, *Collected Works*, 2:499; "Address before the Young Men's Lyceum of Springfield, Illinois," January 27, 1838, *Collected Works*, 1:115.

8. "Address before the Young Men's Lyceum of Springfield, Illinois," January 27, 1838, *Collected Works*, 1:112; "Speech at Peoria, Illinois, October 16, 1854, *Collected Works*, 2:255; Lewis E. Lehrman, *Lincoln at Peoria: The Turning Point* (Mechanicsburg, PA: Stackpole Books, 2008).

9. "Speech at a Republican Banquet," December 10, 1856, *Collected Works*, 2:385.

10. "Speech at Chicago Illinois," July 10, 1858, *Collected Works*, 2:501; Burton, *Age of Lincoln*, 44–48.

11. "Speech in Independence Hall, Philadelphia, Pa.," February 22, 1861, *Collected Works*, 4:240.

12. See White, *A. Lincoln*, 606, on religious significance. See Douglas L. Wilson, *Lincoln's Sword: The Presidency and the Power of Words* (New York: Knopf, 2006), 203, 206, on the rewriting of the opening lines.

13. Burton, *Age of Lincoln*, 181; LeeAnn Whites, *Gender Matters: Civil War, Reconstruction, and the Making of the New South* (New York: Palgrave MacMillan, 2005), 36.

14. "To Henry W. Halleck," July 7, 1863, *Collected Works*, 6:319; Peter Parish, *The American Civil War* (New York: Holmes and Meier, 1975), 501–3; Allen Nevins, *War for Union* (New York: Scribner's, 1959), 3:155.

15. "Preliminary Emancipation Proclamation," September 22, 1862, *Collected Works*, 5:433–6; "Emancipation Proclamation," January 1, 1863, *Collected Works*, 6:28–31.

16. Burton, *Age of Lincoln*, 161–83, 212–15; Foner, *Fiery Trial*, 256. The Siege of Fort Hudson lasted from March 22 to July 9, 1863; the heroic and unanticipated participation of the black Louisiana Guards who were being used to build bridges and support positions occurred when they were ordered into attack on May 27. The Battle of Milliken's Bend was fought June 7, 1863, as part of the Vicksburg campaign.

17. Lincoln to James C. Conkling, August 26, 1863, *Collected Works*, 6:406–11. See also Lincoln to Conkling *Collected Works*, 6:414 (August 27, 1863), and Lincoln to Conkling, 6:423 (August 31, 1863).

18. Burton, *Age of Lincoln*; "To the Editor of the Sangamo Journal," June 13, 1836, *Collected Works*, 1:48. Some say that Lincoln did not mean that women should have the right to vote, pointing out that women did not pay taxes or serve in the military at that time. John Mack Faragher, *Sugar Creek: Life on the Illinois Prairie* (New Haven, CT: Yale University Press, 1986), 106. Although Lincoln never pursued the issue, he, nevertheless, made the point that if and when they did pay taxes, they should be able to vote.

19. Edward Steers Jr., *Blood on the Moon: The Assassination of Abraham Lincoln* (Lexington: University Press of Kentucky, 2001), 91.

20. "Last Public Address," April 11, 1865, *Collected Works*, 8:399–405; Burton, *Age of Lincoln*, 240; McPherson, *Battle Cry*, 852.

21. See also Burton, *Age of Lincoln*, specifically on positive and negative liberty; James M. McPherson, "Lincoln and Liberty," in *Abraham Lincoln and the Second American Revolution*, by McPherson (New York: Oxford University Press, 1990); Don E. Fehrenbacher, "The Paradoxes of Freedom," chap 10, in *Lincoln in Text and Context*, by Fehrenbacher (Stanford, CA: Stanford University Press, 1987); Paludan, *Presidency of Abraham Lincoln*, 230–31.

22. Wilson, *Lincoln's Sword*, 225; *Illinois State Journal*, November 23, 1863. See also Cincinnati *Daily Gazette*, November 21, 1863.

23. Borrit, *Gettysburg Gospel*, 131–59; Wilson, *Lincoln's Sword*, 230, 239; Burlingame, *Abraham Lincoln*, 2:573.

24. The nine volumes can be accessed at http://quod.lib.umich.edu/1/lincoln/.

25. I put into a text file all of Lincoln's collected works from his inauguration, March 4, 1861, to his last on April 14. I stripped out all headers and annotations, deleted duplications, removed Lincoln's name, and other extraneous materials such as titles (General, Mr., Major, Col.). Then I created two Word document files, one from Lincoln's inauguration through the Gettysburg Address (see fig. 9.3) and one from after the Gettysburg Address to his last communication on April 14, 1865 (see fig. 9.4). I performed the word clouds first with the program Wordle, and then the ones displayed here were created in tagxedo. See tagxedo.com.

26. Initially, the word "new" was very large, then I remembered that the New York draft (race) riots had occurred following Gettysburg. Therefore, I hyphenated New-York, New-Jersey, and so on, so that only when the word "new" is not part of a place does it appear in the word clouds. "New" is still significant among the words beginning with the Gettysburg Address.

10

Seldom Twice Alike:
The Changing Faces of Lincoln

Harold Holzer

*B*etween the last month of 1862 and the first hours of 1863, Abraham Lincoln did nothing less than come to terms with his own immortality. In his annual message to Congress back on December 1, 1862, with the deadline for execution of the final Emancipation Proclamation looming, he had modestly predicted only that: "*[W]e* cannot escape history. We . . . of this administration, will be remembered in spite of ourselves." But on January 1, 1863, he offered a far bolder prediction to the handful of witnesses gathered in his White House office as he picked up his pen to sign the actual document: "If my name ever goes into history, it will be for this act." Significantly, the latter comment was repeated by a prominent journalist of the day and then quoted by an artist working at the White House the following year to paint a tribute to the first reading of the preliminary Proclamation to the cabinet.[1]

In other words, Lincoln had first recounted his statement to a journalist—one of the men responsible for writing what has come to be called "the first draft of history." And then the words served to inspire an artist working to "draft" the same history in pictorial terms. Nothing could have been more fitting and proper, to paraphrase the famous words Lincoln spoke at Gettysburg later that year. To Lincoln, making history had increasingly come to embrace not only the printed word but also the mass-produced image. In an age in which images could be quickly made and widely distributed at affordable prices, American audiences came to

embrace a similar interest in pictorial tributes. They were more than illustrations. They were visualizations of history.[2]

Ever since winning the Republican presidential nomination in 1860,
Lincoln had become accustomed to making himself available to pictorial
as well as documentary reporters. He had proven a cooperative subject for
artists and photographers who descended on his Springfield hometown
that spring and summer to request sittings. Although he had little time
to pose stiffly and formally in the tradition of, say, George Washington,
who devoted hours of his retirement to standing immovably before Gilbert
Stuart and others, Lincoln did permit painters to sketch him while he read
his mail or met with visitors. On one memorable occasion, he had left his
temporary office in the State Capitol, walked across the hall, and sat for
photographer Alexander Hesler beneath its large, sun-drenched windows.

As Lincoln had come to understand, such pictures could be quickly
reproduced and circulated to admirers, usefully answering lingering concerns among potential voters that he was simply too homely to aspire to
the White House. Demand for his images had risen once again when he
grew a beard after Election Day, changing his appearance as no other
president-elect had done before his inauguration. But between 1861 and
1863, while Lincoln occasionally did visit photography studios in Washington to sit for updated poses that painfully document his rapid aging in
office, painters and print publishers generally turned to other, more current subjects—particularly the new generation of military heroes making
their reputations on the battlefields of the Civil War. The production of
Lincoln images declined.

The Emancipation Proclamation, however, should have propelled Lincoln back into the forefront of the American picture industry. His new status as a "great emancipator" seemed to cry out for revised graphic tributes.
For a time, however, the president did little to encourage image-makers,
providing few fresh photographs essential for adaptation into engravings
and lithographs. In the first seven months of 1863, he is known to have
ventured into a photography studio only once, an April 17 visit to Mathew
B. Brady's gallery, where he posed for a rather nondescript full-figure pose.

The president was so tall that the camera operator, Thomas Le Mere,
proved unable to capture his entire frame on the plate. "Can it be taken
with a single negative?" Lincoln was said to have jested as the photographer
arranged the pose. Lincoln recalled once seeing landscape photographs
stitched together to form a single, extra-wide image. "I thought perhaps this
method might be necessary for my full-length landscape." No, Le Mere assured him, he would make three identical images using a multi-lens camera.[3]

But standing next to a chair, his fist on a prop pedestal at his right,
Lincoln is seen only from the calves up (see fig. 10.1). "They look about as

alike as three peas!" the president declared on seeing the resulting three images. But the novelty of posing before such new-fangled cameras apparently wore off quickly. Other poses long ascribed to 1863 sittings have now reliably been redated 1864, which makes sense from a political point of view: Lincoln would naturally have felt more need to provide new images during an election year; in 1863, his possible quest for a second term was still twelve months away.[4]

In August 1863, Lincoln did return to a photograph studio as a friendly gesture to one of Brady's best cameramen, Alexander Gardner, who had split from the Brady operation not long after photographing Lincoln near the Antietam battlefield in October 1862. By summer 1863, Gardner and

Fig. 10.1. Abraham Lincoln, photograph by Thomas Le Mere at Mathew Brady's gallery, Washington, April 17, 1863. (From the Lincoln Financial Foundation Collection, courtesy of the Indiana State Museum [O-769])

his brother James opened their own Washington gallery on Seventh and D Streets, above a book and stationery store.[5] Fitted with what Gardner called "the newest and most improved apparatus," his new headquarters was lit "so as to obviate all heavy and unnatural shadows under the eyebrows and chin."[6] Perhaps intrigued by the advertised promise that poses would now require no more than five seconds, the president agreed to be Gardner's very first customer. In the quiet of a Sunday, August 9, accompanied by his assistant private secretary John Hay, Lincoln inaugurated Gardner's new operation. "This being Sunday & a fine day," Hay recorded in his diary, "I went down with the President to have his picture taken at Gardner's. He was in very good spirits. He thinks that the rebel power is at last beginning to disintegrate that they will break to pieces if we only stand firm now."[7]

The president's anticipation of a military breakthrough proved premature, but Lincoln was amply rewarded by the photographs Gardner took that day: four cartes de visite well suited for mass production and three Imperial-camera photographs that were more ambitious but less successful. Several images taken that day showed him holding a copy of John Wein Forney's newspaper, the *Washington Chronicle* (see fig. 10.2), which he no doubt read between poses. Another succeeded in capturing the president standing, from head to toe (see fig. 10.3). One picture in particular seems to have caught Lincoln's fancy, and it was a surprising choice for his admiration: The Imperial camera showed him awkwardly slouched over a marble-topped table, the swallow tail of his frock coat billowing like a drape beneath his hip, and his face resting on his clenched hand (see fig. 10.4). Worse, the shot was vaguely out of focus; the sharp detail evident in the cartes was absent. Yet, this is the pose that prompted Lincoln to send a thank-you letter to the photographer after Gardner sent all the prints to the White House. On August 18, Lincoln signed the following acknowl-edgment, drafted in John Hay's hand:

Fig. 10.2. Lincoln seated, photograph by Alexander Gardner, Washington, August 9, 1863. (Library of Congress [O-71])

Fig. 10.3. Lincoln standing, photograph by Alexander Gardner, Washington, August 9, 1863. (Library of Congress [O-75])

My Dear Sir Allow me to return my sincere thanks for the cards and pictures which you have kindly sent me. I think they are generally very successful. The Imperial photograph in which the head leans upon the hand I regard as the best that I have yet seen. I am very truly Your Obt Servt A. Lincoln[8]

Declarations that offered opinions about his own images are so rare that this one, however misguided, automatically ranks as important. Yet, it makes one wonder: Did Abraham Lincoln really understand what kind of images appealed to customers? Apparently not. While other shots from the Gardner series of August 9, 1863, were widely circulated, no attempt was ever made to reproduce and sell the misfocused and informal Imperial that Lincoln so inexplicably admired.

Gardner and Lincoln both achieved far better results three months later. On Sunday, November 8, the president returned to Gardner's to pose for a fresh series of portraits. This time the circumstances were different. As John Hay recorded it: "Went with Mrs Ames to Gardner's gallery & were soon joined by Nico & the Prest. We had a great many pictures taken. Some of the Presdt. the best I have seen. Nico & I immortalized ourselves by having ourselves done in group with the Presdt."[9]

Fig. 10.4. Lincoln seated, elbow on book, photograph by Alexander Gardner, Washington, August 9, 1863. (Library of Congress [O-74])

What did Hay's shorthand mean? For one thing, his diary entry notes that Lincoln arrived at Gardner's accompanied by his principal White House secretary, John G. Nicolay—"Nico" in Hay's description. Hay had apparently gone separately to pick up a "Mrs. Ames" and bring her to join this photographic rendezvous. And while the result of the secretaries' convergence at Gardner's is well known—as Hay described it, the three posed for their only photograph together, a souvenir both secretaries treasured ever after (see fig. 10.5). But who was the mysterious "Mrs. Ames"? In fact, she was the key to why these particular Gardner photographs turned out to be some of "the best" Hay had ever seen.

Fig. 10.5. (*Left to right*) John G. Nicolay, Abraham Lincoln, and John M. Hay, photograph by Alexander Gardner, Washington, November 8, 1863. (Library of Congress [O-76])

Sarah Fisher Clampitt Ames (1817–1901) was a sculptor seeking a commission to honor Lincoln the emancipator with a marble bust sculpture for a U.S. Capitol competition. Although little else is known about her life or career, she had been an antislavery activist and a nurse in a hospital temporarily established during the war at the Capitol building. She likely met Lincoln in the latter capacity and began sketching him. The pioneering Lincoln art historian Rufus Rockwell Wilson dismissed her as "an amateur sculptoress [sic]," but there is evidence that she was very much a professional.[10] Her husband was the noted portrait painter Joseph Ames, and she had studied art herself in both Rome and in her adopted city of Boston.[11] Her other portrait works included busts of Lincoln contemporaries Anson Burlingame and Ulysses S. Grant.[12] At one point, she had produced a portfolio of preparatory sketches of Lincoln, which sadly perished in the fire that destroyed Washington's Patent and Trademark building.[13]

Like many artists before and after her who grew frustrated by Lincoln's inability or refusal to sit still even for the artists he welcomed into his presence, Ames elected to lean on the crutch of photographic models to supplement her life sittings.[14] This explains her presence at the Gardner series, although historians have underestimated her role. For too long, the poses have been described in chronological terms—that is, works meant to capture Lincoln as he looked just before delivering his Gettysburg Address. But there is no evidence to suggest that the president visited Gardner's specifically to provide visual accompaniment to the words he would speak two weeks later at the dedication of the cemetery for the battle dead; there is scant evidence that he had even begun to crystallize his thoughts for the "few appropriate remarks" he was scheduled to deliver.[15] The only hint that Gettysburg may have been on his mind at all that day is the presence of a white manuscript visible on Brady's table in some of the poses at Gardner's that day: "a two-page supplement of 'The Boston Journal' in which was printed Everett's Gettysburg oration which Mr. E. had sent him."[16]

That testimony was offered by journalist Noah Brooks, who did more than any other man to feed the stubborn myth that the November 8 poses were designed as Gettysburg mementoes.

> One November day—it chanced to be the Sunday before the dedication
> of the national cemetery at Gettysburg—I had an appointment to go
> with the President to Gardner, the photographer, on Seventh Street,
> to fulfill a long-standing engagement. Mr. Lincoln carefully explained
> that he could not go on any other day without interfering with the
> public business and the photographer's business, to say nothing of his
> ability to be hindered by curiosity-seekers 'and other seekers' on the
> way thither. . . . The President suddenly remembered that he needed a

paper, and, after hurrying back to his office, soon rejoined me with a long envelop [*sic*] in his hand in which he said was an advanced copy of Edward Everett's address to be delivered at the Gettysburg dedication. ... In the picture which the President gave me, the envelope containing Mr. Everett's oration is seen on the table.[17]

Brooks's widely quoted postwar recollection has value in that it placed yet another prominent figure on the scene (Hay, who may have regarded Brooks as a rival for Lincoln's attention, failed to acknowledge his presence). But it entirely missed the point. Lincoln's spectacular poses that November day were attributable not to any flush of excitement over his approaching destiny at Gettysburg but to the presence of a formally trained artist who knew how to pose her subjects. Sarah Ames's hand is particularly visible in the two close-up pictures taken that day. One especially majestic shot from the chest upwards (but often cropped into a face-only portrait in reproductions made after 1909) has become one of the most frequently reproduced images in the entire Lincoln archive (see fig. 10.6). Yet, it survives in relatively few circa 1863 prints—because Mrs. Ames probably took the original with her to serve as a model for her sculpture.

Another curious pose, showing Lincoln in such dramatic profile that he is nearly turned away from the camera, focuses on his brawny arm

Fig. 10.6. Lincoln, photograph by Alexander Gardner, Washington, November 8, 1863. (Library of Congress)

and shoulder but could not have been taken to serve as a commercially reproducible photograph at the time (see fig. 10.7). Again, the explanation lies with Mrs. Ames. Determined to sculpt Lincoln from the chest up, she clearly required this additional photograph as a model for her project. Eventually, her painstaking research paid off. In 1867, pioneering American art historian Henry T. Tuckerman offered his opinion that "Mrs. Ames, wife of the portrait-painter, has executed a bust of Lincoln, from memory, which many familiar with his expression regard as a most successful portrait."[18] Unaware of her invaluable experience at Gardner's

Fig. 10.7. Lincoln in profile, photograph by Alexander Gardner, Washington, November 8, 1863. (Collection of the New-York Historical Society [O-80])

three years earlier, Tuckerman erred only in asserting that the sculptor had worked from memory alone.

Not until 1868 did Congress purchase Ames's thirty-six-inch-high draped marble bust portrait for $2,000. Today, it sits in a niche near the Senate's public gallery, not far from Francis Bicknell Carpenter's mammoth canvas of the *First Reading of the Emancipation Proclamation*, which fills a nearby stairwell. Although the bust is little known to modern visitors, who understandably have far more familiarity with Vinnie Ream's full-length statue in the Rotunda, Washington observer Mary Clemmer Ames—no relation to the sculptor or her husband—clearly thought Mrs. Ames's work superior when she compared them in the early 1870s. In the author's opinion, the Ames bust "transfixed more of the soul of Lincoln in the brows and eyes of his face than Mrs. Ream has in all the weary outline of her many feet of marble," adding, "[A]ny one who ever saw . . . his living humanity must thank Mrs. Ames for having reflected and transfixed it in the brows and eyes of this marble."[19]

Lincoln sat for no further photographs universally ascribed to 1863. Ironically, a photographer on the scene at Gettysburg missed the once-in-a-lifetime opportunity to capture the president on November 19 as Lincoln addressed the crowd gathered at the dedication of the Soldiers' National Cemetery. By legend, a cameraman positioned near the speakers' platform was busy adjusting his focus when Lincoln unexpectedly concluded his remarks and resumed his seat; his speech had proven so brief, the photographer had missed it entirely. But this story is hard to accept at face value. For one thing, had a photographer indeed been present in the front row on this occasion, he surely would have made a preliminary picture of the principal orator of the day, Edward Everett, who held the stage for two hours before Lincoln rose for his own immortal two minutes. Yet, none exists. Alternatively, had a photographer been truly frustrated by Lincoln's brevity, he surely would have taken a picture instead of Lincoln in his chair on the platform, either before or after. Neither picture is known. All that survives are a distant scene showing a top-hatted man from behind as he arrives at the ceremony (see fig. 10.8) and a sweeping shot of the audience, taken from the very back of the crowd, which, when enlarged many times, shows the blurry face of a bare-headed Lincoln as he sits and awaits his turn to speak (see fig. 10.9). A recently discovered companion shot is believed to show the president on horseback, also from a considerable distance, and from behind, as he arrives on the scene for the ceremonies. The indistinct figure appears to wear a black band around the brim of his stovepipe hat, just as Lincoln did on November 19. But the modern viewer cannot help concluding that the art of photography had missed a great opportunity that unforgettable day.

Fig. 10.8. Top-hatted man believed to be Lincoln (*right*) arriving on horseback at the Gettysburg ceremony. Photograph by an unknown camera operator, Soldiers' National Cemetery, Gettysburg, November 19, 1863. (National Archives)

Fig. 10.9. This detail shows a bare-headed Lincoln (*center*) after taking his seat on the speaker's platform, surrounded by other dignitaries. Photograph by an unknown camera operator, Soldiers' National Cemetery, Gettysburg, November 19, 1863. (National Archives)

The fine arts and popular graphics responded in ways of their own to Lincoln in 1863. Unquestionably, the greatest Lincoln painting of 1863 was the work of Edward Dalton Marchant, one of the few portraitists in the year of Emancipation to act quickly to commemorate its issuance with a portrait of Lincoln (see fig. 10.10). Marchant had started his career as a portraitist in New York back in the 1840s, later moving on to Philadelphia, where for the next thirty years, he established himself as one of that city's leading painters. As the due date of Lincoln's final Emancipation Proclamation drew near, leaders of Philadelphia's Union League, a prominent, pro-Republican, pro-abolition organization, asked Marchant to create a portrait of Lincoln as emancipator for placement in Philadelphia's most famous building—Independence Hall. Once again, publisher John Wein Forney, the *Washington Chronicle* editor who also owned a Philadelphia paper, played a role in the project. In the waning hours of 1862, he wrote the letter of introduction that the artist carried to the White House:

> My dear Mr. President—the bearer, Mr. E. D. Marchant, the eminent Artist, has been empowered by a large body of your personal and political friends to paint your picture for the Hall of American Independence. A generous subscription is made—and he visits you to ask your acquiescence, and to exhibit his testimonials. He will need little of your time. There is no likeness of you at Independence Hall. It should be there; and as Mr. Marchant is a most distinguished Artist, and is commanded by the most powerful influences, I trust you will give him a favorable reception.[20]

Lincoln immediately agreed to grant Marchant extended sittings. He had visited Independence Hall en route to his inauguration on Washington's birthday, 1861, toured its public rooms, no doubt saw its historic portraits of leaders of the American Revolution, and understandably would have relished the idea of seeing his likeness added to such a gallery. As he declared in a speech the day of his visit to Independence Hall, "I would rather be assassinated on this spot than to surrender it."[21] Now he would do something else: He would see he was enshrined there along with heroes of another age.

Marchant began work on his composition in March. "My studio was for several months in the White House," he recalled, "where I was in daily communication with the remarkable man whose features I sought to portray." It was, he said, "more truly a labor of love than I am often permitted to perform." Marchant's vision tended to artistic traditions of old. In an attempt "to symbolize on canvas, the great, crowning act of our distinguished President," Marchant dressed him in an uncharacteristic white tie and portrayed him clutching an out-of-date quill as he signs the document ending slavery in the rebellious states. In the background, the

Fig. 10.10. *Abraham Lincoln*, by Edward Dalton Marchant, oil on canvas, portrait from life, Washington, D.C., signed and dated: "E. D. Marchant. / From Life. 1863." (Courtesy of the Abraham Lincoln Foundation of the Union League of Philadelphia)

chain beneath a classical-looking Liberty statue shatters in metaphorical acknowledgment of Lincoln's act.

Though he was compelled to consult an outdated 1861 photograph as a model—unlike Mrs. Ames, he apparently did not convince the president to visit a photography studio for new pictures—Marchant proudly recalled that his finished work elicited a "rather enthusiastic" response from those who first viewed it.[22] Still, he later admitted of Lincoln, "He was seldom twice alike. Hence the endless variety observable in the photographs of him." Lincoln was, Marchant conceded, "the most difficult subject who ever taxed" his skills as an artist.[23]

Although the final painting was exhibited most briefly at Independence Hall—it was soon relocated to, and remains in, the superb Civil War–era art collection of the Union League—Marchant probably regarded his experience with profoundly mixed emotions. During his work on the picture, he evidently asked Lincoln to issue a temporary furlough to his son, Henry, a major in General Joseph Hooker's army. The younger Marchant had experience of his own as a painter of miniatures, but the father probably yearned for a reunion more than he needed an assistant. Lincoln obligingly requested a pass on February 27, asking for the officer's release "for four or five days" if "it will be no detriment to the service." When the project proceeded more slowly than expected, Lincoln sought an extension for Henry "for business purposes, hoping that it will not interfere with the public service." The major later died on campaign—adding a poignant layer of meaning to their Lincoln project.[24]

It was common for the best paintings of the day to inspire reproductions as popular prints. Marchant's picture proved no exception. One of Philadelphia's most prominent engravers, John Sartain, engraved a print.[25] But it is instructive that the adaptation did not appear until 1864—a year after the painting was completed, and only once Lincoln's reelection campaign increased public demand for new portraits. The Marchant-Sartain collaboration remained unique even in the year 1864. As much as the New Year's Day issuance of the proclamation stimulated Lincoln's belief that his name would go down in history, the act did not stimulate visual accompaniment to editorial praise until 1864 at the earliest and only then in the midst of a political race.

Another example of the limited appeal of the genre was a chromolithographic adaptation by Ehrgott, Forbriger, & Company of Cincinnati of expressionistic painter David Gilmour Blythe's painting *President Lincoln Writing the Proclamation of Freedom, January 1st. 1863* (see fig. 10.11). The considerable rarity of the print—only a handful of copies have surfaced over the years—suggests that its symbolic touches (a bust of James Buchanan hanging by its neck from a bookcase, and a room cluttered with such accoutrements as scales of justice and a rail-splitter's maul, not to mention the sight of a barefoot Lincoln wearing a nightshirt) seemed too obscure to appeal to audiences of the day. The painting itself was rarely exhibited.[26]

African Americans and progressive Republicans may have joyfully welcomed emancipation, but their enthusiasm did not convince profit-minded picture publishers that mass-produced tributes to the document or its author would achieve robust sales. They may have judged the document radical, controversial, and dangerous. Did it require the portrayal of people of color? Would white customers display such images on their walls, even if they showed liberated slaves as ragged and subservient? Such

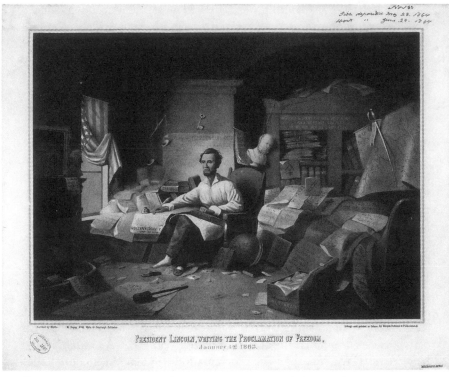

Fig. 10.11. *President Lincoln Writing the Proclamation of Freedom, January 1st. 1863*, after a painting by David Gilmour Blythe, 1863, published by M. Dupuy, Pittsburgh, 1864. (Library of Congress)

unanswerable questions kept emancipation visuals a surprising rarity until Lincoln's death and martyrdom made the genre safe for a broad public. In 1863, emancipation went all but unnoticed—at least in art.

Instead, the separate-sheet display prints that Lincoln did inspire that year tended to address other issues, usually comically and often derisively. *The Four Years Contract and Its Progress* by E. W. T. Nichols was one of the Boston lithographer's series of critical satires showing Lincoln enduring criticism from the Committee on the Conduct of the War, while sitting on a log labeled "Fredericksburg"—scene of the Union military disaster in the waning days of 1862. In a companion piece, *The Great American WHAT IS IT? Chased by Copper-heads*, giant snakes representing Democratic opposition pursue Lincoln and a group of ragged ex-slaves (see fig. 10.12). Lincoln is tearing up the "Constitution & the Union as it was" and revealing a "New Black Constitution [signed] A. L. & Co."

Such roiling domestic political issues, of course, did not noticeably affect Lincoln's rarely seen image overseas. In 1863, however, Paris publisher

Charles Chardon the elder issued Ferdinand Delannoy's *Lincoln Recevant les Indiens Comanches* (see fig. 10.13), a fascinating pictorial account of the American president's White House meeting with Indian chiefs—of several tribes, not just Comanche, as it happened—at which he told his visitors, "It is the object of this Government to be on terms of peace with you, and with all our red brethren."[27] The piece is unique in the Lincoln pictorial canon: No American-made image of Lincoln alongside Native Americans was ever created on America's own shores.

Perhaps the most powerful of all pro-Lincoln images of 1863 did not even identify the president by name. Dominique Fabronious's lithograph *The Mower*, which was copyrighted as the year came to a close on December 15, showed a bearded farmer clearing grass with a large scythe, which is snaring a snake writhing in the grass (see fig. 10.14). The snake is the same "copperhead" that plagued Lincoln in politics and in other prints of the day, but here the bearded figure triumphs over the danger. Moreover, the farmer bears an unmistakable resemblance to the president, even if he is not specifically so identified. But the poetic tribute in the print's

Fig. 10.12. *The Great American WHAT Is It? Chased by Copper-heads*, by E. W. T. Nichols, lithograph, Boston, 1863. (Library of Congress [LC-USZ62–89615])

Fig. 10.13. *Lincoln Recevant les Indiens Comanches*, by Ferdinand Delannoy, engraving, published by Charles Chardon the elder, Paris, ca. 1863. (From the Lincoln Financial Foundation Collection, courtesy of the Indiana State Museum [L-172])

caption is surely meant to evoke respect for Lincoln's ongoing fight with the antiwar Democrats:

> We have battles to fight, we have foes to subdue,
> Time waits not for us, and we wait not for you!
> The mower mows on, though the adder may writhe
> And the copperhead coil round the blade of his scythe.[28]

Not all Lincoln pictures elicited similarly rapturous analysis in 1863. Emancipator or not, Lincoln still provoked partisan reactions, often ardently expressed. At their most powerful, portraits could arouse not only reverence but hostility. On July 11, for example, in the midst of the convulsive New York City draft riots, a mob made its opposition to Lincoln known by literally abusing his image. Breaking into a town home on Lexington Avenue between Forty-Fourth and Forty-Fifth Streets, marauders ransacked the residences of its two occupants, a clothing merchant and a coach manufacturer known to be pro-Lincoln in their politics. An eyewitness to the scene watched: "One fellow appeared at a window with a picture of the President, spat on it, split it over his knee and hurled it into the street, where it was quickly trampled into atoms."[29]

This powerful recollection speaks volumes about the emotional response audiences might provide in extreme cases to Lincoln's image in 1863, however rarely it was put on view. An admirer was likely to hang a print portrait in a place of honor in his parlor or add a carte-de-visite photograph to his family album—where it might share space with religious icons and family members. On the other hand, a violent foe might as easily destroy such a picture as a demonstration of opposition. What is known for sure about the face of Lincoln in 1863 is that it was seldom put on display, but when it was, it pleased his supporters and incited his enemies. That Americans remained bitterly divided was clearly demonstrated by their decidedly mixed reaction to such pictures.

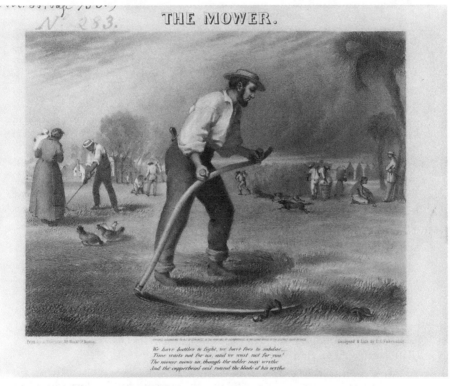

Fig. 10. 14. *The Mower*, by Dominique Fabronius, lithograph, printed by A. Trochsler, Boston, 1863. With caption in verse: "We have battles to fight, we have foes to subside / Time waits not for us, and we wait not for you! / The mower mows on, though the adder may writhe / And the copperhead coil round the blade of his scythe." (Library of Congress [LC-USZ62–55538])

Notes

1. Lincoln, annual message to Congress, December 1, 1862, in Roy P. Basler, ed., *The Collected Works of Abraham Lincoln*, 9 vols. (New Brunswick, NJ: Rutgers University Press, 1953–55), 5:537, hereafter cited as *Collected Works*; Francis B. Carpenter, *Six Months at the White House with Abraham Lincoln: The Story of a Picture* (New York: Hurd and Houghton, 1866), 269. The journalist was John Wein Forney, editor of the *Washington Chronicle*, a Lincoln administration organ in all but name.

2. This chapter does not consider cartoons published on the pages of the weekly pictorial press, a subject that has been widely covered by other books. Rather, it treats the pictures that people retained, treasured, and displayed—photographs and popular prints—that during the Civil War achieved the status of secular icons in American homes.

3. Thomas Le Mere quoted in Lloyd Ostendorf, *Lincoln's Photographs: A Complete Album* (Dayton, OH: Rockywood Press, 1998), 129.

4. For the old attributions of a series of Brady photographs to 1863, see, for example, Stefan Lorant, *Lincoln: A Picture Story of His Life*, rev. ed. (New York: Norton, 1969), 320–21.

5. For a photo of the new gallery, see ibid., 123.

6. *Washington Daily Intelligencer*, May 26, 1863, reprinted in D. Mark Katz, *Witness to an Era: The Life and Photographs of Alexander Gardner* (New York: Viking, 1991), 51.

7. Michael Burlingame and John R. Turner Ettlinger, eds., *Inside Lincoln's White House: The Complete Civil War Diary of John Hay* (Carbondale: Southern Illinois University Press, 1997), 70.

8. Lincoln to Alexander Gardner, August 18, 1863, in Roy P. Basler, ed., *The Collected Works of Abraham Lincoln: Supplement, 1832–1865* (Westport, CT: Greenwood Press, 1974), 199.

9. Burlingame and Ettlinger, *Diary of John Hay*, 109.

10. Rufus Rockwell Wilson, *Lincoln in Portraiture* (New York: Press of the Pioneers, 1935), 179.

11. George C. Groce and David H. Wallace, *The New-York Historical Society's Dictionary of Artists in America, 1564–1860* (New Haven, CT: Yale University Press, 1957), 8.

12. Charles E. Fairman, *Works of Art in the United States Capitol Building, Including Biographies of the Artists* (Washington, DC: GPO, 1913), 7.

13. William Kloss and Diane K. Skvarla, *United States Senate Catalogue of Fine Art*, ed. Jane R. McGoldrick (Washington, DC: GPO, 2002), 258.

14. For other examples, see Van Deren Coke, *The Painter and the Photograph from Delacroix to Warhol* (Albuquerque: University of New Mexico Press, 1964).

15. David Wills to Lincoln, November 2, 1863, Abraham Lincoln Papers, Library of Congress.

16. Michael Burlingame, ed., *Lincoln Observed: Civil War Dispatches of Noah Brooks* (Baltimore: Johns Hopkins University Press, 1998), 89.

17. Noah Brooks, quoted in Lorant, *Lincoln*, 322–23.

18. Henry T. Tuckerman, *Book of the Artists: American Artist Life Comprising Biographical and Critical Sketches of American Artists* (1867; New York: James F. Carr, 1967), 603.

19. Mary Clemmer Ames, *Ten Years in Washington: Life and Scenes in the National Capital, as a Woman Sees Them* (Hartford, CT: Worthington, 1873), 112.

20. John Wein Forney to Abraham Lincoln, December 30, 1862, Abraham Lincoln Papers, Library of Congress.

21. Lincoln, Speech at Independence Hall, Philadelphia, February 22, 1861, *Collected Works*, 4:240.

22. "Lincoln's Growth as Portraits Tell It," *New York Times Magazine*, February 7, 1932; *Vineyard Gazette*, August 26, 1887.

23. *New York Times Magazine*, February 7, 1932.

24. Lincoln to Joseph Hooker, February 27, 1863, and March 5, 1863, *Collected Works*, 6:118, 125.

25. For an example, see Harold Holzer, Mark E. Neely Jr., and Gabor S. Boritt, *The Lincoln Image: Abraham Lincoln and the Popular Print* (New York: Scribner's, 1984), 108.

26. Ibid., 105–6.

27. Speech to Indians, March 27, 1863, *Collected Works*, 6:152. The *Washington Daily Chronicle* for March 28, 1863, identifies the chiefs as representing the Cheyenne, Kiowa, Arapaho, Apache, and Caddo tribes. For the image and a discussion, see Harold Holzer, "An American Hero in Prints Abroad: The European Image of Lincoln," in Richard Carwardine and Jay Sexon, eds., *The Global Lincoln* (New York: Oxford University Press, 2011), 58–59, 61.

28. Bernard F. Reilly Jr., *American Political Prints, 1766–1876: A Catalog of the Collections in the Library of Congress* (Boston: Hall, 1991), 511. Reilly's exhaustive catalogue points to a noticeable drop-off in the production of political prints in 1863. It counts forty-four prints in 1860, forty-one in 1861, eighteen in 1862, and fifteen in 1863. In 1864, the number jumped back to forty-four.

29. *New York Daily News*, July 14, 1863.

Appendixes

Contributors

Index

Appendix A: The Emancipation Proclamation and the Gettysburg Address

The Emancipation Proclamation

The text of Abraham Lincoln's most important piece of writing boasts none of the narrative brilliance for which his other famous manuscripts are celebrated. In fact, the deadening legalese of the Emancipation Proclamation has been subjected to much criticism by generations of historians—not to mention antislavery leaders of Lincoln's own time—some of whom have insisted that its numbing tone revealed its author's indifference to black freedom.

Frederick Douglass, for example, who had yearned for such a proclamation for years, conceded when it was finally issued, "It was not a proclamation of 'liberty throughout the land, unto all the inhabitants thereof,' such as we had hoped it would be, but was one marked by discrimination and reservation." And from Europe, Karl Marx admitted that the document reminded him of "the trite summonses that one lawyer sends to an opposing lawyer."

In more recent times, scholar Henry Louis Gates Jr. acknowledged that the document was crafted with only "the precision of a constitutional legal brief." Lerone Bennett Jr. complained that it boasted "no new-birth-of-freedom swagger, no perish-from-the-earth pizzazz." And Richard Hofstadter famously derided the Proclamation with the devastating observation that it boasted "all the moral grandeur of a bill of lading."

What many observers, then and now, have failed to comprehend is that Lincoln intentionally chose a legal, rather than a moral, proclamation for very practical reasons: He dearly wanted the document to withstand any potential future court challenges—immediately and ever after. He hoped to persuade conservative, war Democrats to support it by couching it as a military necessity, not an act of philanthropy. And to avoid constitutional doubt, he based his order on his powers as a commander in chief in times of war, not as one with a quest to liberate. Eventually, Lincoln did, in fact, provide the poetic rhetoric to adorn this prose thunderbolt—in speeches like the Gettysburg Address, which he delivered eleven months later.

In a sense, the Emancipation Proclamation was so unprecedented and so revolutionary that it did not need the help of Lincoln's literary skills to assure its monumentality. As the president himself noted the day he signed this document, "If my name ever goes into history, it will be for this act." In this regard, even critics of its spare and formal literary style have never disagreed.

The Emancipation Proclamation
January 1, 1863

By the President of the United States of America:
A Proclamation.

Whereas, on the twentysecond day of September, in the year of our Lord one thousand eight hundred and sixty two, a proclamation was issued by the President of the United States, containing, among other things, the following, towit:

"That on the first day of January, in the year of our Lord one thousand eight hundred and sixty-three, all persons held as slaves within any State or designated part of a State, the people whereof shall then be in rebellion against the United States, shall be then, thenceforward, and forever free; and the Executive Government of the United States, including the military and naval authority thereof, will recognize and maintain the freedom of such persons, and will do no act or acts to repress such persons, or any of them, in any efforts they may make for their actual freedom.

"That the Executive will, on the first day of January aforesaid, by proclamation, designate the States and parts of States, if any, in which the people thereof, respectively, shall then be in rebellion against the United States; and the fact that any State, or the people thereof, shall on that day be, in good faith, represented in the Congress of the United States by members chosen thereto at elections wherein a majority of the qualified voters of such State shall have participated, shall, in the absence of strong countervailing testimony, be deemed conclusive evidence that such State, and the people thereof, are not then in rebellion against the United States."

Now, therefore I, Abraham Lincoln, President of the United States, by virtue of the power in me vested as Commander-in-Chief, of the Army and Navy of the United States in time of actual armed rebellion against authority and government of the United States, and as a fit and necessary war measure for suppressing said rebellion, do, on this first day of January, in the year of our Lord one thousand eight hundred and sixty three, and in accordance with my purpose so to do publicly proclaimed for the full period of one hundred days, from the day first above mentioned, order and designate as the States and parts of States wherein the people thereof respectively, are this day in rebellion against the United States, the following, towit:

Arkansas, Texas, Louisiana, (except the Parishes of St. Bernard, Plaquemines, Jefferson, St. Johns, St. Charles, St. James[,] Ascension,

Assumption, Terrebonne, Lafourche, St. Mary, St. Martin, and Orleans, including the City of New-Orleans) Mississippi, Alabama, Florida, Georgia, South-Carolina, North-Carolina, and Virginia, (except the fortyeight counties designated as West Virginia, and also the counties of Berkley, Accomac, Northampton, Elizabeth-City, York, Princess Ann, and Norfolk, including the cities of Norfolk & Portsmouth[)]; and which excepted parts are, for the present, left precisely as if this proclamation were not issued.

And by virtue of the power, and for the purpose aforesaid, I do order and declare that all persons held as slaves within said designated States, and parts of States, are, and henceforward shall be free; and that the Executive government of the United States, including the military and naval authorities thereof, will recognize and maintain the freedom of said persons.

And I hereby enjoin upon the people so declared to be free to abstain from all violence, unless in necessary self-defence; and I recommend to them that, in all cases when allowed, they labor faithfully for reasonable wages.

And I further declare and make known, that such persons of suitable condition, will be received into the armed service of the United States to garrison forts, positions, stations, and other places, and to man vessels of all sorts in said service.

And upon this act, sincerely believed to be an act of justice, warranted by the Constitution, upon military necessity, I invoke the considerate judgment of mankind, and the gracious favor of Almighty God.

In witness whereof, I have hereunto set my hand and caused the seal of the United States to be affixed.

Done at the City of Washington, this first day of January, in the year of our Lord one thousand eight hundred and sixty three, and of the Independence of the United States of America the eighty-seventh.

[L.S.]

By the President: ABRAHAM LINCOLN

WILLIAM H. SEWARD, Secretary of State.

"Emancipation Proclamation," January 1, 1863, in Roy P. Basler, ed., *Collected Works of Abraham Lincoln*, 9 vols. (New Brunswick, NJ: Rutgers University Press, 1953–55), 6:28–30.

The Gettysburg Address

The draft printed below may be the closest text we have to the address Abraham Lincoln actually delivered at Gettysburg.

Roy P. Basler, editor of Lincoln's collected works, published all six known copies of the speech: the first draft; the second draft, reprinted below; a newspaper version; the so-called Edward Everett Copy; the George Bancroft Copy; and Lincoln's version of the final text. The first page of the first draft was written on official Executive Mansion stationery prior to November 19, 1863. However, there is some speculation that both the second page and the entire second draft were finished in Gettysburg, either during the evening of November 18 or the morning of November 19. Lincoln probably read his address from this second draft or from yet another copy since lost, although some eyewitnesses claimed he did not read verbatim at all.

Reporters composed the newspaper version, based on both shorthand notes and a copy of the text Lincoln invited them to quickly consult on the scene. It is unique in that it indicates the points at which the audience applauded. Some obvious errors are in this version, however, especially an almost comical reference to "refinished" rather than "unfinished" work. However, only minor errors in punctuation and capitalization otherwise mar the *New York Tribune*, *Times*, and *Herald* versions. Significantly, the newspaper texts added "under God" to the final sentence—reflecting the fact that Lincoln probably ad-libbed the phrase at the time he delivered the speech. All subsequent versions contain this wording.

Basler refers to the Edward Everett Copy as a "careful revision." Everett, the principal orator at Gettysburg, sent a gracious note to the president the day after their appearance, noting, "I should be glad, if I could flatter myself that I came as near to the central idea of the occasion, in two hours, as you did in two minutes." On January 30, 1864, he wrote again to Lincoln to request a copy of the Gettysburg Address for inclusion, with his own oration, in a volume to be sold at the New York Sanitary Fair. Lincoln generously complied.

The fourth, the so-called George Bancroft Copy, was prepared at the famous historian's request. An interesting side note is that in this copy Lincoln changed "upon this continent" to "on this continent." This revision is also reflected in the final text. Bancroft asked for the copy so it could be included in a proposed "Autograph Leaves of Our Country's Authors," which was to be sold at the Baltimore Sanitary Fair to raise funds for the war wounded. Lincoln sent the requested text to Bancroft on February 29, 1864.

The final text, also known as the Bliss Copy, was required because Lincoln made a fatal error in the copy he prepared for Bancroft, writing it on both sides of one page, and so it could not be pasted into the "Autograph Leaves" album. With considerable patience, Lincoln agreed to rewrite the speech on two separate sheets sometime after May 1864. The only manner in which this text differs from the Bancroft Copy is that Lincoln omitted the word "here" from the original "for which they here gave the last full measure of devotion."

Over the years, historians have speculated that Lincoln used an altogether different text for his actual speech. If so, the copy has vanished, although in the late twentieth century, a disputed text was "discovered," allegedly given at the scene as a souvenir to David Wills, Lincoln's host at Gettysburg. An overwhelming majority of scholars quickly cast doubt on its authenticity. No other Lincoln speech in the Lincoln canon has stirred so much interest. The most famous of all Lincoln's writings from 1863—or any other year—remains the holy grail of Civil War history.

The Gettysburg Address
(Second Draft)
November 19, 1863

Four score and seven years ago our fathers brought forth, upon this continent, a new nation, conceived in Liberty, and dedicated to the proposition that all men are created equal.

Now we are engaged in a great civil war, testing whether that nation, or any nation, so conceived, and so dedicated, can long endure. We are met here on a great battle-field of that war. We have come to dedicate a portion of it as a final resting place for those who here gave their lives that that nation might live. It is altogether fitting and proper that we should do this.

But in a larger sense we can not dedicate—we can not consecrate—we can not hallow this ground. The brave men, living and dead, who struggled here, have consecrated it far above our poor power to add or detract. The world will little note, nor long remember, what we say here, but can never forget what they did here. It is for us, the living, rather to be dedicated here to the unfinished work which they have, thus far, so nobly carried on. It is rather for us to be here dedicated to the great task remaining before us—that from these honored dead we take increased devotion to that cause for which they here gave the last full measure of devotion—that we here highly resolve that these dead shall not have died in vain; that this nation [under God]* shall have a new birth of freedom; and that this government of the people, by the people, for the people, shall not perish from the earth.

  * Eyewitnesses remembered and the extant newspaper transcript confirms that Lincoln added "under God" as he was reading from this copy of the address.

"Address Delivered at the Dedication of the Cemetery at Gettysburg," November 19, 1863, Second Draft, in Basler, *Collected Works*, 7:18–19.

Appendix B: Timeline, 1863

January 1   President Lincoln signs Emancipation Proclamation.

January 3   First drawing of Santa Claus (by Thomas Nast) is published in *Harper's Weekly*.

January 8   Construction (in California) of the first transcontinental railroad begins, to be completed in 1869.

January 20   General Ambrose Everett Burnside leads his troops in what would become known as the disastrous "Mud March" to cross the Rappahannock River following defeat at Fredericksburg.

January 25   Lincoln names General Joseph Hooker to replace General Burnside as commander of the Army of the Potomac.

February 10   P. T. Barnum promotes the marriage of Tom Thumb and Lavinia Warren.

February 16   Kansas State is established as the first land-grant college under the 1862 Morrill Act.

February 24   Arizona is organized as a Territory of the United States.

March 3   Congress approves removal of all Indians from Kansas.

March 3   Lincoln signs first conscription (draft) act.

March 14   Admiral David G. Farragut leads federal naval squadron past Port Hudson, Louisiana.

April 2   "Bread riot" occurs in Richmond.

April 5–6   Lincoln visits General Hooker at headquarters of the Army of the Potomac near Falmouth, Virginia.

April 13   William Bullock is granted a patent for continuous-roll printing, using both sides of a sheet.

May 1   Confederate Congress permits enslavement or execution of captured African American Union soldiers.

May 1–4   Battle of Chancellorsville. Robert E. Lee defeats Union army but loses General Thomas J. "Stonewall" Jackson to friendly fire (Jackson dies May 10).

May 5   Arrest in Ohio of antiwar "Copperhead" Democrat, former Congressman Clement Laird Vallandigham. "Valiant Val" is tried and convicted by military tribunal.

May 19   General Ulysses S. Grant tries frontal assault on Vicksburg, Mississippi, without success.

May 28   The famous 54th Massachusetts Regiment, one of the first African American volunteer units, leaves Boston for the front.

June 27   Lincoln replaces General Hooker with General George Gordon Meade.

July 1–3   Union forces under General Meade defeat Lee and his forces at Gettysburg, Pennsylvania. Meade fails to pursue the retreating Confederates.

July 4   Grant and his troops force the Confederates to surrender Vicksburg, Mississippi.

July 8   Port Hudson, Louisiana, surrenders to the Union.

July 10   Clement C. Moore, author of *A Visit from St. Nicholas*, dies.

July 13   New York City Draft Riots begin—worst civil disturbance in U.S. history save for Civil War itself.

July 18   The 54th Massachusetts Regiment assaults Battery Wagner, near Charleston, South Carolina. The fortress is not taken, but the courage and sacrifice of the African American troops bring national recognition. White commander Robert Gould Shaw is killed in action.

June 20   West Virginia is admitted to the Union as the thirty-fifth state.

July 26   Sam Houston, first president of the Republic of Texas, dies.

August 9   Lincoln urges General Grant to welcome black troops in order to "close the contest."

September 19–20   Confederates turn back Union forces at Chickamauga.

October 3   President Lincoln proclaims a national Day of Thanksgiving.

October 13   Republican John Brough soundly defeats Democrat Clement Vallandigham in closely watched race for governor of Ohio. Under terms of his conviction, Vallandigham had been banished to Confederacy but fled and waged the race from Ontario, Canada.

October 16   Lincoln establishes new, consolidated military Department of Mississippi, putting Grant in command.

October 29   Representatives of sixteen countries meet in Geneva, Switzerland, and form the Red Cross.

November 19   President Lincoln and Edward Everett give speeches at dedication of Soldiers' National Cemetery at Gettysburg.

November 20   Lincoln suffers bout of smallpox and tells persistent favor-seekers, "Now I have something I can give everyone."

November 23 Battle of Chattanooga waged.

November 24 Battle of Lookout Mountain, Tennessee, occurs.

December 7 Congress convenes in Washington (Confederate Congress opens on the same day in Richmond).

December 8 Lincoln issues Proclamation of Amnesty and Reconstruction. He transmits annual message to Congress, summing up the year 1863. He pays tribute to the army and navy, "to whom, more than to others, the world must stand indebted for the home of freedom disenthralled, regenerated, enlarged, and perpetuated."

Also in 1863

Edward Everett Hale publishes *Man without a Country.*

Henry Wadsworth Longfellow writes "Tales of a Wayside Inn."

T. H. Huxley writes "Evidence as to Man's Place in Nature."

J. S. Mill writes *Utilitarianism.*

Whistler paints *Little White Girl.*

Ebenezer Butterick develops the first paper dress pattern.

The National Academy of Sciences is founded in Washington, D.C.

Travelers Insurance Company is founded.

Roller skating is introduced in the United States.

John D. Rockefeller establishes an oil refinery in Cleveland.

In Washington, the Capitol dome is completed.

France sends troops to Mexico City. In 1864, Archduke Maximilian of Austria will become Emperor of Mexico.

Signal Corps is created as a special branch of the army.

Allan Pinkerton organizes the Secret Service.

George Pullman invents a folding upper berth for trains.

Popular music includes "When Johnny Comes Marching Home," "Just Before the Battle, Mother," and "Sweet and Low."

CONTRIBUTORS

Michael B. Ballard has been an archivist at Mississippi State University's Mitchell Memorial Library for thirty years. He currently serves as coordinator of its Congressional and Political Research Center and as associate editor of the publishing projects of the Ulysses S. Grant Association. He is the author of twelve books.

Orville Vernon Burton is the Distinguished Professor of Humanities, the director of the Clemson Cyberinstitute, and a professor of history and computer science at Clemson University. He is the author of *The Age of Lincoln* and editor of *The Essential Lincoln: Speeches and Correspondence*. Burton is a board member of the Abraham Lincoln Bicentennial Foundation.

Catherine Clinton holds a chair in U.S. history at Queen's University Belfast in Northern Ireland. She is the author of *Mrs. Lincoln: A Life*, along with a number of articles for scholarly journals on the Lincolns and their marriage. Her other books include *Harriet Tubman: The Road to Freedom* and *Fanny Kemble's Civil Wars*.

William C. Davis is a professor of history at Virginia Tech University. He has written forty books, including *Lincoln's Men: How President Lincoln Became Father to an Army and a Nation*; *"A Government of Our Own": The Making of the Confederacy: Jefferson Davis, the Man and His Hour*; and the Pulitzer Prize nominee *The Battle of Bull Run*.

Sara Vaughn Gabbard (coeditor) is executive director of Friends of the Lincoln Collection of Indiana. She is editor of *Lincoln Lore* and coeditor (with Harold Holzer) of *Lincoln and Freedom: Slavery, Emancipation, and the Thirteenth Amendment* and (with Joseph Fornieri) of *Lincoln's America, 1809–1865*. With Richard Etulain and Sylvia Frank Rodrigue, she is currently editing the Southern Illinois University Press series *The Concise Lincoln Library*.

Harold Holzer (coeditor) is chairman of the Abraham Lincoln Bicentennial Foundation, successor organization of the U.S. Lincoln Bicentennial Commission, which he cochaired for ten years. He is also the author, coauthor, or editor of forty-three books on Lincoln and the Civil War. Among his many honors, he won a second-place Lincoln Prize for *Lincoln at Cooper Union*, numerous awards for history, research, and children's literature, and the National Humanities Medal from the President of the United States.

John F. Marszalek is executive director of the Ulysses S. Grant Presidential Library, Mississippi State University. He is editor of *The Papers of Ulysses S. Grant* and author of many books, including *Sherman: A Soldier's Passion for Order*. He is editing an annotated edition of Grant's *Memoirs*.

Edna Greene Medford is chair of the history department at Howard University. She is a coauthor of *The Emancipation Proclamation: Three Views* and a member of the boards of the Lincoln Forum and the Abraham Lincoln Bicentennial Foundation. A frequent guest on C-SPAN, she served as a member of the board of Borders Group.

Barnet Schecter is an independent historian and the author of *The Devil's Own Work: The Civil War Draft Riots and the Fight to Reconstruct America* and *The Battle for New York: The City at the Heart of the American Revolution*. His most recent work is *George Washington's America: A Biography through His Maps*.

Craig L. Symonds is emeritus professor of history at the U.S. Naval Academy. He recently concluded a year back in the classroom as its Class of '57 Distinguished Professor. The author of *The American Heritage History of the Battle of Gettysburg* and *The Civil War at Sea*, he won the Lincoln Prize for *Lincoln and His Admirals*.

Frank J. Williams is a retired chief justice of the Rhode Island Supreme Court. He is the founding chairman of the Lincoln Forum, president of the Ulysses S. Grant Association, and former president of the Abraham Lincoln Association. His many books include *Judging Lincoln* and *The Mary Lincoln Enigma*.

Bob Zeller is cofounder and president of the Center for Civil War Photography and a leading authority on Civil War images. He is the author or coauthor of ten books, including *The Blue and Gray in Black and White* and *The Civil War in Depth*, the first 3-D photographic history of the conflict. He has also authored novels and sports books.

Index

Italicized page numbers indicate figures.